DEFENDERS
of the
FAITH

DEFENDERS
of the
FAITH

Religion and Politics
from the Pilgrim Fathers
to Ronald Reagan

Wilbur Edel

New York
Westport, Connecticut
London

Copyright Acknowledgments

The author and publisher are grateful for permission to reprint from the following sources:

Leonard Bushkoff, "Intelligence Memoirs and Scandalous Occasions," *Foreign Intelligence Literary Scene,* October 1984, p. 7.
"Church and Bomb," *The Economist,* 5 February 1983, p. 19.
Richard Cohen, "Prayer," Washington *Post,* 21 October 1982. Copyright © 1982, Washington Post Writers Group, reprinted with permission.
"Jerry Falwell's Crusade," *Time,* 2 September 1985, p. 49.
People for the American Way, "The Gospel According to Four Religious Leaders," advertisement in the New York *Times,* 10 May 1982.
James Reston, "Politics and the Press," New York *Times,* 9 April 1986. Copyright © 1986 by The New York Times Company. Reprinted by permission.
United Nations Association of the United States of America, *Nuclear Proliferation: Toward Global Restraint,* printed as part of the record of U.S. Senate Hearing 98-909, "United Nations Association Report on Nuclear Nonproliferation" (27 June 1984), p. 47.

Library of Congress Cataloging -in-Publication Data

Edel, Wilbur.
    Defenders of the faith.

    Bibliography: p.
    Includes index.
    1. Church and state--United States--History.
2. Religion and state--United States--History.
3. Christianity and politics--History.
4. Religion and politics--United States--History.
5. United States--Church history. 6. United States--
Religion. I. Title.
BR516.E42 1987   322'.1'0973   87-2367
ISBN 0-275-92662-1 (alk. paper)

Library of Congress Catalog Card Number: 87-2367
ISBN: 0-275-92662-1

First published in 1987

Praeger Publishers, One Madison Avenue, New York, NY 10010
A division of Greenwood Press, Inc.

Printed in the United States of America

∞

The paper used in this book complies with the Permanent Paper Standard issued by the National Information Standards Organization (Z39.48-1984).

10 9 8 7 6 5 4 3 2

Acknowledgments

Assistance provided by the staff of the Bucknell University Library, whose excellent collections I was permitted to use at will, greatly facilitated this study. Special thanks go to Tom Mattern, whose intimate knowledge of government documents and reference materials saved me many hours of searching. I also appreciate the help of Bucknell University students Laurie Weissinger and Rochelle Peterson in gathering, listing, and copying documents. Last, but only in a chronological sense, was the efficient and untiring performance of Irene Klushin, who turned a very rough collection of sheets into a beautifully typed manuscript.

Contents

Introduction

The "faith of our fathers" has long been a favorite theme in political speeches as well as in church sermons. Almost invariably, the focus of such a discourse is on the religious principles that underlie the American way of life. Frequently overlooked, or glossed over, are the serious differences that divided the original settlers of this country and that have fragmented the religious community in the United States ever since. Perhaps more serious are the vastly different notions as to how even agreed-upon principles should be translated into public policy.

Most of the fundamentals of modern U.S. political practice have evolved with little church influence or input. This was not always so. The concept of an established (official, government-supported) church was an inheritance that came to America with immigrants from every country of Europe. With few exceptions, the colonies had their established churches, although no one church dominated the entire country as in England. Independence did not eliminate this condition, but as the doctrine of separation of church and state came to be accepted, the influence of religious organizations on the design of public policy faded.

Notwithstanding the traditional character that the principle of separation of church and state has come to assume, this concept has not been interpreted uniformly over the past 150 years—that is, since direct public support of churches was eliminated in all states of the Union. Disagreement as to the meaning and extent of separation raised relatively few hackles in the late nineteenth and early twentieth centuries. In recent years, however, this has become a national issue, which has drawn church officials, civic organizations, political parties, and state and national legislators—even the president of the United States—into a series of disputes on subjects ranging from prayer in public schools to defense against external aggression. Where, formerly, political decisions were rarely evaluated in religious terms, it has become commonplace to find the defense of Christianity associated with the election or defeat of particular candidates for public office, or even with such unchurchly questions as giving up the Panama Canal or supporting revolutionary or counterrevolutionary uprisings. At the same time, there has been a growing movement, led by fundamentalist preachers and their sympathizers in public office, to reinstate as the law of the land religious precepts reminiscent of the colonial era.

This revivalist approach to political decision making comes at a time when the world is torn by both religious and anti-religious fanaticism. It completely ignores the fact that the threat to freedom is greatest when individuals are judged by their adherence to a particular creed or dogma, religious or otherwise. Those in the United States who apply such judgments do so in the belief that their standards are those of all true Americans, and that the enforcement of such standards will ensure a return to the faith of our fathers. This attitude reflects an abysmal ignorance of the nation's history and the significance of the changes that have raised the country from its colonial heritage of religious bigotry to a democratic society with the greatest measure of individual freedom ever achieved on this earth. It also ignores or misinterprets the experience of other countries in the centuries of struggle when good and evil were represented by such symbols as the cross, the star and crescent, the hammer and sickle, and the swastika.

To dispel the myths and historical misunderstandings perpetrated, knowingly or unknowingly, by those who seek this country's political leadership on the basis of the greater purity of their religious belief is the purpose of this book.

DEFENDERS
of the
FAITH

A Nation
Is
Molded

1

Religion and Politics
in the World of Our Ancestors

For as long as human beings have lived together in organized society, belief in a supernatural power has been a major influence on their notions of good and evil and of acceptable and unacceptable behavior. In tribal society, worship—or, more often, fear—of the supernatural stemmed from the conviction that spirits inhabited the winds, rain, rocks, and trees, and that humans could guard against these essentially antagonistic forces by protective rituals and symbols. Today we label these beliefs superstition, forgetting that such holy days as Christmas and Easter were Christian adaptations of early pagan rites celebrating the birth of the sun-god and the rebirth of life among plants and animals each spring.[1]

As tribes grew into nations and more complex political and religious organizations evolved, the distinction between political and religious decision making sharpened. For thousands of years, however, these two processes went hand in hand, with little thought given to the question of separation of church and state. On the contrary, any suggestion that the two be divorced would have been considered both heretical and treasonable: heretical in its challenge to established religious doctrine; and treasonable in its challenge to the authority of the ruler, whose position was based on the will of the god or gods that he and his people worshiped.

It was in this sense that the rulers of the Roman Empire reacted to the doctrine preached by Jesus of Nazareth and those dissident Jews who called themselves Christians. The Emperor Tiberius and his successors during the first three centuries A.D. took little comfort in the instruction to "render unto Caesar the things which are Caesar's" knowing full well that to "render unto God the things that are God's" struck at the very

core of Roman authority.[2] By the time Christ's message had begun to circulate, rulers of the empire were claiming that they themselves were gods;
and, as such, they were the chief defenders of the family of deities believed by Romans to control human affairs.

Although worship of non-Roman gods was tolerated in many con-
quered areas, the persecution and martyrdom of early Christians reflected
Roman resistance to—and fear of—the belief in one supreme deity who
would acccept "no other gods before me."[3] Roman governors knew, of
course, that the concept of one all-powerful god had been preached by
Jewish leaders for centuries. Prior to the coming of Christ, the more
rebellious Jews had been hounded and executed, but they were considered
only a minor irritant, their influence being limited to the general area of
Palestine. On the other hand, Christianity, although adopted by relatively
few Jews, seemed a more ominous threat when it spread throughout the empire, even to the Roman capital.

As the Roman Empire crumbled under the impact of barbarian invasions and internal corruption, Christianity gained strength. However, the
church's eventual triumph over the forces of persecution resulted in
political entanglements never anticipated or desired by its founders. The
practice of Christianity was legalized in 313 A.D., by an official edict of
co-emperors Constantine and Licinius.[4] In the subsequent contest for
political power, Constantine emerged the victor. Announcing his conversion to Christianity, he moved the capital of the empire from Rome to
Byzantium, renamed Constaninople (now Istanbul, in Turkey). Before his
death in 337, Constantine adopted Christianity as the official state
religon. This action had several important effects: first, it established
what was to become the Orthodox Eastern church, whose influence still
predominates among Christian communities in the Middle East, the
Balkans, and Russia. Second, and politically more significant, it clinched
the tie between the Orthodox community and the emperor, who assumed
leadership of both church and state. As the Viceroy of God, responsible
for designing his government "according to the pattern of the divine
original," the emperor's word was law for the church as well as for the
organs of government. This association became traditional in regions
dominated by the Eastern church, most notably in Russia under the
tsars.[5]

Although the Roman Empire was not divided politically between
East and West until the death of Theodosius I in 395 A.D., the western
church never acknowledged the emperor's jurisdiction over its affairs. It
insisted that the ultimate authority in all spiritual matters was the Bishop

of Rome. As successor to Saint Peter, who was considered the founder of the church, the bishop of the Holy See of Rome automatically assumed the title of pope. Notwithstanding this initial desire for a clear distinction between spiritual and temporal responsibilities, the growing strength of the papacy resulted in part from de facto alliances with western monarchs who dominated the European scene after the fall of the Roman Empire in the fifth century. These alliances not only widened the ecclesiastical influence of the church, they also extended its temporal power enormously. As the western empire recovered from the devastating assaults of the Goths, the Huns, and other invaders, aspirants to political leadership looked to the church to legitimize their claims. Thus, Charlemagne, the first European monarch to head the new Holy Roman Empire, received his crown from Pope Leo III in Rome. As a landowner, the church came to control a substantial region in central Italy known as the Papal States. In later years that territory was gradually reduced to the present confines of Vatican City, but the church's dominant position in religious affairs remained secure throughout Europe until the sixteenth century.

THE CHURCH GOES TO WAR

Even as the Church of Rome was building a political power base in western Europe, a new savior was campaigning in the Middle East under the banner of Islam. Born in Mecca and raised in Arab tradition, Mohammed at age forty felt the call to preach the "true religion." His message, unlike that of Jesus, called upon believers not only to accept "what is revealed to Mohammed," but to "fight for his cause," which is the cause of Allah. No vision of the meek inheriting the earth appears in the Koran. Nor is the true believer called upon to "love thine enemy." On the contrary, the command is: "Prophet, rouse the faithful to arms." For those who fall in battle there is this assurance:

> You must not think that those who were slain in the cause of Allah are dead. They are alive, and well provided for by their Lord; pleased with His gifts and rejoicing that those whom they left behind and who have not yet joined them have nothing to fear or to regret; rejoicing in Allah's grace and bounty.

Although Allah is characterized as "the Compassionate, the Merciful," He expects his followers to fight all unbelievers and to "make war on them until idolatry is no more and Allah's religion reigns supreme."[6]

Despite fundamental differences that separate Muslim and Christian conceptions of the nature and purposes of the deity, both accept the Old Testament version of the origin and early development of man, up to and including the birth of Jesus Christ. However, the Koran departs from Christian belief in denying the divine origin of Jesus, declaring him to have been simply another prophet like Moses and Abraham. "Allah forbid that He Himself should beget a son," the Koran says. "When He decrees a thing He need only say 'Be,' and it is."[7] The Koran goes on to describe in great detail, for its followers, the rules of conduct that govern all social and political activities and relationships. In this all-encompassing concept of religious obligations, the idea of separation of church and state has no place.

Following the command of the Koran and the leadership of Mohammed and his successors, Muslim Arabs began a conquest that ultimately took them from the Middle East across North Africa and into Spain. When in 1095 the Christian Byzantine emperor appealed to Pope Urban II for assistance against the Muslim Turks, the pope responded by calling for a crusade to free the Holy Land from the infidels. For more than a century after that, Jerusalem, the city that both Muslims and Christians considered holy, became the focus of bloody warfare by armies convinced that they were acting in the name of God—or Allah.

Thousands of the war's victims had nothing to do with the military contest. The first crusade to answer Pope Urban's call was led by Peter the Hermit, whose followers were mainly "simple pilgrims determined to brave every danger for love of the Holy Land." Joined by soldiers and adventurers, Peter's army became involved in battles from Hungary to Asia Minor. One group of Christian soldiers "stormed a fortified village inhabited by Greek peasants and, mistaking the Christian villagers for Saracens, the 'crusaders' butchered them with unheard-of refinements of cruelty."[8] In retaliation, as the pilgrims moved onward, a Turkish army attacked and slaughtered all but a few thousand pilgrims.[9]

Later crusades were conducted by professional soldiers, led by kings and nobles well-versed in the arts of war. For the most part these armies fought with no more than the normal degree of barbarity in that barbarous age; but when aroused by religious fanatics, soldiers killed with a frenzy that was frightening even to their own leaders. Having finally succeeded in routing the enemy from the Holy City of Jerusalem, the "soldiers of Christ" found only a small group of survivors, who surrendered to the Count of Toulouse when he promised that they would not be killed. As for the rest, one historian reports that "the massacre perpetrated by the Crusaders in Jerusalem has long been reckoned among the greatest crimes in history."[10] For two days, "they scoured the streets and alleys, gardens and courtyards, killing all who fell in their path . . . men, women, children and old people." Arab soldiers and civilians were not the only victims. The entire Jewish community of the city was slaughtered, "as many as the building would hold were shut up in the synagogue, which was then set afire."[11]

During the next century, despite the Crusaders' success in establishing Christian kingdoms in Jerusalem and a few other cities, Muslim armies had more than one opportunity to demonstrate their own savagery. Ultimately, as the Christian armies dwindled in size and strength, their ability to defend Jerusalem vanished. Sultan Saladin promised "to treat Jerusalem as the Christians dealt with it when they took it from the Moslems ninety-one years ago." In fact, he agreed to a negotiated surrender in which "more than three-fourths of the inhabitants were able to purchase their freedom," the remainder being taken as slaves.[12] Repeated attempts by Christian armies to retake Jerusalem failed, and enthusiasm for wresting the Holy Land from the infidels at any cost paled gradually. Before it was over, literally hundreds of thousands of men, women, and children had been butchered or enslaved, or had died of disease or exposure, all in the name of religion.

ANOTHER KIND OF BATTLE

Three centuries after the last Christian army had been driven from the Holy Land, the Church of Rome was stunned by a blow from another direction. In 1517 Martin Luther, a German Catholic priest and professor of theology, shocked the western world by the boldness of his attack on the laxity of church officials and the widespread abuse of the practice of granting "indulgences"—forgiveness of sin—principally to those who could pay liberally for such favors. Originally intended only as a means of initiating a discussion on the practices requiring correction, Luther's Ninety-five Theses brought such violent recrimination from the church hierarchy that he was led ultimately to challenge some of the most basic elements of papal doctrine. This caused his excommunication in 1521, which did not still the revolt.

Spreading first through German cities and states, the cause of reform was taken up by a French cleric, John Calvin, whose uncompromising view of God's will as the determining factor in all human activity dominated reform efforts for years to come. As other theologians—and princes—entered the debate, the movement known as the Protestant Reformation convulsed the Catholic world in a way that was far more significant than the earlier break between Rome and the Orthodox Eastern Church. Moreover, the impact of Protestantism was felt not only throughout Europe but also in the newly discovered American continents, where exploration and colonization proceeded even as the Reformation, spurred by a rising spirit of nationalism, continued to spread through western Europe.[13]

For the colonists who were later to found a new nation in North America, the events that had the greatest influence on both their political development and church–state relations occurred in England. The first ecumenical (world-wide) council called at Arles by Constantine in 314 A.D. was attended by three bishops and a priest from Britain. Nine hundred years later, and before the famous Magna Carta was drawn up, King John, "by the common consent of our barons" surrendered "to our Lord the Pope Innocent and his catholic successors, the whole realm of England and the whole realm of Ireland ... receiving back and holding these, as a feudal dependant, from God and the Roman Church."

The following year King John was obliged by these same barons to sign the Magna Carta. This historic agreement, concluded three centuries before the religious revolt initiated by Martin Luther, forced the king to guarantee the civil and political rights that form the basis of what the English came to think of as their constitution. Essentially a political document, the Carta (Charter) nevertheless contained a strong element of religious doctrine, asserting that the compact had been drawn "by God's inspiration and for the safety of our soul and those of our ancestors and heirs, for the honour of God and the exaltation of Holy Church," which was then the Church of Rome. Following this introductory statement of purpose, the Carta listed as its first condition "that the Church of England be free, and have her rights intact and her liberties uninjured." The document concluded with the explanation that the charter had been confirmed by "the lord the Pope Innocent III."[14]

From 1215 A.D., when the Magna Carta was signed, until the reign of Henry VIII, England's monarchs accepted and enforced Catholicism as the nation's religious creed. Henry himself was named by the pope as Defender of the Faith for his stirring rejection of Martin Luther's demands for reform. His disavowal of papal authority occurred after the pope refused to invalidate Henry's first marriage so that he could discard his wife (who had failed to provide him with a male heir) and marry again. England's break with Rome became official in 1533 when Henry, on his own authority, dissolved his marriage to Katherine of Aragon, married Anne Boleyn, and was excommunicated by Pope Clement VII. Henry did not, however, give up the title "Defender of the Faith." On the contrary, he saw to it that the Act of Supremacy passed by Parliament in 1534 not only confirmed the king's place as head of state but established his position as "supreme head on earth of the Church of England." To ensure nationwide acceptance of this unification of church and state, the law defined as treason any person's denial of the king's ecclesiastical supremacy.[15]

All through the two centuries of colonization that followed Henry's break with the papacy, Britain was torn by conflicts over the direction the Church of England should take. Henry had sought no important change in religious practice or theology, only freedom from domination by the pope. However, his successors were involved in a continuing struggle between those who desired a return to Catholicism and others who supported one or another variety of Protestantism. The fortunes of each faction changed according to the preference of the reigning king or queen, a preference demonstrated not only by appointments of favored public and church officials but also by direct action against religious opponents. Although methods used to defend the faith never reached the level of persecution accorded heretics by the Spanish Inquisition, or Protestant Huguenots by the French, imprisonment, execution—even burning at the stake—were penalties applied by both Catholic and Protestant rulers of England.[16]

On the political side, the struggle was between the Crown and Parliament, each determined to have the last word in determining national policy on all issues. Ultimately, Charles I was dethroned and beheaded, not simply because of religious differences with Parliament, but because of his uncompromising adherence to the doctrine of the divine right of kings. This concept he had inherited from his predecessor, James I, who once declared that "Kings are not only God's lieutenants upon earth . . . but even by God himself they are called gods . . . for that they exercise a manner or resemblance of divine power on earth."[17] Charles did his cause no good by marrying the Catholic daughter of the king of France at a time when the overwhelming majority of English people were Protestants. This act by the presumed Defender of the Faith was regarded by both Presbyterian and Puritan members of Parliament as further evidence of the king's disregard for constitutional principles. By 1642 it was clear that the contest for power could be resolved only by force of arms.

The civil war that shook the British Isles in the 1640s came more than a century after Henry VIII's rejection of papal authority. During that period religious reformers who were not satisfied with Henry's modest changes in church procedure, which included introduction of the first official Bible printed in English, had increased their influence in government as well as among the general population. Foremost among those urging greater attention to personal salvation, and less to pompous church ritual, were the Puritans, so called for their insistence on what many regarded as an extremist approach to purification of the church. Persecution of these Calvinistic religious radicals drove many into exile in Holland and Germany. Some abandoned Europe altogether and sought refuge in America. In England, as the reform movement continued to grow, Puritans took the lead in both parliamentary and military opposition to the king.

The conflict that ended with the execution of Charles I in 1649 was far more revolutionary in character than the so-called Glorious Revolution that occurred almost forty years later. The government established after Charles' death was a republic, devoid of both king and House of Lords. Royalty having been cast out, Parliament assumed all authority for designing the laws of the land—all, that is, except for decisions made by the military under Oliver Cromwell. Lord Protector of the Commonwealth was the title eventually assigned to Cromwell, but it might as well have been Defender of the Faith, for he represented the Puritan view that English Protestantism needed to be purified to eliminate all vestiges of Catholic theology and ceremony from the Church of England. Actually, Cromwell was more tolerant of political and religious differences than his more radical followers. That tolerance, however, did not extend to his opponents in Parliament or to Catholic rebels in Ireland. The former he dealt with by driving them out of the legislature; the latter were slaughtered unmercifully by Cromwell's armies. With the governing power firmly in the hands of the Protector, it is no wonder that the Commonwealth Parliament failed to resolve what one historian calls ''two of the most pressing problems of the seventeenth century: the constitutional problem of deciding where sovereignty lay, in the executive or legislature . . . and, secondly, the problem of whether or not religious toleration was compatible with political stability.''[18]

Reaction to the dictatorial government led by Cromwell until his death in 1658, and for a year afterward by his son, brought a movement for restoration of the monarchy. Intended as a means of restoring stability after two decades of military and civil turmoil, the short reign of the last two Stuart kings failed to settle either the political or the religious problem. Tentative resolution of both came a short time later when, in the Glorious (and bloodless) Revolution of 1688, James II was deposed and the Dutch husband of James's eldest daughter was offered the crown on the condition that he reject the absolutist theory of the monarchy and agree to a set of political reforms contained in a bill of rights drawn up by Parliament.

The British Bill of Rights of 1689 was hailed by most English people, at home and abroad, as the victory of representative government over monarchial despotism. This it certainly was. However, it also marked the ultimate triumph of Protestantism in England, the mother country of the 13 colonies already established in North America. For the guarantees of free speech, regular elections, and so forth, were accompanied, not by a simple declaration of religious freedom but by a denunciation of popery and adoption of Protestantism as the official state religion.

Setting a pattern for the later American Declaration of Independence, the British Bill of Rights was introduced by a long list of grievances. The first element of dissatisfaction was that "the late King James II . . . did endeavor to subvert and extirpate the Protestant religion and the laws and liberties of this kingdom." Suppression of Protestantism, the complaint continued, had been accomplished by persecution of the clergy, prosecution of dissidents in a court created specifically to deal with ecclesiastical matters, and the disarming of Protestants "at the same time when Papists were both armed and employed contrary to law." These conditions, the document stated, were to be remedied by the new king, William of Orange, "whom it hath pleased Almighty God to make the glorious instrument of delivering this kingdom from popery and arbitrary power." William also agreed to support all of the reforms listed in the Bill of Rights. Most of these had to do with political and civil rights, but included were provisions to declare the ecclesiastical court "and all courts of like nature" illegal, and to permit Protestants—not Catholics—to have "arms for their defense."[19]

By the close of the seventeenth century, Protestantism of one sort or another had been established as the dominant religion, not only in England but in the north German states, the Netherlands, and Scandinavia, while Catholicism retained the allegiance of most people and rulers in Poland, France, and the countries of southern Europe. Among Protestants, however, sharp differences in both theology and ritual had emerged. The range of reforms and views is seen in the development of sectarian organizations as far apart as the rigidly intolerant followers of John Calvin, who believed in the subordination of state to church, and the pacifist Quakers, who rejected not only the notion of a state church but the trappings and authority of the clergy as well. Despite the often bitter contests for predominance among Protestant sects, there was near unanimity in the belief that the word of God was the source of all natural law and the basis of good government. Thus, political decision making in every country was in the hands of men firmly attached to the established church, whatever church that might be.

Furthest removed from church-related centers of political power were groups like the Quakers and Mennonites. Even in Protestant countries, their rejection of the concept of a state church and refusal to take oaths or perform military service subjected them to greater discrimination than more moderate Protestant dissenters. William Penn, for example, was expelled from Oxford University for questioning the tenets of the religious establishment, and later was imprisoned in the Tower of London for his writings on behalf of the Society of Friends. The tract of American land given Penn by Charles II in 1681 was in recognition of the services that Penn's loyal, anti-Quaker father had rendered the Crown, rather than to advance Penn's scheme for establishing a refuge for religious dissenters.

The lot of non-Christians changed little during and immediately after the Reformation. With the expulsion of the Mohemmedan Moors from Spain and the Turks from southeastern Europe, those groups ceased to have any part in either the political or religious development of the West. Jews remained in almost all parts of Europe; but from the time of the Crusades, they had been subjected to persecution in most countries, some of which capped persecution with forced migration to other lands. Even where their presence was tolerated, Jews were not permitted to participate in any phase of the political process. Moreover, they were commonly forbidden to own land or to engage in any economic activity except small, non-professional businesses and the despised practice of moneylending.

This, in brief, is the background against which the opening of the American continents must be viewed. Given the close tie between church and state in the major colonizing nations, it comes as no surprise that religion played a significant part in the colonizing effort. Explorers from the Catholic nations of Spain, Portugal, and France carried their priests as well as their flags to lands from Florida on the east coast and California on the west down to the farthest tip of South America, and from Canada down the Mississippi to New Orleans.

Settlers in the 13 colonies that ultimately formed the United States came largely from the Protestant countries. Dutch, English, and Swedish explorers led the way to that part of the New World. Those who came to stay, rather than simply to open trading posts, brought a variety of religious views. Some were tied closely to the established churches of their homelands, and others were more concerned with economic security than with religious freedom. However, many immigrants belonged to sects that had experienced both social and legal discrimination, if not persecution; and it was these newcomers who assumed positions of leadership in the major English settlements. The emotionally charged history of church–state relations in those 13 colonies, and in the nation that evolved from them, is the subject of the following chapters.

2

Church and State
in Colonial America

Looking back at this country's growth from a coastal fringe of primitive settlements to a continentwide giant among the nations of the earth, Americans sometimes find it difficult to distinguish between the history and the mythology of that extraordinary development. One of the most persistent myths is the long-popular notion that the first settlers came to this continent to establish communities in which there would be complete religious freedom. It is true that the religious persecution practiced in most of the countries of Europe led many early immigrants to the New World, seeking refuge. Discrimination ranged from simple harassment or ostracism to arrest, trial, imprisonment, and either formal execution by government officials or murder by fanatical followers of doctrinaire clerics.

What is not true is that the founders of the first permanent settlement in Virginia, and the pioneers who established the Massachusetts Bay Colony—later called the "cradle of liberty"—proclaimed the principle of religious freedom for this new land. Quite the contrary: 9 of the 13 colonies had official, government-supported churches and sociopolitical establishments that discriminated against dissenters in much the same way as nonconformists were treated in Europe. A look at some of these New World settlements quickly dispels the myth that a major objective of the colonists was to establish a government free from religious ties and religious intolerance.

THE ROYAL GRANT OF AUTHORITY

Governments in all of the 13 colonies derived their authority from grants or charters from the mother country. In most cases, this meant a formal franchise from the reigning English king or queen. Most frequently, charters were issued to favored, loyal subjects of the Crown, not to religious or political malcontents. Many grants were to proprietors, who assumed full responsibility for every aspect of colonial operation: political, economic, and religious. Others went to commercial companies formed by individuals who were well connected with the royal family and whose principal interest was economic gain.

The first of these favors was bestowed by Henry VIII's daughter, Queen Elizabeth, "by Grace of God of England, Fraunce and Ireland Queene, defender of the faith," whose benevolence was extended to "our trustie and welbeloved servant Walter Ralegh, Esquire."[1] Expeditions organized by Walter Raleigh in 1585 and 1587 placed a handful of pioneers on Roanoke Island, off the coast of North Carolina. The first group abandoned the site after one torturous year, and the second contingent of 108 souls had vanished by the time a relief ship appeared in 1591.

In 1606, new interest in the region, named Virginia by Raleigh in honor of the "Virgin Queen" Elizabeth, produced a charter from King James I to eight "Gentlemen, and divers others of our loving subjects." The purpose of these gentlemen was "to deduce a colony of sundry of our people into that part of America commonly called Virginia, and other parts and Territories in America . . . which are not now actually possessed by any Christian Prince or People."[2] The "other parts" were identified as all the lands from 34 degrees to 45 degrees north latitude, an enormous tract that included the Atlantic shore from present-day Wilmington, North Carolina, to the mouth of the St. Croix River on the most northern point of the Maine coast. As clarified by subsequent charters in 1609 and 1620, these lands were to be divided between "Knights, Gentlemen, Merchants," and others—the representatives of two commercial companies operating out of London and Plymouth, England. The southern sector, centering about Virginia, was assigned to the London Company; New England was designated Plymouth Company territory.[3]

The first permanent English settlement in the New World was established by the London Company on May 14, 1607. In honor of the king, it was named Jamestown, located a short distance upstream from the mouth of the James River in present-day Virginia. The colony soon gained a revised charter, which, a century and a half later, gave the colonists one of their most potent arguments against continued English rule. In extending greater management powers to the London Company, the king declared that his subjects in the Virginia colony and "their children and posterity" would have all the rights and liberties of Englishmen, "as if they had been abiding and born within this our realm of England."[4]

In the northern territory assigned to the Plymouth Company, the first landing was made, not, as most Americans believe, by the Pilgrims at Plymouth, Massachusetts, but by a group under the leadership of George Popham, who put ashore at the mouth of the Kennebec River in Maine on August 19, 1607.[5] Like the first attempt to plant a colony on Roanoke Island, Popham's effort failed: he and his companions returned to England after only a year on American soil.

In 1609, permission to "streach out the Bounds of our Dominions" in present-day New England was granted by King James I to Sir Ferdinand Gorges and "Certain Knights, Gentlemen Adventurers and divers other Persons of Quality."[6] This favored group still did not include the first contingent of English citizens to brave the wilds of Massachusetts. That hardy band, known to history as the Pilgrims, were actually squatters in a region not assigned to them. In 1620 the Pilgrims received a grant of land from the London South Virginia Company. Instead, they changed their minds and headed for New England, which was under the jurisdiction of the Plymouth Company. The famous Mayflower Compact was an agreement, not with the Crown or the Plymouth Company, but among the Pilgrims themselves. They jointly pledged to enact "such just and equal Laws, Ordinances, Acts, Constitutions, and Officers . . . as shall be thought most meet and convenient for the general Good of the Colony."[7] The document was typical of such early agreements in that it was signed only by the leading male members of the colony. Nine years later, the area was first designated the Massachusetts Bay Colony by royal charter from Charles I to the Plymouth Company, as before, rather than to the settlers. Company officers were given full authority to govern an enormous tract of land, extending from 40 degrees to 48 degrees north latitude—roughly from midway up the New Jersey coast to the Gaspé Peninsula in eastern Canada.[8]

In between Massachusetts and Virginia, Dutch and Swedish explorers preceded the British in many places. New York and parts of New Jersey were opened in 1613 by Dutch traders who governed the Hudson River valley under charter from the government of the Netherlands. The Dutch West India Company ran this private preserve as a strictly commercial enterprise, showing little concern for the views of its settlers until the latter petitioned the Lords States-General of the United Netherlands to grant them "suitable burgher government, such as their High Mightinesses shall consider adapted to this province, and resembling somewhat the government of our Fatherland." All this came to nought in 1663, when the English took the entire region from the Dutch by force. The following year, a royal grant gave to the Duke of York all the land between the west bank of the Connecticut River and the east bank of Delaware Bay.[9] To no one's surprise, the duke renamed the northern portion, calling it New York. He gave the section south of what had been the Dutch town of New Amsterdam to Lord John Berkeley and Sir George Carteret. For thirty-eight years, Berkeley and Carteret administered their proprietary colony, New Jersey, under concessions to the settlers, after which the province was returned to the Crown.[10]

A similar pattern of grants to members of the British peerage led to the formation of colonies in Maryland and the Carolinas. In 1632, a charter for Maryland was issued by Charles I to Caecilius (Cecil) Calvert, Lord Baltimore.[11] Later, the two Carolinas were carved out of land originally granted to Sir Walter Raleigh but assigned in 1630 by Charles I to his attorney general, Sir Robert Heath. When Heath failed to develop the area as planned, his grant was terminated and a new charter was issued by Charles II to a group of nobles led by the Earl of Clarendon and Duke of Albemarle.[12]

Even Pennsylvania, justly known as a haven for religious dissidents, was given by Charles II to William Penn in 1681 to discharge a financial obligation owed by the Crown to Penn's father, an admiral with long and distinguished service in the British navy. The Pennsylvania charter made no reference to the monetary debt, but declared that the grant was made with "regard to the Memorie and Meritts of his [William Penn's] late Father. . . . and perticulerly to his Conduct, Courage and Discretion . . . in that Signall Battell and Victorie fought against the Dutch Fleete."[13]

Exceptions to the usual procedure of making New World grants to Court favorites can be found in colonies that were formed by breaking off from those with early charters. Connecticut and Rhode Island, for example, were organized as separate colonies after migrants from Massachusetts appealed to England for recognition of the need for local governments. In the case of Rhode Island, the initial patent for Providence Plantations was authorized by an act of Parliament during the Cromwell Protectorate. Later the grant was confirmed by royal charter from Charles II, after the monarchy had been restored.[14]

Connecticut residents also organized their own local governments, provisionally under authority from the Massachusetts General Court, as the legislature was called. Subsequently, a charter was granted by Charles II

in recognition of the valiant efforts of John Winthrop and others in opening this region, "a considerable Enlargement and Addition of Our Dominions and Interest there." In effect, the Crown confirmed the Fundamental Orders of Connecticut, a compact written by the town officials of
Windsor, Hartford, and Wethersfield and signed January 14, 1639.[15]
Thanks to these organizing initiatives on the part of the settlers, Connecticut and Rhode Island were the only colonies permitted by the Crown to
elect their own governors.

Like Connecticut and Rhode Island, New Hampshire was first
populated by settlers from Massachusetts. In 1629, Charles I approved an
agreement between the Plymouth Company's Council for New England
and Captain John Meson of London, to develop and govern an area along
the coast north of Massachusetts. The colony was never formally chartered by the Crown, but in 1679 Charles II appointed a president and
council to govern the "tract of land called The Province of New-
Hampshire."[16]

Delaware (named after the first royal Virginia governor, Baron De
La Warr) was one of the colonies born of assignment by its first proprietor to someone else. Initially, the area was included in the grant to
the Duke of York. It was ceded by the Duke to William Penn in 1682 to
provide Pennsylvania with access to the Atlantic Ocean. The colony was
unique, recognition of its right to function as a separate province having
been obtained from the proprietor rather than from the British Crown.
In 1701 William Penn made good on an earlier promise to give the
residents of the counties of "New-Castle, Kent and Sussex, upon
Delaware" a charter, which entitled them to an elected assembly and
the same guarantees of freedom accorded to the people of Pennsylvania.[17]

Establishment of the last of the 13 English colonies came in 1732,
when George II issued a charter to "John, lord-viscount Purcival of our
kingdom of Ireland," along with 19 "gentlemen and such other persons
as shall be elected" in accordance with the grant. One of these gentlemen
was James Oglethorpe, whose colonial purposes were unlike those of any
other explorer, proprietor, or commercial company interested in the New
World. As the charter acknowledged, Georgia was intended to "extend
our fatherly compassion even to the meanest of our subjects" and to provide an opportunity for the poor of England to make a new start in a new
land. Administration of the colony by Oglethorpe's company continued
until 1752, when a provincial government was established with the traditional royal governor and council.[18]

THE AMERICAN INHERITANCE

In their introductory history courses nowadays, young people in the United States learn about the partnership between the Catholic church and the armies of Spanish, Portuguese, and French kings, conquering American lands by force of arms. Students remember that the church presumed to divide the New World between two of the major contenders for its riches. A year after Columbus landed on the Caribbean island of San Salvador (modern Watling Island), Pope Alexander VI drew a line "from the Arctic pole to the Antarctic pole," giving Portugal the South American bulge containing Brazil and adjacent lands east of the line, and assigning to Spain everything farther west.[19] Maybe a few high school graduates still recall that, as a matter of policy, Spain forbade colonization by heretics or non-Christians.

If this mental picture of Catholic colonization seems oversimplified, it is no more so than the common perception that the Protestant invasion of North America was an effort to establish communities completely free of religious bias. Quite the reverse was true. For a century and a half, settlers in the British colonies designed and operated local governments in which participation was limited to God-fearing Christians—even, in some settlements, to members of a particular Protestant church. This was entirely consistent with the political history of the mother country and of all the countries of Europe. With the exception of the Georgia charter, every authorization for the exploration and settlement of land in the New World included in its statement of objectives the desire to advance the cause of Christianity.

Given this background, it is not surprising that the transplanted tie between church and state took root in most of the English colonies. If such a tradition has left no firm impression on the modern generation, perhaps it is because there was no *one* established church in the colonies, as in England, and no central authority in North America to enforce ecclesiastical decisions on the entire colonial population, as the monarchy did in England. Nevertheless, competition for predominance among religious sects was far less violent in the colonies than in England, where each succeeding monarch defined church policy differently and most treated heretics unmercifully. Throughout these tumultuous 155 years, the English church, as well as the government, was a battleground on which Catholics fought Protestants and strict Puritan moralists vied with more moderate Protestant groups for control of both ecclesiastical and political affairs.

In the process, separate churches were established to reflect the different Protestant approaches to religious observance. The Episcopal church, directed by a central episcopate, disavowed papal authority but retained much of the pomp and ceremony of Catholicism. Presbyterians provided for administration of church affairs by presbyteries made up of preachers and nonpreaching elders elected by the parishioners. The Congregational church of the Puritans, most dogmatic of the Protestant sects in religious doctrine, was even more decentralized. Denying the need for bishops or presbyteries, each Puritan congregation selected its own leaders and ran its own affairs, acknowledging only Christ as the one common leader of all. The distinguishing characteristic of the Baptists was the rite of washing away sin by immersion, as Jesus had experienced at the hands of John.[20] Methodism—to live and worship by John Wesley's "rule and method"—was a later development, carried abroad by itinerant evangelists. Least concerned with the trappings of organized religion was the Society of Friends, dubbed Quakers by Church of England Protestants who gibed at the Friends' "trembling at the word of the Lord." Having dispensed with churchly rites, symbols, and ordained ministers, Friends relied on the "inner light" of each individual to establish union with God.[21]

The American colonies reacted in a variety of ways to the shifting fortunes of the several Protestant and Catholic churches in England, but they did not follow the mother country's practice of replacing an established religious hierarchy with one of a different persuasion. Colonists were influenced by the diversity of beliefs and practices they had inherited, largely from England but also, to an important extent, from countries on the European mainland. Lutherans from the Netherlands and Sweden, for example, were among the earliest settlers in the middle colonies from New York to Maryland. Dutch and German Mennonites, Scotch-Irish Presbyterians, French immigrants (both Catholic and Huguenot Protestants), and many others added to the melting-pot area between Puritan New England and the southern colonies where Britain's established church gained an early foothold.

COLONIAL GOVERMNENT: FOR GOD-FEARING CHRISTIANS ONLY

Not only was Virginia the initial testing ground for English settlers, it led the other colonies in other important respects also. The first permanent settlement dates from May 13, 1607, when a group sponsored by the London Company arrived. Government of this tiny community was the responsibility of a council of six, including the indefatigable John Smith. Full control was assumed by the colony's first governor, Baron De La Warr, but the later political structure of the province began to take shape in 1624 when the company charter was canceled and Virginia became the first royal colony. Although this suggests the imposition of tight dictatorial supervision, another first was achieved by royal acceptance of an elected legislature—the House of Burgesses—establishing the principle of self-rule. Finally, the Virginia colony was the first to adopt the Church of England as the established church of the province.[22]

Virginia's colonial charters, like most others, indicated the advancement of Christianity as a major goal of colonization. It was understood that the particular cause to be advanced was that of the Church of England. However, occasionally the terms of a grant were more specific. The second (1609) charter of Virginia, for example, concluded with this outright ban against the intrusion of Catholics:

> Because the principal Effect which we can desire or expect of this Action is the Conversion and Reduction of the People in those Parts unto the true Worship of God and Christian Religion, in which Respect we should be loath that any person should be permitted to pass that we suspected to affect the Superstitions of the Church of Rome, we do hereby Declare, that it is our Will and Pleasure that none be permitted to pass in any Voyage from Time to Time to be made into the said Country, but such as first shall have taken the Oath of Supremacy.[23]

This Oath of Supremacy acknowledged the English monarch as both chief of state and head of the Church of England.

Notwithstanding Virginia's long history of rule by an aristocracy loyal to both the Crown and the Anglican church, over the years the land attracted a variety of dissidents including Scottish Presbyterians, Welsh Baptists, German Lutherans, French Huguenots, and, before William Penn opened his sanctuary, English Quakers. All contributed to the growth of a more liberal view of self-government and, ultimately, to the revolutionary fervor that made Virginia one of the leaders in the struggle for independence.

Neighboring Maryland was different. Envisioned as a separate colony by Sir George Calvert, the first Lord Baltimore (who was also a

Catholic member of the royal commission responsible for governing Virginia), the plan was bitterly opposed by those Virginians who "made no distinction between an English adherent of the Church of Rome and an out-and-out enemy."[24] King Charles' sympathy with Calvert led him to issue the requested charter in 1632; but by that time George Calvert had died, leaving the project in the hands of his son Cecil. The Maryland charter vested almost unlimited authority in the proprietor, but provided also for an elected assembly of freemen "for the framing of laws."[25] In a remarkably short time the assembly drew up an Act for the Liberties of the People, which declared that "all the Inhabitants of this Province being Christians (Slaves excepted) Shall have and enjoy all such rights, liberties, immunities, priviledges and free customs within this Province as any naturall born subject of England."[26] This act, a brief two-paragraph statement of principle, was approved in 1639—two years before enactment of the Massachusetts Body of Liberties. It anticipated by more than a century the revolutionary demand for recognition of colonists' rights as Englishmen.

Equality of treatment for Catholics did not set well with many of Maryland's Protestant settlers, any more than it did with their Virginia neighbors. The colony experienced constant friction and periodic changes in the laws respecting religious freedom, as one side or another prevailed. Often this depended on conditions in England and Lord Baltimore's standing with the home government. The Puritan Revolution, which culminated in the execution of Charles I in 1639, destroyed Lord Baltimore's base of support. That same year Maryland passed an Act Concerning Religion, which was intended to guarantee full rights for both Protestants and Catholics. In the process, this law narrowed religious freedom to those who believed in the divinity of Jesus and made all others subject to death if they denied this principle or otherwise blasphemed the one true God.[27] When the number and influence of Puritan settlers increased, the Act Concerning Religion was repealed. Lord Baltimore, out of favor in England, lost his proprietorship. Although the colony was restored to the Calverts in 1688, the final triumph of Protestantism, which brought William of Orange to the British throne, resulted also in the conversion of Maryland to a royal colony with the Church of England ensconced as its established church. Still another restoration of the proprietorship, after the turn of the century, brought little change in the character of the provincial government or the privileged position of the Anglican church. However, discriminatory religious treatment added fuel to the fires ignited during the 1760s and 1770s by British tax and trade policies.

Farther south, the breakup of the original Virginia territory was influenced more by the vastness of that grant than by religious conflict. When a charter for Carolina was issued by Charles II to a group of his favorites, it was for "parts of America not yet cultivated or planted and only inhabitated by some barbarous people, who have no knowledge of Almighty God."[28] The first Carolina constitution was drafted in 1669, before the separation of that province into north and south. This remarkable document was framed by the English philosopher John Locke, whose writings later exerted a powerful influence on the leaders of the American Revolution. Though never fully adopted, Locke's constitution reveals the importance of religion in New World politics. His detailed prescription for colonial government provided not only an executive and legislative structure but a host of rules for relationships among the various segments of society. Avoiding the concept of an established church, Locke's constitution nevertheless reflected many of the concerns of officials throughout the English colonies. No fewer than 16 of the 120 articles dealt with religion. In one section of the constitution Locke made these points:

- "No man shall be permitted to be a freeman of Carolina, or to have any estate or habitation within it, that doth not acknowledge a God; and that God is publicly and solemnly to be worshipped."
- "Jews, heathens and other dissenters," including native Indians, are to be converted, not abused because of their non-Christian ways.
- The form of oath taken in the presence of a government official must be prescribed by the church.
- Only church members shall have "any benefit or protection of the law, or be capable of any place of profit or honor."
- All churches should be free from attack or abuse, but the church should not be used to attack the government or government policy.[29]

The author of this document was far more tolerant than the colonial governors and local committees who designed the laws under which the colonists would live. Equality of treatment for all churches and all Christians, for example, was not widely accepted or practiced. Nor was there general aceptance of Locke's assumption that even slaves were entitled to church membership (but not freedom). On the other hand, most settlements agreed with his stand that if a group failed to meet the test of what constituted a Christian church, their assemblies "shall not be esteemed as churches, but unlawful meetings, and be punished as other riots."

Notwithstanding Locke's cautious introductory statement that the fundamental law he proposed would "avoid erecting a numerous democracy," his notions of free expression, which were generally within the bounds of Christian belief, did not take root in colonial society. In fact, even those portions of his system that were adopted provisionally were abandoned when the Carolina proprietors abrogated the constitution in 1693, only 24 years after it had been written.[30] In many colonies the religious tolerance recommended by Locke was applied more effectively than in the Carolinas. This was true of Rhode Island, most of the middle colonies, and, to a lesser extent, the southernmost colony of Georgia.

Last to be established, the Georgia proprietorship was returned to the Crown after only 20 years of inefficient administration by the proprietors' company representatives, who acted without benefit of any representative assembly. Nevertheless, insofar as religion was concerned, all groups except Catholics were tolerated. Even a party of 42 Jews found homes in Savannah and "shamed the Christians by the exemplary quality of their lives."[31] Although the Church of England was established by Georgia law in 1758, neither membership nor attendance was enforced. Moreover, some non-Anglican churches were granted glebes (land for church use) by the royal government.

Pennsylvania and Delaware, both governed under laws established by William Penn, led the central states in adopting the principle of religious freedom. This does not mean that Penn intended to separate religion from politics. On the contrary, despite his Quaker rejection of an established (state) church, Penn's 1682 Frame of Government of Pennsylvania, opened with a lengthy preface relating man-made law to the word of God. Having established the religious basis of the rules of society, he concluded: "This settles the divine right of government.... So that government seems to me a part of religion itself."[32] Essentially an essay on the common qualities of mankind and government, the principal political conclusion expressed in this preface was that—be it monarchy, aristocracy, or democracy—"any government is free to the people under it (whatever be the frame) where the laws rule, and the people are a party to those laws." On this basis Penn constructed the operational framework of Pennsylvania's government, which consisted of a governor (himself or his designee), a legislative council elected by the freemen of the province, a general assembly with limited powers, and a system of courts. Refusing to accept the common concept of one form of Christianity as superior to all others, he provided only that voters and officeholders "shall be such as profess faith in Jesus Christ, and that are not convicted of ill fame, or unsober and dishonest conversation, and that are of twenty-one years of age, at least." The equally important Pennsylvania Charter of Privileges, issued by Penn in 1701, gave full legislative responsibility to the general assembly while continuing the freedom of religious belief expressed in his earlier Frame of Government.[33]

Delaware came directly under Penn's supervision in 1682 when the Duke of York ceded him the territory. Therefore, Delaware's form of government was basically the same as that designed for Pennsylvania. This meant a significant element of self-government and a degree of religious liberty matched only by that offered the residents of Rhode Island. Although this did not entirely satisfy the settlers in Delaware, most of whom were members of the Church of England, no established church ever dominated that colony. The "Christians only" rule for officeholders was not quite so broad as it would appear: the oath of office required candidates to deny papal authority, which in effect debarred Catholics from public service. In time, new waves of immigrants and the missionary efforts of non-Anglican ministers brought increasing numbers of Methodists and Presbyterians, the latter group strengthened by many Scotch-Irish among the new arrivals.[34]

New Jersey never was part of Penn's royal proprietorship, but many Quaker colonists settled in the territory. Just as important to the colony's development were Puritans from New England and Dutch settlers (who had explored and settled from New York to Maryland, challenged early on only by the Swedes). Under concessions from its proprietors, self-government became the rule in New Jersey. Most towns permitted participation by freemen of any denomination. A subproprietorship purchased by Quakers, in what they called "the Province of West New Jersey in America," went even further, providing for annual elections by secret ballot and placing "almost unlimited political power in an assembly elected by all the proprietors, freeholders and inhabitants." On the other hand, Puritan communities followed the New England tradition, allowing only to members of the Congregational church the privilege of participating in local government, a practice that did not square with the intent of the original proprietors whose concessions guaranteed freedom of religion to all. When the proprietorship was terminated in 1703, a royal governor was installed with authority to appoint all important officials, and the power of the provincial legislature was curtailed. However, the general assembly continued to function until the time of the Revolution.[35]

As in New Jersey, the colonial population of New York included a variety of nationalities and religious sects. New York perhaps had the strongest Dutch influence, having been populated and controlled by Dutch patroons for over 30 years before being subjugated by the English. While still in Dutch hands, the area attracted many religious dissidents, because the Netherlands sheltered many such groups—such as the Pilgrims, whose flight from English persecution took them to Holland before they set out for America on the Mayflower. As a result, although the Dutch West India Company favored the Reformed church, Puritans, Lutherans, Quakers, and even a few Jews found a haven in this part of the New World.

New Netherlands became New York with relatively little change in either religious or political practice. Freemen of various faiths participated in local councils permitted under the Duke of York's proprietorship. However, unlike the Dutch West India Company and the English companies that held governing rights to most of New England, the Duke of York was reluctant to see laws and policies for the entire colony decided by an elected legislature. Finally in 1683 he agreed to the formation of a provincial assembly, mostly so as to make the colony self-supporting. To the Duke's dismay, the focus of the first General Assembly was not on revenues but on colonists' rights. The formulation of a Charter of Libertyes and Priviledges, very like that devised by the Massachusetts legislature some 40 years earlier, so enraged the Duke that he ordered his New York governor to repeal it immediately. When the Duke became King James II, in 1685, he canceled the colony's charter. By then, turmoil in England created by James' Catholicism had reduced his effectiveness in the colonies. When, after only three years, his reign ended, New York—and most other colonies as well—felt their constitutional rights and freedoms to be more secure.[36]

In sharp contrast to the religious permissiveness of some colonial governments, those dominated by New England Puritans were rigidly intolerant. Strongest and most tenacious in their effort to define and enforce standards of morality were the Congregational churches of Massachusetts and Connecticut. Although the very nature of their organization ruled out the kind of central authority that directed the affairs of the Church of England, there was a unifying force in the harsh Puritan sense of right and wrong, of good and evil. Massachusetts was the center of Congregationalism in the colonies, the earliest settlements being governed by men whose faith was as firm as their morals were strict. To ensure continuation of such leadership, public office was limited to freemen who were "21 years of age, and possessed of local town endorsement, sober, peaceful and orthodox in religion, and with a ratable estate of £20."[37] A further restriction was imposed by the Charter of 1629, which provided that the colony be administered by a governor, deputy governor, and 18 assistants "elected and chosen out of the Freemen of the [Plymouth] Company," the corporate body in England to which colonizing rights had been granted.[38] By agreement (but of doubtful legality), the company moved the seat of government from England to Massachusetts, where for all practical purposes it remained thereafter.[39]

One effect of the move was to stimulate an interest in local government by colonists "who were not of the churches" and who "crossed the ocean reather to better their worldly condition than for religious reasons." However, the Puritan leadership was not about to relinquish control to those who, as one churchman put it, "go and come chiefly for the matter of profit" in contrast to the founders who "came to abide here, and to plant the gospel." The Puritans retained administrative authority by convincing the freemen of the province to place all lawmaking power in the hands of their elected governor and assistants and to approve a rule "that for time to come no man shall be admitted to the freedom of this body politic but such as are members of some of the churches within the limits of the same." One historian sums up the impact of this early legislation as follows:

> The restriction of political rights thus inaugurated remained in force until after the English Restoration [in 1689], and did much from the very beginning to stiffen the social life and atmosphere of Massachusetts into that rigid theocratic mould which characterized it throughout the seventeenth century. Hereafter there might be contests between freemen and magistrates, between General Court and Assistants; but they would be contests within the bosom of the church, and the church members as a class would be bound together against outsiders by their interest in preserving their monopoly of political power. Thus the leaders, by sharing a portion of their power with the element in the population in which they had the greatest confidence, solidified their own position and laid the basis for a peculiar type of religious aristocracy.[40]

In 1641, without jeopardizing its theocratic powers, the provincial legislature approved a Body of Liberties that set forth explicit protections to be afforded individuals in relationship to government. Remarkable for its detailed exposition of political philosophy and legal procedures, the document stressed personal protections first and foremost. Many articles opened with the phrase "No man shall be compelled [restrained, or punished]." As in the Mayflower Compact, the liberties were devised by men and for men. The place of women can be appreciated from the associations made in Article 14:

> Any Conveyance or Alienation of land or other estaite what so ever, made by any woman that is married, any childe under age, Ideott, or distracted person, shall be good if it be passed and ratified by the consent of a generall Court.

Only 2 other articles (out of 98) dealt with the Liberties of Women: these referred to a wife's entitlement to a share in her deceased husband's estate, and to her right to be "free from bodilie correction or stripes by her husband unless it be in his owne defence upon her assault." By comparison, Liberties of Children were defined in four articles, Liberties of Forreiners and Strangers in three, and Liberties of Bruit Creatures in two.

Religious influence is evident in every section of the Body of Liberties (which was drafted by Nathaniel Ward, an English minister who later became pastor of the Congregational church in Ipswich, Massachusetts). The tie between church and state, though limited, is suggested by the initial assertion that the plan was based on "humanitie, Civilitie, and Christianitie." Another provision noted that "Civill Authoritie hath power and libertie to see the peace, ordinances and Rules of Christ observed in every church according to his word, so it be done in a Civill and not in an Ecclesiastical way." Rules for capital punishment called for the death penalty for worship of "any god but the lord god" and for "any man or woeman" found to be a witch. The concluding pages dealt with "the Liberties the Lord Jesus hath given to the Churches." Declaring that this section was not intended to be "in the exact form of Laws or Statutes," the authors nevertheless called upon "all that are and shall be in Authoritie to consider them as laws, and not to faile to inflict condigne and proportionable punishments upon every man impartiallie that shall infringe or violate any of them."[41]

Witchery was a punishable offense in many colonies, as it was in England. Even the tolerant Quaker state of Pennsylvania is known to have brought at least two persons to trial on such a charge. However, only in Massachusetts was there so frenzied an outbreak of trials and executions as occurred in Salem in 1692, when 125 people were charged with witchcraft and 20 of them—13 women and 7 men—were put to death. All but one had pleaded innocent. Nineteen of those executed were hanged. The twentieth was executed by pressing, described in one record as "a barbarous practice sanctioned by English law for those who refused to plead."[42]

As in Massachusetts, personal freedom within the constraints of Puritan morality characterized the early governments of Connecticut and New Hampshire. Both were settled by a combination of migrants from Massachusetts and newcomers from Europe. The political framework in both colonies was designed and administered largely by Puritan leaders.[43] Resistance to Puritan domination was stronger in New Hampshire, but pressure from Massachusetts (with claims to New Hampshire territory) kept the "desparately wicked" opponents of Puritan influence at bay. Not until 1679 was New Hampshire declared a separate royal colony with its own provincial government.[44]

At a much earlier date, Connecticut established itself as a separate entity under the domination of Puritan migrants from Massachusetts. Even before the Bay Colony enacted its Body of Liberties, Connecticut produced a document that is celebrated today on every Connecticut license plate bearing the slogan "Constitution State." In January 1639, the followers of Reverend Thomas Hooker adopted what can accurately be described as the first written constitution in the history of the United States. Though it contained no bill of rights, the Fundamental Orders of Connecticut established a framework of government modeled on the Puritan sense of order and morality. Its tone was set by the introduction, which stated that "where a people are gathered togather, the word of God requires that to mayntayne the peace and union of such a people there should be an orderly and decent Gouvernment established according to God." In that spirit, the founders declared their purpose "to mayntayne and presearve the liberty and purity of the gospell of our Lord Jesus . . . also the disciplyne of the Churches which . . . is now practised amongst us." In civil affairs, the Fundamental Orders provided that all public officers, including a governor and members of the legislature, were to be elected annually under these simple rules: only freemen admitted by a majority of the townsmen of their community could vote for governor and other executive officers; all admitted inhabitants could vote for deputies to the legislature; all voters were required to take an "oath of Fidellity" to the province; no one could be elected to any office except "a Freeman of this Commonwelth"; and, in addition, "the Governor [must] be always a member of some approved congregation."[45]

Many of the Puritans who left Massachusetts for Connecticut and New Hampshire did so because of their differences with the ruling elite in the Bay colony. Those who chose Rhode Island as their sanctuary had been so strident in their criticism of Massachusetts Puritanism that they were invited to leave or face prosecution for heresy.

First among these expatriates was Roger Williams, a Congregational minister. His views on the distinction between ecclesiastic and civil authorities so enraged church leaders that he was banished from Massachusetts by act of legislature, and a ship's captain was ordered to take him back to England. Forewarned of this plan, Williams fled to Rhode Island, where he founded the town of Providence. In 1643 he obtained from Parliament "a free and absolute Charter of incorporation" for the Providence Plantations. Unusually brief for such a document, the charter granted the inhabitants of the Plantations "full Power and Authority to rule themselves." Even the usual caution that provincial laws "be conformable to the Laws of England" was eased by the phrase "so far as the Nature and Constitution of the place will permit."[46]

On this foundation, Rhode Island proceeded to organize what it characterized as a "democratical" government, a phrase abhorred by most American leaders until long after the Revolution. Although falling short of modern standards of democracy by virtue of its completely male electorate, Rhode Island was nevertheless far less restrictive in its voting qualifications than any of its neighbors. Its tolerance of diverse religious groups caused it to be referred to by Massachusetts Puritans as Rogues' Island. Yet the dissident Congregationalists, Quakers, and Anabaptists who populated the colony were as faithful to their religious beliefs as were members of the more acceptable churches in other provinces. Given the force of religion in colonial society, it is remarkable that any province under a European monarch could establish, as Rhode Island did, what one historian refers to as "the first secular state of modern times."[47]

THE GREAT AWAKENING

The "excess of freedom" permitted in Rhode Island was only one evidence of what strict churchmen regarded as a general decline in morality. As early as 1628, officials in Plymouth, Massachusetts, took it upon themselves to capture and deport the leader of a neighboring community who tolerated drunkenness and licentious revelry around a maypole.[48] In New England, even the opening of an Episcopal church was regarded as a sacrilege: Cotton Mather warned against "those unwarrantable Ceremonies which the Land of Our Fathers' Sepulchres has been defiled with."[49] Similarly, an observer of the Connecticut scene deplored the "decline as to the life and power of godliness . . . a general ease and security in sin."[50] Complaints of this kind were repeated in other colonies, particularly where ministers were few and far between and frontier life forced settlers to concentrate on the harsh problems of daily existence. Even among the more educated members of society, religious beliefs faced growing competition from emerging concepts of "science, reason, and nature—the trinity of the oncoming Enlightenment."[51]

In reaction to this supposed moral decline, ministers endeavored to convince backsliders of the need to be saved by rededication to the principles and practices of Christianity. Led by the emotional entreaties of charismatic preachers, the colonies experienced a revival of religious fervor in the 1730s and 1740s that was unmatched in any other period of American history. The first of these awakeners was Jonathan Edwards, a Yale graduate whose sermons in Northampton, Massachusetts, in 1734 initiated the first wave of religious enthusiasm among New Englanders. Other evangelists followed, attacking the secular trend of the early eighteenth century and those ministers tolerant of the trend. The persuasive powers of Edwards, Gilbert Tennent, George Whitefield, and others even caught up skeptics in the emotional surge. The power of these speakers is illustrated by this report of an incident involving one of the leading scientists and intellectuals of the revolutionary age:

> Benjamin Franklin, although not one to be taken in by the antics of a religious pitchman, out of curiosity once attended a sermon by a famous revivalist in favor of a cause which Franklin disapproved. Having resolved in advance to contribute nothing to that cause, when the sermon was over he emptied the gold and silver as well as the coppers from his pockets into the collection plate.[52]

Challenged on all sides, from New England to Georgia, traditionalists in the established churches joined with rationalists to contain the effects of the evangelists. By 1745 the fervor of the Great Awakening had subsided, but it left its mark in the divisiveness that split congregations in all sects and in the creation of an evangelist tradition that has reappeared at intervals throughout U.S. history. Whether or not the Great Awakening had any bearing on the subsequent revolt against England is a matter of conjecture, although one historian believes it awakened "the spirit of American democracy."[53]

3

Impact of the Revolution

For 150 years the colonies grew and prospered as part of the expanding British Empire. Although loosely controlled by their allegiance to the Crown and by the executive power of a proprietor or governor designated by the British monarch, they were left largely to their own devices insofar as day-to-day affairs were concerned. Decision making in these matters was in the hands of local or colonial assemblies, elected, in most cases, by the landowners of the region. Larger issues, such as foreign trade and defense, remained under the control of the Crown and Parliament.

Until the 1760s, England's colonial policies generated no separatist sentiment: the interests of the colonies were closely tied to those of the mother country in its contest with the rival empires of France and Spain. That rivalry frequently erupted into open warfare; and every time England became embroiled in a power struggle, the contest spilled over into the New World. "King William's War" was what the colonists called the European War of the League of Augsburg, in which England joined the Netherlands and the German states in an effort to curb French ambitions on the continent. Spanning the decade from 1688 to 1697, that conflict reoccurred only a few years later as the War of the Spanish Succession, or "Queen Anne's War," as the colonists referred to it, and continued from 1701 to 1713. Again in 1740, France was the enemy when the nine-year War of the Austrian Succession broke out; it was fought in America as King George's War. Finally, Britain's Seven Years' War with France concluded what Americans called the French and Indian Wars, a bitter struggle that plagued American settlements from 1756 to 1763.

In each of these conflicts the colonies were subjected to repeated attacks along their northern and western borders, where French troops combined with Indian tribes in an attempt to break Britain's hold on the continent. The ultimate British victory in the French and Indian Wars removed France from Canada; but the financial drain of the war, and irritations arising from the quartering of English troops in colonial cities, had much to do with the worsening of relations between the colonies and England. Having contributed heavily to their own defense with locally raised militia, the colonists did not take kindly to the continued presence of British troops after the war was over. They were even more reluctant to accept the burden of taxation that England felt was only fair to apply to colonial trade and business activities. As the pressure for enforcement of royal decrees and parliamentary acts increased, colonial leaders began to question the legal foundation of British actions, delving into detailed analyses of the world's political systems as well as England's constitutional history. The king's own advocate general for Massachusetts Bay actually abandoned his post to contest the legality of the Writs of Assistance, which authorized customs officers to search homes and businesses for goods on which taxes had not been paid. This action by Boston attorney James Otis gave courage to others in resisting British authority and stirred a new kind of patriotism throughout the colonies. What was new was the use of the term "patriot" to mean a person whose first loyalty was to the colonies, rather than to the Crown.[1]

Subsequent complaints addressed to the king continued to stress the colonists' right to the same protections they would have if they resided in England. Acts of Parliament aimed specifically at activities in the colonies gave American settlers a common grievance and fostered a unity of purpose that grew firmer with each repressive action by British authorities. As friction mounted throughout the 1760s and early 1770s, the need for a common front was pressed by articulate and influential Americans, from John and Samuel Adams in Massachusetts to Patrick Henry and Richard Henry Lee in Virginia.

CONTRIBUTIONS OF THE CLERGY

From the earliest rumblings of revolt to the Declaration of Independence, clergymen in the colonies were embroiled in the controversy over the reasonableness of British rule, the need or desirability of independence, and the nature of the government that would take over the responsibilities of king and parliament. The closeness of church and state in almost every colonial community made this involvement inevitable. Furthermore, the most renowned American ministers of the time were among the best educated citizens and were acknowledged leaders of their communities. If their sermons did not deal directly with such inflammatory issues as the Writs of Assistance or the Stamp Tax, they often addressed the broader questions of the purpose of government and the rights of the people. Congregationalist ministers in New England were particularly vocal on these subjects. Even as James Otis was declaiming against the Writs of Assistance as an unconstitutional abridgment of fundamental English law, Reverend Abraham Williams was preparing a sermon in which he declared to the governor and legislature of Massachusetts that the principal end of government was "to secure the rights and properties" of all members of society, and that governing authorities were not entitled to use "arbitrary, illegal measures" in fulfilling their function.[2]

Laymen and clergy alike stressed the religious and moral basis of organized society. Letters to newspapers often made the same point made by sermons preached in church: that what was frequently referred to as natural law emanated from the word of God, and human conduct must be guided by rules and laws based upon God's word.[3] Theoretical discussion did not stop there, however. As conflict between British administrators and American colonists grew, the analyses offered by leaders in the New World often concerned the rights of the people versus the authority of government. Discussion of the theories of Locke, Montesquieu, and other philosophers well-known to educated Americans led, in turn, to consideration of the more immediate problems of colonists' rights and the limits of England's powers. A Rhode Island lawyer and a Congregationalist minister, both writing in 1768, struck the same chord. Theirs was not a call for revolt but a plea for recognition of the need for individual freedom in the tradition of English law.[4]

When pleas of this sort produced no basic change in Britain's attitude, American activists demonstrated their opposition to the character of English rule by defiance of trade and tax laws and by organizing events like the Boston Tea Party, in which a band of local citizens disguised as Indians boarded three ships of the British East India Company and threw the entire cargo of tea into Boston Harbor.

Some ministers, less inclined toward confrontation, began to suggest that, when rulers whose authority derives from the people misuse that authority, the people have a right to "transfer it to others."[5] One

Congregational clergyman used a more belligerent tone when he preached resistance to evil and the justice of defensive war. Taking his text from the command in Galatians 5:1 to "Stand fast therefore in the liberty wherewith Christ hath made us free," this Harvard-educated minister assured his audience—a company of colonial artillery—that a proper reading of the Bible made clear "the consistency of war with the spirit of the gospel."[6]

The views expressed in these sermons did not by any means represent the opinions of most colonial clergy in the early 1770s. Nor were lay leaders advocating rebellion or separation from Britain. Nevertheless, when Britain responded to the Boston Tea Party by closing the port of Boston and revoking the Massachusetts charter, these "Intollerable Acts" were protested not only by New Englanders but by residents of almost every other colony.[7]

The Quebec Act of June 22, 1774 added fuel to the fire by legitimizing the practice of Catholicism in that heavily French-populated Canadian province. According to William Lee of London, writing in September 1774 to his brother, Richard Henry Lee of Virginia, British troops and warships were being dispatched not only to subdue the New England rebels but to reinforce Britain's position in Canada. "General Carleton," Lee reported, "the ablest officer in the British service, is sent to his Government of Quebec to embody 30,000 Roman Catholics there." Stressing this aspect of the threat, Lee asserted that "as the first blow is struck by the Ministry [the King's cabinet ministers] and every tie of allegiance is broken by the Quebec Act . . . the compact between the King and the people is totally done away with."[8]

Before William Lee's letter reached America, discontent had become sufficiently widespread to generate a call for a meeting of delegates from each of the colonies, to determine how best to present their common grievances to the Crown and obtain relief from the onerous taxes and restrictive laws known collectively as the Intollerable Acts. As records of the First Continental Congress attest, the purpose of the delegates who convened in Philadelphia on September 5, 1774, was to accomplish this task within the framework of English law and without disavowing allegiance to the Crown. James Duane of New York put the matter concisely, proposing that "In the resolves to be adopted, the prerogatives of the Crown, the interest of Great Britain, and the rights of the colonies ought each to have their proper influence, and our proceedings to be tempered not only with a regard to justice but a desire of reconciliation."[9]

Though reconciliation with Britain was the avowed purpose of Congress, the heat generated by the first day's debates over voting procedures led Thomas Cushing of Massachusetts to suggest that a more serene atmosphere might be achieved if each morning session was opened with a prayer. This, too, became a matter of controversy. Finally, Cushing's Massachusetts colleague, Samuel Adams, proposed and won approval for an invitation to Jacob Duché, an Anglican clergyman, to open the next day's session with a suitable prayer.

The diary of John Adams glows with praise for the minister's performance on the morning of September 7. No reference is made to debate on the religious issue, although Adams outlined the previous day's critical discussion as to whether voting in Congress should be by colony, or weighted by each colony's population, or determined by "a compound of numbers and property." James Duane, however, after recording the actions taken on procedural matters—including the decision that each colony was to have one vote—noted that the suggestion for an opening prayer brought a number of objections. "Those who favored the proposal," he said, asserted "the propriety of a Reverence & Submission to the Supreme Being & supplicating his Blessing on every Undertaking, on the practice of the Romans, the British Parliament & some of the Assemblies on the Continent." Opponents cited the differences among the religious beliefs of the delegates, the possible interpretation of such a practice as mere show, the private nature of devotions, the lack of any effort to find a commonly accepted form of prayer, and "the Hazard of submitting such a Task to the Judgement of any clergy."[10]

If members of Congress were not in full agreement on the desirability of a religious introduction to their duties, they did, almost to a man, asociate good government with Christian morality. This did not mean that they welcomed direct participation of the clergy in the political process. As strict a moralist and devout a churchgoer as John Adams had some misgivings about Georgia's selection of John Joachim Zubly as one of its delegates. "He is the first Gentleman of the Cloth who has appeared in Congress," Adams wrote to his wife, adding, "I can not but wish he may be the last." Adams found churchmen "too little acquainted with the World" and "too much loaded with vanity to be good Politicians."[11]

These generalizations certainly did not apply to Zubly, whose grasp of the political situation between England and the colonies was revealed in his pamphlet, *The Law of Liberty*, and in his correspondence with Lord Dartmouth, a member of the British House of Lords. Writing to the British peer in 1775, Zubly put the major issue clearly: "Whether the

Parliament of Great Britain has a right to lay taxes on Americans who are not and cannot there be represented." He went on to suggest that if Parliament would enact a law stating that "America is entitled to all the common rights of mankind and all the blessings of the British Constitution," the conflict would be resolved. Zubly's insightful conclusion is worthy of note. Referring to the colonies' share in the financial burden of the British Empire, Zubly advised—and warned—Lord Dartmouth in this fashion: "Let Americans enjoy, as hitherto, the privilege to *give* and *grant* by their own representation, and they will give and grant liberally; but their liberty they will never part with but with their lives."[12] Along with the pleadings of other Americans, this advice fell on deaf ears. Zubly continued to argue for reconciliation with Britain, but his loyalist leanings finally forced him to retire from Congress and, later, to leave America for England.

Reservations about minister-politicians did not prevent Congress from using the clergy to heal rifts among the colonists, which might have weakened the united front they needed for an effective appeal to Britain. When a backcountry revolt in North Carolina threatened to play into the hands of loyalist opponents of the Congress, North Carolina's congressional delegates asked the Presbyterian ministers of Philadelphia to "use their pastoral influence to work a change in the disposition of the people of that province." Showing as much concern for the established power structure as for a peaceful settlement of differences, the letter of invitation gave the ministers this picture of the situation in North Carolina:

> [The dissidents], by the Artifices of wicked and designing men have been led astray from the path of duty & taught to believe that the contest which at present subsists betwixt America & the parent State owes its origin to factious & seditious men in these Colonies who aim at Independence of Great Britain & are desirous to establish a system of democracy in America, thereby to rise to power & to build up themselves upon the ruin of the British Constitution.

This artfully designed missive ignored the true nature of the problem, which was the refusal of the wealthy landowners in the eastern part of North Carolina to grant western settlers an equal voice in the political affairs of the province. Nevertheless, Congress not only approved the plan for clerical mediators but authorized the payment of $40 per month for each of two ministers to travel and spread the word among the disaffected people of North Carolina.[13]

Like other social groups in the colonies, clergymen were far from united in their attitudes toward either British–American relations or more local problems. Anglican ministers associated with the Church of England remained, for the most part, loyal to the mother country. This earned them the scorn of other sects—scorn mounting to outrage over the question of establishing an Anglican episcopate in America to oversee Church of England affairs throughout the colonies. This "plot" stirred Presbyterian minister Francis Alison and two other Pennsylvanians to write a series of "Centinel" essays which, according to one modern author, were responsible for arousing the colonists to the threat of both religious and political domination of American affairs by an oppressive British establishment. Other accounts of the Revolution give less weight to the "Centinel" articles, notwithstanding John Adams' post-revolutionary reminiscence that "the apprehension of Episcopacy contributed ... as much as any other cause, to arouse the attention, not only of the inquiring mind, but of the common people, and urge them to close thinking on the constitutional authority of Parliament over the colonies."[14]

Even within the Anglican brotherhood the colonies had their sympathizers. As one historian points out, some were influenced by the local people "who supported and paid them," while others reacted to the proximity of their parishes to the Philadelphia meeting place of Congress.[15] When, in 1775, a bishop in England refused to ordain an applicant for the ministry "because he was a rebellious American," a Virginia congressman and member of the Church of England expressed his disgust, showing un-Anglican tolerance in his inclination to "let every man worship God under his own fig tree."[16]

More aggressive in their presentation of colonial complaints, Congregational and Presbyterian ministers used both the pulpit and the press to denounce Britain's unrighteous rule in America. One of the most politically active clergymen was John Witherspoon, the Presbyterian president of the College of New Jersey. His election to the Second Continental Congress could not have displeased even the likes of John Adams. Other ministers were content to limit their activities to their parishes. However, the volume of patriotic sermons and essays by members of the clergy during the years immediately preceding the Declaration of Independence has prompted historian Arthur Schlesinger to conclude that the clergy, "knowing from long practice how to insinuate politics into sermons and sermons into prayers," carried almost as much weight as the legal profession in propagandizing the colonial cause.[17]

In between the staunchly loyalist and overtly rebellious churchmen were many with less firm attachments to either political point of view. Many of these, including Quakers, wanted simply to be left alone and were amenable to any government that would permit them to go their own way unmolested. Among such groups, loyalists worked diligently to recruit support for the British cause. Joseph Galloway, whose insistence on accommodation with Britain eventually led the Pennsylvania Assembly to accept his request to be relieved of his duties as a delegate to Congress, claimed to find support for his "moderate measures" among "Quakers, the high and low Dutch, the Baptists, Mennonites, Dumplers, etc."[18] Quaker pacifism aroused the ire of more aggressive critics of British policy, particularly after the uproar produced by the first military engagement at Lexington and Concord in April 1775, which brought widespread demands for armed resistance.

Antipathy toward Catholics, evident in most of the colonies for more than a century, was heightened by passage of the Quebec Act in 1774. The annual celebration of Pope Day on every 5 November, when effigies of the pope were burned in many Massachusetts towns, "spread as far south as Charleston" after news of the Quebec Act reached America.[19] This liberalization of religious controls by Parliament infuriated the more anti-Catholic sects in America, particularly those in New England who saw the strengthening of Catholicism in neighboring Canada as a threat to their way of life. The threat took on military significance when Britain went abroad to recruit troops to help quell the American mutiny. In addition to German mercenaries (Hessians), Irish Catholics were induced to enter British service by what one irate Virginian called "the high premiums given by the Popish towns." He warned that "the establishment of Popery will no doubt be the reward of the exertions of the Roman Catholics." Feeling on this score ran so high that when Europeans with military experience began to volunteer their services to the Continental Congress, some members of Congress protested that they "did not approve of employing in our Service Foreign Papists."[20] However, as the strain of military needs bore more heavily on colonial resources, these objections faded; and military talent from such Catholic strongholds as France and Poland was welcomed without the embarrassment of debate as to the religious qualifications of the volunteers.

ALL MEN ARE CREATED EQUAL

The American Revolution, unlike the later upheaval in France, was almost exclusively a political revolt. Almost, but not quite. The moment the colonists asserted the belief that "all men are created equal," social structure change was inevitable. That philosophical bombshell did not appear in any of the appeals addressed to King George III by the Continental Congress, but the first of those petitions laid the groundwork for such a proposition. "The immutable laws of nature, the principles of the English constitution, and the several charters or compacts" granted to the colonies were cited to prove that the right of all Americans to "life, liberty and property" could not be abridged by either the King or Parliament. This was the sense of the resolutions approved by the First Continental Congress on October 4, 1774, as incorporated into an address to the king from "Your Majesty's most loyal subjects." Despite the petitioners' assurances of loyalty, the tone of challenge, together with multiple incidents of deliberate flouting of British authority, caused King George to conclude in November 1774 that, because "the New England governments are in a state of rebellion, blows must decide whether they are to be subject to this country or independent."[21] Another five months passed before armed Massachusetts farmers challenged British troops at Lexington and Concord. Although delegates to the Congress continued for another year to talk of a peaceful settlement with their acknowledged sovereign, the King's official Proclamation of Rebellion in August 1775 signaled his government's intent to suppress all resistance by force of arms.[22]

As the military confrontation spread throughout most of the colonies, Congress' efforts to find a peaceful resolution of its differences with England gave way to recurring demands for independence. By May 1776 the pressure for separation from Britain brought to an end any effective movement for reconciliation. On May 10 Congress approved a resolution calling upon each colony to replace British governmental agencies with "such Government as shall in the opinion of the Representatives of the People best conduce to the happiness and safety of their Constituents in particular, and America in general." On May 15, after three days of "vigorous, intermittant debates," Congress voted to add a preamble to the May 10 resolution, written by hawkish John Adams; it laid all responsibility for the break on the king and Parliament and declared that "the exercise of every kind of authority under the Crown should be totally suppressed."

Elated by his success in winning approval of the statement, which many thought too strong, Adams wrote to a friend that passage of his proposal was "the most important Resolution that ever was taken in America."[23] He may well have been right, for there was no stopping the independents from that point on. A formal Declaration of Independence was introduced by Richard Henry Lee on June 7; and, despite a final effort by moderates to delay any irrevocable decision, a revised statement, written by Thomas Jefferson, was approved after three days of debate and was announced on 4 July.[24]

The social implications of the concept of equality as incorporated in the Declaration of Independence were slow to develop. Few of the revolutionary leaders believed that the self-evident truth "all men are created equal" meant any more than that all were created by the same God. Similarly, few desired the kind of social leveling advocated by the likes of Thomas Paine, the fiery pamphleteer who years later became Citizen Tom Paine, member of the revolutionary French Chamber of Deputies. Most viewed the revolt against Britain as a means of wresting from the king and Parliament control of the governmental process in the American provinces. Once that had been accomplished, they assumed that lawmaking and administration would remain with those most capable of governing—the educated elite, whose stake in society was measured principally in land ownership. The anti-elite approach to government evident in Paine's *Common Sense* was acknowledged to be effective as a rallying cry but was derided by John Adams as characterized by "some whims, some sophisms, some artful addresses to superstitious notions." Adams considered Paine's concept of government to be "so democratical, without any restraint or even an attempt at any equilibrium or counterpoise, but that it must produce confusion and every evil work."[25] In this he was joined by an overwhelming majority of colonial leaders who, as later efforts to design a constitution demonstrated, were content to leave in state hands all decisions as to how "consent of the governed" was to be interpreted.

With the break from England, given the chance to put into practice their beliefs as to the best form of government, most Americans argued that a republic was the most "virtuous" and therefore the most likely to ensure happiness for the people. Virtue was the key. Carter Braxton of Virginia, addressing his state's constitutional convention, put it very directly: "The happiness of man, as well as his dignity, consists in virtue." Braxton added that "virtue is the principle of a republic, therefore a republic is the best form of government."[26] John Adams made the same point in his declaration that "Public virtue cannot exist in a nation without private [virtue], and public virtue is the only foundation of republics."[27] After the fashion of philosophers dating back to ancient Greece, Adams noted that the most desirable government faces constant danger, for "its Principles are as easily destroyed as human Nature is corrupted. Such a Government is only to be supported by pure Religion or Austere Morals." Certainly the colonies had no more austere moralist than Adams, who went so far as to declaim—in private—against the activity that had supported much of the country's growth. "The Spirit of Commerce," he wrote to Mrs. Warren, "which even insinuates itself into Families and influences holy Matrimony, and thereby corrupts the Morals of Families as well as destroys their happiness . . . is incompatible with that purity of Heart and Greatness of soul which is necessary for an happy Republic."

During the Revolutionary War, despite all their letters, essays, speeches, and sermons about the ideal form of government, few colonial leaders pressed for implementation of their theories at the national level. However, they reacted enthusiastically to Congress' suggestion that the states replace the political structures imposed by England with governments of their own design. Thus, at the state level, political theory was first put to the test of practical application.

THE STATES TAKE THE LEAD

When the Second Continental Congress approved Richard Henry Lee's resolution of May 10, 1776, recommending that each colony form a new government responsible to the people rather than to the Crown, it gave the signal that independents had long awaited. In a matter of months, most of the 13 colonies called conventions or convened their legislatures to prepare constitutions that would provide a governmental framework independently of Great Britain. In the drafting of each state's fundamental law, the influence of religion reasserted itself, for belief in "one true God" was still considered basic to a properly ordered society. However, the way in which this concept was expressed varied considerably from one state to another.

Two colonies drew up constitutions months before the call came from Congress, and both took the precaution of leaving the door open to reconciliation with the mother country. Delegates to New Hampshire's constitutional convention did no more than set up the basic framework for political operation. No bill of rights was included until 1784, when a 38-paragraph list of protections was added. In that later revision, prefaced by a general guarantee of "the rights of conscience," was a lengthy section on the individual's "natural and unalienable right to worship God according to the dictates of his own conscience." Not content with the simple principle of free choice, however, the convention gave the legislature power to authorize use of public funds "for the support and maintenance of public protestant teachers of piety, religion and morality." Furthermore, all previous agreements for support of the ministry were to continue "as if this constitution had not been made."[28]

New Hampshire's constitution was adopted on January 5, 1776. Two months later, the colonial legislature of South Carolina prepared its, more comprehensive, document. Intended to be effective "until an accommodation of the differences between Great Britain and America shall take place," the constitution included a statement of grievances that indicated the strength of the religious factor, both in the revolt against English rule and in the sociopolitical system preferred by the colonists. Prominent among the protested actions was restoration of French law and the Roman Catholic religion in Quebec, and the expansion of that territory westward "through a vast tract of country so as to border on the free Protestant English settlements, with a design on using a whole people differing in religious principles." Two years later, the South Carolina legislature rewrote its constitution, acknowledging the separation from Britain effected by the Declaration of Independence and incorporating into that state's fundamental law a lengthy exposition of the religious principles that were to be observed. To begin with, Article 38 announced that "the Christian Protestant religion . . . is hereby constituted and declared to be the established religion of this State."[29] All existing Protestant societies, including local branches of the Church of England, were recognized as part of the Protestant community. New Protestant churches were to be given the same rights, if the organizers agreed in writing to the following principles:

1st. That there is one eternal God, and a future state of rewards and punishments.
2d. That God is publicly to be worshiped.
3d. That the Christian religion is the true religion.
4th. That the holy scriptures of the Old and New Testaments are of divine inspiration, and are the rule of faith and practice.
5th. That it is lawful and the duty of every man being thereunto called by those that govern, to bear witness to the truth.

Virginia proved to be a major battleground for the contest between leaders of the established church and those who argued that religious conviction is a personal matter and should not be imposed or infringed by

government. Most influential among the Virginians who supported freedom of religion were Thomas Jefferson, James Madison, and George
Mason. Seldom does the third member of this group receive proper
recognition for the ultimate victory of the concept of religious freedom;
but Mason was the author of the first Virginia Declaration of Rights,
which laid the foundation for Madison's and Jefferson's later campaign
to erect a barrier between church and state. The last section of the
Declaration, approved on June 12, 1776, by the Virginia legislature, with
only minor changes in Mason's original draft, reads as follows:

> That Religion, or the duty which we owe to our Creator, and the man-
> ner of discharging it, can be directed only by reason and conviction,
> not by force or violence; and, therefore, all men are equally entitled
> to the free exercise of religion, according to the dictates of con-
> science; and that it is the mutual duty of all to practise Christian
> forbearance, love, and charity, toward each other.[30]

Legislative approval of this bill of rights, and the formal structure of
government contained in the state constitution that was proclaimed two
weeks later, did not end debate on the relation between church and state.
Less than a decade after adopting the above article Virginia became embroiled in a bitter controversy over a bill that proposed to use a property
tax "to restore and propagate the holy Christian religion." Intended by
its sponsors to provide support for the Episcopal church, the bill was
defeated when Madison (among others) pointed to its dangers by present-
ing a Memorial and Remonstrance Against Religious Assessments. Quot-
ing the 1776 Declaration of Rights, Madison argued that the individual's
duty to God can be expressed only in terms of his own belief, and that his
membership in civil society is a "subordinate association" in which
"religion is wholly exempt from its cognizance."[31] This defense against
state intrusion into the sphere of religion, set forth in 1785, was followed
a year later by a stronger move, this one initiated by Thomas Jefferson.

Jefferson's Act for Establishing Religious Freedom was vigorously
resisted by his opponents, just as vigorously as Jefferson had fought the
earlier attempt to reinstate public funding of churches. Although passage
of the bill did not end all facets of the struggle, it did settle the basic question of church–state relations (in Virginia), by declaring:

> [N]o man shall be compelled to frequent or support any religious wor-
> ship, place, or ministry whatsoever, nor shall be enforced, restrained,
> molested, or burthened in his body or goods, nor shall otherwise

suffer on account of his religious opinions or belief; but that all men shall be free to profess, and by argument to maintain, their opinions in matters of religion, and that the same shall in no wise diminish, enlarge, or affect their civil capacities.[32]

New Jersey was the last of the colonies to hold a constitutional convention before the Declaration of Independence was issued. It completed deliberations in June and publishing its state constitution on July 3, 1776. Concentrating on the structure, functions, and method of choosing the executive, legislature, and judiciary, the convention devoted several sections to individual rights but did not follow the more popular procedure of attaching a separate bill of rights. Significantly, the question of religion was given full attention in the body of the constitution, as is evident from these provisions:

That no person shall ever, within this Colony, be deprived of the inestimable privilege of worshipping Almighty God in a manner agreeable to the dictates of his own conscience; nor, under any pretence whatever, be compelled to attend any place of worship contrary to his own faith and judgment; nor shall any person within this Colony ever be obliged to pay tithes, taxes, or any other rates for the purpose of building or repairing any other church or churches, place or places of worship, or for the maintenance of any minister or ministry, contrary to what he believes to be right or has deliberately or voluntarily engaged himself to perform.

Although the constitution went on to assert that "there shall be no establishment of any one religious sect ... in preference to another," it did not abandon the traditional Protestant bias. Immediately after the ban against an established church came this assurance:

No Protestant inhabitant of this Colony shall be denied the enjoyment of any civil right merely on account of his religious principles; but ... all persons professing a belief in the faith of any Protestant sect who shall demean themselves peaceably under the government, as hereby established, shall be capable of being elected into any office of profit or trust, or being a member of either branch of the legislature.[33]

The four colonial constitutions discussed above, adopted prior to the Declaration of Independence, demonstrate the differences in attitudes toward religion that existed throughout what were soon to become 13 independent states. Connecticut's brief constitution of 1776 retained the tradition of public support of Protestant churches by avoiding all reference to religion, leaving the matter in local hands. Continuing "the ancient Form of Civil Government contained in the charter from Charles the Second," the Connecticut legislature simply amended the charter by adding a series of protections for its citizens—creating, in effect, a bill of rights, although not labeled such. No guarantee of religious freedom was included in the state's fundamental law until 1818, when a convention was called to write a new constitution to replace the colonial charter.

Massachusetts struggled with constitutional problems for almost four years before reaching a settlement that included a religious clause similar to that approved by New Hampshire. Earlier efforts failed because the state legislature was deaf to outside opinion. One memorable protest came from a convention of delegates chosen by the towns of Exeter County. Along with other complaints, they cited the legislature's one reference to religion as objectionable "because the free exercise and enjoyment of religious worship is there said to be allowed to all the protestants in the State, when in fact, that free exercise and enjoyment is the natural and uncontroulable right of every member of the State."[34]

Popular rejection of the legislature's proposal led to a statewide constitutional convention in September 1779. First on the agenda was the framing of a Declaration of Rights, a task that, with one exception, was completed with relatively little difficulty. That exception, the article on religious freedom, was largely debated time after time, with final action repeatedly postponed to permit further consideration of "so important an article." Debaters posed such questions as whether freedom for "Christians of all denominations" should be modified to exclude "Papists," or whether such freedom should be limited to churches "whose avowed principles are not inconsistent with the peace and safety of society" (whatever that might mean). Finally, after endless haggling over details, the convention approved an article that opened with the declaration that "the Happiness of a People and the good order and preservation of Civil Government essentially depend upon piety, religion and morality." From this basic premise the delegates went on to authorize the state legislature to require the towns in Massachusetts "to make suitable provision, at their own expense, for the institution of the publick worship of God, and for the support and maintenance of publick Protestant Teachers of piety, religion and morality." The article concluded with a guarantee of equal protection of the law for all Christians who conduct themselves as good citizens, and an assurance that no law would permit one church to be shown preference over others.[35]

Protestant bias was less obvious, but still apparent, in other areas. Some states, including New Jersey, North Carolina, and South Carolina, showed their partiality by making seats in the legislature and executive offices available to Protestants only, or by phrasing the guarantee of full civil rights in such a way as to make it appear that only Protestants would be protected. North Carolina put this limitation in no uncertain terms:

> No person who shall deny the being of God or the truth of the Protestant religion, or the divine authority of either the Old or New Testaments, or who shall hold religious principles incompatible with the freedom and safety of the State, shall be capable of holding any office or place of trust or profit in the civil department within this State.[36]

Delaware and Maryland showed no preference for Protestantism, guaranteeing equal protection to "all persons professing the Christian religion." However, Maryland made a declaration of Christian faith a requirement for officeholding. Pennsylvania's approach was broader still. In the Quaker tradition, that state offered freedom of worship, full civil rights, and eligibility for public office to "any man who acknowledges the being of a God."

New York's position, like Virginia's, was unequivocal in declaring that the free exercise of religion, "without discrimination or preference, shall forever hereafter be allowed." This unrestricted guarantee was not reached easily. At one point in the convention deliberations, John Jay offered an amendment to the religious clause that would have denied all civil rights, including the right to own land, to "professors of the religion of the Church of Rome." This penalty—sponsored by the man who later became the first chief justice of the U.S. Supreme Court—would have applied to all Catholics who would not renounce the pope's authority to absolve men from sin or from allegiance to New York State. Only after Jay's motion was voted down did the convention agree on the broader freedom sought by more farsighted members.[37]

Fear of clerical influence on the formulation of public policy led a few states to adopt constitutional restrictions that today would be considered a kind of reverse discrimination. Three of the earliest state constitutions barred clergymen from elective office. In the bare-bones style that characterized many of Georgia's declarations of principle, one article in its constitution stated that "no clergyman of any denomination shall be allowed a seat in the legislature." North Carolina broadened the proscription to exclude the clergy from executive as well as legislative posts, while New York went all the way, denying ministers eligibility for any civil or military office. New York's rationale for barring all clergymen from public office was that "whereas ministers of the gospel are, by their profession, dedicated to the service of God and the care of souls, [they] ought not to be diverted from the great duties of their function."[38] This disenfranchisement was not removed until 1846, when a constitutional convention made a number of changes, one of which was to eliminate this provision altogether.

In Rhode Island, the principal problem was with Puritans who wanted their Congregational church restored to the dominant position it still held in the rest of New England. Rhode Islanders however, retained their maverick tendencies throughout the colonial period, the Revolution, and the early years of independence; and they came closest to achieving complete separation of church and state. One of the most interesting aspects of this state's early history is that it won its freedom from domination by the Massachusetts theocracy by a grant from the same Puritan Parliament that turned England from a monarchy to a commonwealth and sent the spirits of New England Puritans soaring. Parliament's 1643 patent for Providence Plantation named the Earl of Warwick governor of the colony, but it gave the inhabitants of Rhode Island "full Power and Authority to rule themselves." When England's revolution was over and the monarchy restored, Rhode Island lost none of the autonomy it had gained from Parliament. A new charter from Charles II gave to the settlers "the free exercise and enjoyment of all their civill and religious rights." The full import of this extraordinary grant can best be perceived by reading the king's own words, in which he explained that

> because some of the people and inhabitants of the colonie cannot, in theire private opinions, conforme to the publique exercise of religion according to the litturgy, formes and ceremonyes of the Church of England . . . our royall will and pleasure is that noe person within the sayd colonye, at any time hereafter, shall bee any wise molested, punished, disquieted, or called in question, for any differences in opinione in matters of religion [which] does not actually disturb the civill peace of our sayd colony; but that all and everye person and persons may . . . at all tymes hereafter freelye and fullye have and enjoye his and theire owne judgments and consciences in matter of religious concernments . . . they behaving themselves peaceablie and quietlie, and not useing this libertie to lycentiousnesse and profaneness, nor to the civill injurye or outward disturbeance of others; any law, statute, usage or customs of this realme to the contrary . . . notwithstanding.[39]

This was the pledge of a Stuart king whose family was denounced for its religious toleration, especially toward Catholics, and whose brother James II was deposed and replaced by William of Orange, an avowed defender of the Protestant faith.

Like Connecticut, Rhode Island saw no need to improve on its charter's guarantee of local autonomy in all matters. The American Revolution did not alter that attitude. Nor did it bring any modification of Rhode Island's fundamental law. Not until 1842—66 years after the Declaration of Independence—did the state decide that it was time to prepare a new constitution.

Reviewing the experiences of the thirteen colonies during their revolt against British rule, the twentieth-century observer becomes unconvinced that one of the goals of the American Revolution was to achieve complete freedom of religion. The evidence clearly demonstrates that the only area of unanimity on this score was belief that faith in God was essential to a moral society. Absence of agreement beyond that fundamental consensus fostered a cautious approach to the religious question on the part of the men who designed the federal constitution.

A Century
of
Change

4

What the Constitution Did—
and Didn't Do

In one respect, the American Revolution was conducted in a fashion never witnessed before or since, anywhere on earth. Thirteen independent states, each with its own government, combined their resources to challenge a world power and, in the process, permitted the war to be directed by a group of more than 60 state representatives—called a Congress—whose authority over the states was limited to *requesting* contributions of men, money, and supplies needed to support the military effort. Even this limited power was based on no formal treaty or agreement, only on the common goal of freedom and the certain knowledge that, as Benjamin Franklin so aptly put it, "We must all hang together, or assuredly we shall all hang separately." Hang together they did, although not without long and sometimes acrimonious wrangling over questions of military, economic, and political strategy.

The miracle is that, from the Declaration of Independence on July 4, 1776, to within seven months of the surrender of Cornwallis at Yorktown in 1781, the war was fought and won under the direction of a government that was little more than a coordinating committee. Eighty-two delegates were selected by the 13 state legislatures to participate in the Congress that approved the Declaration of Independence. Some delegates never appeared at the designated meeting place in Philadelphia, others attended for relatively brief periods. Only 56 signed the Declaration. Then, in the war years, it was not uncommon for fewer than half the members of Congress to be present at any particular time. Occasionally, the presiding officer was forced to write to state legislatures reporting the absence of their delegates and demanding that at least one representative be sent, so that Congress could conduct its business properly. For all practical purposes, it was the dedicated minority of this extraordinary body that constituted the wartime government of these imperfectly united states.[1]

A MORE PERFECT UNION:
THE FIRST ATTEMPT

Even before the Continental Congress abandoned reconciliation in favor of separation from England, its members recognized that something more than a coordinating committee was needed to demonstrate to the world their intention to remain united under a formally constructed constitutional government. On June 11, 1776, the day after Congress had adopted a resolution for independence, it acted on a suggestion made four days earlier by Richard Henry Lee of Virginia and appointed a committee "to prepare and digest the form of a Confederation to be entered into between the colonies."[2]

Considering the importance of its assignment, the committee completed its task in a remarkably short time, submitting a plan of confederation to Congress on July 12. Each of the states had a representative on the committee, but, as in every such group, the real work was done by a few. The first drafts were prepared, not by such revolutionary stalwarts as Samuel Adams of Massachusetts or Roger Sherman of Connecticut, but by Pennsylvania's most ardent advocate of reconciliation, John Dickinson, and New Hampshire's Josiah Bartlett.[3] We know very little about the committee members' reactions to these drafts. However, what few records remain indicate the problems remained the subject of bitter debate for the next 12 years, until the Articles of Confederation were superseded by a new constitution.

Most hotly debated were the division of powers between state and federal governments and the manner of voting in the new Congress. As to the latter, there was very little prospect of change from the system used by the Continental Congress, which was to ensure absolute equality among the states by allowing one vote to each. The only challenge to that concept arose in connection with the states' share of federal expenses. Some argued for contributions based on number of inhabitants; others suggested that the value of a state's property was the appropriate measure of its ability to pay. How to count number of inhabitants sparked a dispute, revealing the depth of feeling that was to surface every time the matter of slavery entered into congressional discussions. After the dust cleared, it was decided to ignore population differences and to divide the costs of government "in proportion to the value of all land within each state."

No such compromise was reached in the matter of voting. Discussion of this problem had scarcely begun when Samuel Chase of Maryland warned that, of all the items in the draft agreement, "this article was the most likely to divide us." His summary of the problem was short and to the point:

> The larger colonies had threatened they would not confederate at all if their weight in Congress should not be equal to the numbers of people they added to the confederacy; while the smaller ones declared against a union if they did not retain an equal vote for the protection of their rights.[4]

The question of federal authority was equally sensitive. The document submitted by the drafting committee indicated a determination on the part of most delegates to regain state jurisdiction over all matters except those considered absolutely essential for "the common defense" of the 13 states and "their mutual and general welfare"—a phrase closely associated with defense of the American system, in 1776, and having none of the social connotations that evolved in the twentieth century. For these limited purposes, all that seemed necessary was a congress of state delegates, chosen by the state legislatures in the same fashion they had selected members of the Continental Congress. To ensure against any broadening of federal powers, the Articles provided that no modification would be permitted "unless such alteration be agreed to in a congress of the united states, and be afterward confirmed by the legislature of every state."[5]

The Articles were just as unequivocal in the language used to guarantee states' rights, which made up the largest part of both the preliminary drafts and the final document. After an opening that identified the new confederacy as the United States of America, the very next article announced that "Each state retains its sovereignty, freedom and independence, and every Power, Jurisdiction and right which is not by this confederation expressly delegated to the United States in Congress assembled." Subsequent paragraphs clarified this sweeping declaration to mean that the states would have complete control over all their civil, political, and economic affairs. Even the conduct of trade with other states and nations was considered a local matter, restricted only by the stipulation that "no state shall lay any imposts or duties" that would conflict with the terms of treaties Congress was then negotiating with France and Spain. Further, each state would devise its own system of elections, tax programs, and guarantees of individual freedom.

Nowhere was resistance to federal intrusion more evident than in the area of civil liberties. The only place in which the phrase "freedom of speech" appeared was in a clause intended to protect a delegate's right to speak his piece in Congress. An attempt by John Dickinson to include a reference to freedom of religion stirred no enthusiasm in any quarter. His draft contained a lengthy article that would have eliminated religious tests or oaths for public office and would have guaranteed freedom of religious belief as well as relief from any obligation to support an established church. In only one respect did this article go beyond similar protections embodied in some state constitutions. This radical element appeared in the opening statement, which read: "No person in any Colony living peaceably under the Civil Government, shall be molested or prejudiced in his or her person or Estate for his or her religious persuasion, Profession or practice." The unusual treatment of women equally with men in the phrase "his or her," repeated several times in the article, may or may not have had a bearing on the quick deletion of this section by Congress. In any case, the entire article was rejected out of hand, despite the fact that Dickinson included a reservation that the guarantees would only apply to state laws enacted after the Revolution began and would leave in place "the usual Laws and Customs Subsisting at the Commencement of this War."[6]

As the record clearly indicates, the notion of federal protection of civil rights made little headway in the framing of the Articles of Confederation. One major concession recognized, in effect, state supremacy in this area, by providing that the "free inhabitants" of any state—"paupers, vagabonds and fugitives from justice excepted"—would be entitled to all the privileges and immunities of free citizens in other states. The almost universal feeling among delegates from all parts of the country was that their state constitutions provided all the individual protections necessary, and that references to civil liberties in the Articles of Confederation would open the door to federal intervention in matters that were the exclusive province of the states. As a result, comments relating to personal freedom were few and far between in the debates over this first constitution.

Those debates continued sporadically for months. After repeated clashes over voting procedures, methods of representation, and disposition of western lands, the end product was more like a treaty than a constitution. Every state retained its sovereignty, freedom, and independence; and the confederation was declared to be no more than "a firm league of friendship," entered into principally for purposes of defense.[7] Notwithstanding the victory of the small states in securing agreement on the principle that each state would have but one vote in Congress, final approval by all 13 states dragged on for three years after November 1777, when Congress thought that it had a finished document. Maryland conditioned its acceptance on congressional action to preserve the lands west of the Appalachian Mountains for the benefit of the country as a whole. This was accomplished in October 1780, and on March 1, 1781 Maryland gave its assent.[8]

A MORE PERFECT UNION: "WE THE PEOPLE" REPLACES "WE THE STATES"

Two potential disasters drove Congress to complete the Articles before the close of 1777. One was the fear that without a firm interstate compact no foreign power would recognize or give overt aid to the fledgling country. The second was the widespread conviction that in the absence of a pledge to use state taxes to "reestablish the publick credit & the value of our paper money" the Revolution would end in bankruptcy.[9] The urgency of the situation was also revealed by the condition of the army, which had camped at Valley Forge for the winter of 1777–78 after successive defeats at Brandywine and Germantown. Volumes have been written about the torturous conditions suffered by Washington's troops at Valley Forge, which were described by the president of Congress as "half in rags & half without blankets." In these circumstances, a compact that was considered "deformed" by some and "a monster" by others was approved, even by those who urged that Congress be considered no more than "a Grand Council of America" with extremely limited powers.[10]

If ratification of the Articles signified the unity of the states in a defensive alliance, it did little to resolve the shortages, high prices, and tumbling value of the currency that arose principally out of the states' insistence on protecting and fostering their individual commercial interests, regardless of the effect on the country as a whole. Even after the peace treaty with England was signed in September 1783, the states continued to act in accordance with their sovereign right to decide all economic matters for themselves. However, as chaotic financial and trade conditions continued to deteriorate, members of Congress and leaders in several states urged their legislatures to seek resolution of the problem. Proposals made periodically in Congress to give that body authority to restrict or levy tariffs on imports were turned down every time they were made.[11]

Meanwhile, as Rufus King reported later, Congress could not pay its debts because many states "shamefully neglected to pay their quotas."[12]

Virginia and Maryland took the first positive step by sending delegates to a conference at Mount Vernon to work out some agreement on the conduct of commerce along their Potomac River border. The most important result of this meeting was the suggestion that other states be invited to consider the overall trade problem on a nationwide basis. In January 1786, the Virginia legislature proposed a gathering of commissioners from the states "to consider and recommend a federal plan for regulating commerce."[13] Nine of the thirteen states—all except Connecticut, Georgia, Maryland, and South Carolina—appointed commissioners, but the only representatives to appear at the meeting in Annapolis were those from Delaware, New Jersey, New York, Pennsylvania, and Virginia. Significantly, those who did attend included Alexander Hamilton, John Dickinson (formerly of Pennsylvania, now representing Delaware), Edmund Randolph, and James Madison—all advocates of constitutional reform.

Like the Mount Vernon conference, the Annapolis convention failed to reach any agreement on the subject for which it was called. However, it was a notable success in stimulating a more comprehensive review of interstate problems. Acknowledging that their instructions limited them "to consider how far an uniform system in their commercial intercourse and regulations might be necessary to their common interest and permanent harmony," the commissioners quickly decided that, with only five states represented, there was no possibility of achieving even this modest goal. Rather than abandon the effort altogether, they took the bolder course of appealing to Congress, as well as to their own state governments, for an investigation of ways to strengthen the confederation. Their cleverly designed report (drafted by Alexander Hamilton, the foremost advocate of strong central government) was addressed to the legislatures of the five states that had sent delegates to Annapolis. However, to ensure maximum effect, the commissioners distributed copies to Congress and the nonparticipating states as well.[14]

The message conveyed by the report was that the country's critical condition was due to defects in the federal system that went far beyond the tangled mess of commercial rivalry. Pointing to instructions given by New Jersey to its delegates at Annapolis, instructions authorizing them to deal not only with trade but with "other important matters," the report concluded that a closer examination of the entire federal system might reveal defects "greater and more numerous" than those relating to commerce.

"With most respectful deference," the commissioners recommended a meeting of representatives from all states "to take into consideration the situation of the United States, to devise such further provisions as shall appear to them necessary to render the constitution of the Foederal Government adequate to the exigencies of the Union." In short, their proposal was that the states reconsider the entire system of government established by the Articles of Confederation.

Given the implications of the Annapolis report, Congress acted with unusual alacrity to the suggestion for a complete review of the Articles. Within five months the matter had been turned over to a special committee, studied, returned to the whole house, debated there, and a resolution approved, which stated that a convention to remedy "the defects in the present Confederation" appeared to be "the most probable means of establishing in these states a firm national government." The reference to a *national* government, rather than a confederacy, was a harbinger of things to come, although discussion of the resolution in February 1787 gave no hint of the storm of controversy that would later be raised by this concept of a strong central authority. The final statement of purpose, which is most frequently quoted only in part in modern arguments as to its intent, reads as follows:

> Resolved that in the opinion of Congress it is expedient that on the second Monday in May next, a Convention of delegates who shall have been appointed by the several states be held at Philadelphia for the sole and express purpose of revising the Articles of Confederation and reporting to Congress and the several legislatures such alterations and provisions therein as shall, when agreed to in Congress and confirmed by the states, render the federal constitution adequate to the exigencies of Government & the preservation of the Union.[15]

Students of early American history have long been aware of the furor raised by the radical solution designed by the Philadelphia convention. Some of the more vehement defenders of state sovereignty, like Patrick Henry of Virginia, viewed the very calling of the convention with suspicion. Henry was one of the delegates chosen to represent Virginia, but he refused to serve, growling that he "smelt a Rat."[16] Similar forebodings were expressed in other states, but only in Rhode Island was opposition to constitutional change so deep-seated that the state refused to send any representatives to the convention.[17]

Present-day opponents of a modern constitutional convention resemble Patrick Henry in only one respect: in their suspicion that such a gathering might undermine the existing constitution. Two centuries ago, the convention method of dealing with basic legal questions was well known and frequently used. Most of the states had relied on such special, popularly elected bodies to draw up their individual constitutions. It was not the procedure that caused concern in 1787, but only the fear that state governments would have their powers sharply curtailed by a strong central authority.

This fear was well founded. Despite subsequent charges that the convention had performed an underhanded sellout of states rights, the legislatures sending delegates to Philadelphia in 1787 were well aware of the convention's broad purpose. All but 2 of the 12 participating states patterned their authorizing resolutions after the letter of invitation from Congress. That letter had stipulated that the convention was not only to revise the Articles of Confederation; it was also charged with designing "such alterations and provisions therein as shall ... render the federal constitution adequate to the exigencies of Government & the preservation of the Union." The only state to add a reservation requiring retention of the one-state-one-vote rule of the Articles of Confederation was Delaware.[18]

Apart from the substantive questions raised at the convention, opponents made much of the secrecy in which meetings were held. Knowing full well that their task would be difficult enough without public badgering of delegates on every issue under discussion, the members adopted as one of the convention rules that "nothing spoken in the House be printed or otherwise published or communicated without leave."[19] No permission to release the official minutes was ever granted, even after the close of the convention, although delegates repeated in public many of the arguments they had made in Philadelphia for or against particular sections of the constitution.

Sensitive also to the possibility (indeed, the likelihood) that opinions expressed and votes cast by each delegate would make him a target of public abuse, the members rejected a rule that would have required their individual votes on particular issues to be recorded in the minutes.[20] Letters, papers and diaries written in 1787 (and published recently) indicate that leaks did occur occasionally; but, on the whole, the secrecy rule was honored to a degree impossible to duplicate—or even to imagine—in today's political arena. This, more than any other factor, enabled the delegates to complete the Herculean task of producing a completely new constitution in just a little more than four months. Today's citizens, accustomed to the comforts of air conditioning, elevators, and rapid transit, could appreciate the quality of this accomplishment if they would remember that the Founding Fathers worked through the steaming Philadelphia summer of 1787 with little to relieve the heat, humidity, and pain of illness—not to mention the strain generated by the conflicting interests and emotions that flared repeatedly during the daily sessions.

To some extent, debates in the 1787 convention were like a replay of those when the Articles of Confederation were under consideration: On both occasions, the principal problems were the extent of authority to be given the federal government, and the system of voting in the federal legislature. The difference lay in the conclusions reached. Whereas the Articles approved only a skeleton government in the form of a Congress with few powers and no means of enforcement, the Constitution established a central structure with executive, legislative, and judicial branches having nationwide authority in many areas formerly reserved to the states—including such vital matters as the regulation of commerce and the levying of taxes. It provided for the kind of structure that its original sponsors most desired and its opponents most feared: a strong national government rather than a loose confederation of sovereign states.

On the whole, most delegates to the Philadelphia convention felt that they had arrived at a reasonable set of compromises on the principal issues. The proposed system would give to voters direct representation in one house of the national legislature, but permitted state legislatures to select members of the new Senate. The latter provision ensured equality of state power in one branch of Congress by specifying that each state would have two senators regardless of its size, wealth, or population. Protection against an "excess of democracy" was provided both by the indirect election of senators and by a screening system that would allow voters to choose presidential electors (presumably the wisest citizens of each state) who would in turn select the president. Although the greatly expanded power of the central government was delineated in relation to all individuals, rather than to the states, federal jurisdiction was set forth in such a way as to exclude police and social functions and to leave authority in the hands of the states as well as with the federal government. Even voting and election procedures were left to the states' discretion, the Constitution specifying only the minimum requirements for candidates for federal office. Finally, the touchy question of slavery was resolved, at least temporarily, by deferring for 20 years any final decision on control of the slave trade and by an agreement that, in the population count used to determine the size of a state's delegation to the House of Representatives, two-thirds of the slaves would be included.

The general agreement reached on these matters may have satisfied most convention delegates, but publication of the proposed constitution set off a countrywide debate more furious than any experienced in the convention. Those who sought to retain the state sovereignty guaranteed by the Articles of Confederation objected, first and foremost, to the substitution of a national government for a federation. This was the point made by Elbridge Gerry of Massachusetts, one of three members of the Philadelphia convention who refused to sign the engrossed copy of the completed constitution. It was also a major objection of Luther Martin of Maryland and of John Lansing and Richard Yates of New York—all of whom left the convention before it had completed its work—and of Patrick Henry of Virginia who had refused to attend at all.[21]

Most vociferous of the so-called Anti-Federalists[22] was Patrick Henry, whose reputation as one of the most vigorous leaders of the Revolution had led to his twice being elected governor of Virginia. When the plan produced by the Philadelphia convention was submitted to a ratifying convention in Virginia, Henry rose time and again to attack almost every aspect of the proposal: it was an illegal attempt to demolish, rather than amend, the Articles of Confederation; the powers granted the national government would destroy the concept of state sovereignty; the authority given the president would inevitably result in tyranny, when a person of less integrity than George Washington assumed the post; and the absence of a bill of rights would mean that there were no protections for the people in such matters as trial by jury, illegal search and seizure, and freedom of religion.[23]

More than any other argument, the demand for a bill of rights appealed to people in every state, including many who favored the new plan of government. Toward the end of the convention, George Mason had raised the issue, insisting that, if the plan were prefaced by a bill of rights, "it would give great quiet to the people." Elbridge Gerry of Massachusetts agreed and moved that a committee be appointed to prepare a bill of rights. Roger Sherman of Connecticut responded with the Federalist view that "The State Declarations of Rights are not repealed by this Constitution and being in force are sufficient." Mason's rejoinder—that this offered no security because "the laws of the United States are to be paramount to State Bills of Rights"—failed to convince the other delegates, most of whom felt that the Constitution did not authorize the federal government to interfere with religion in any way. Put to a vote, Gerry's resolution was defeated, with ten states opposed (including his own state and Mason's) and none recorded in favor.[24]

Despite this setback—or perhaps because of it—the matter became a major issue when the Constitution went before the state ratifying conventions. Eight of the thirteen included with their ratification messages to Congress requests for immediate action to amend the constitution by adding the kinds of protection that had been incorporated into state constitutions years before.[25]

In Massachusetts, New York, and Virginia (three states whose support was vital), ratification was by no means certain. Elbridge Gerry, who was not a delegate to the Massachusetts ratifying convention, created a furor by sending to the convention chairman a letter explaining his refusal to sign the document issued from Philadelphia and offering to respond in person to questions from delegates to the Massachusetts convention. This did not sit well with pro-Constitution delegates, including the chairman, Governor John Hancock, and revolutionary hero Samuel Adams (whose support was reluctant). Ratification eventually won, but not until agreement had been reached on the need for adding a bill of rights to the Constitution. Before putting the matter to a vote, Hancock assured the delegates that he gave his assent to the Constitution "in full confidence that the amendments proposed will soon become part of the system." Even so, the final vote showed that ratification had been approved by the narrow margin of 187 to 168.[26]

More uncertain still was the outcome of the contest in New York, where Governor George Clinton and two of his delegates to the Philadelphia convention challenged the work of that body as a flagrant violation of the amendment provision of the Articles of Confederation. Fearing the worst, Alexander Hamilton conceived the idea of a series of essays, to be published in New York newspapers, setting forth the merits of the new constitution and rebutting its critics. Enlisting the aid of another New Yorker, John Jay, Hamilton opened his campaign with the first of the now-famous papers known as *The Federalist*, published in the New York *Independent Journal* from October 27, 1787, to March 1, 1788, under the pseudonym "Publius." After contributing four pieces, Jay became ill, and Hamilton turned to Madison for help. The Virginian entered the fray with what is regarded as the most masterful of all the Federalist papers, Number 10, which deals with the basis of competing interests in society and the need to "control the violence of faction."[27]

The effect of this extraordinary writing campaign, which, in a little more than four months, produced 85 essays on every aspect of political theory and practice, is difficult to judge. Certainly it was not the only publicity barrage aiming to influence public opinion on the Constitution.

Essays and letters on the proposed system appeared almost daily in newspapers throughout the country during the period when state conventions were considering ratification. Like the authors of *The Federalist*, some of the better-known anti-Federalists preferred to write anonymously. By the spring of 1788, supporters of the Constitution had won ratification resolutions in nine states. However, these nine, although sufficient to bring the Constitution into effect under the terms of Article VII, did not include the key states of Virginia and New York.

In Virginia, debate raged concerning every major issue raised by the proposed Constitution. Relatively little heat was generated by the general concept of republican government, although forms of monarchy and aristocracy had their advocates. William Grayson favored a "president for life" and "a senate for life with the powers of the House of Lords" because, he insisted, "republics, in fact, oppress more than monarchies." John Marshall was one of the few Federalists to speak favorably of democratic government. Assuming that term appropriate to the government outlined in the Constitution, he defined the choice in this fashion:

> I conceive that the object of the discussion now before us is whether democracy or despotism be most eligible . . . We, sir, idolize democracy. Those who oppose it have bestowed eulogiums on monarchy. We prefer this system to any monarchy. . . . We admire it because we think it a well-regulated democracy.[28]

Anti-Federalist forces, led by Patrick Henry, thundered about the impending disaster that a national government of overweening power would cause. Henry's repeated challenge to the sponsors of the new system reveals a major source of anti-Federalist grievances: destruction of state sovereignty as guaranteed by the Articles of Confederation. Starting his attack with the Constitution's Preamble, Henry demanded to know "Who authorized them to speak the language of 'We, the people,' instead of 'We, the States'?"[29] James Madison led the defense on most issues raised by Henry. Without the calmly logical refutations of Madison, plus the renewed (but low-key) support of Edmund Jennings Randolph, ratification would have been defeated in Virginia. Pro-Constitution forces finally won the day, voting their approval on June 27.

All through the Virginia contest, Madison kept a wary eye on events in New York where Governor George Clinton reinforced Henry's arguments against adoption of the Constitution, stressing the need for a bill of rights even if this had to be accomplished by a second national convention.

In April Madison wrote to a colleague: "Conditional amendments or a second general Convention will be fatal.... The circumstances under which a second Convention composed even of wiser individuals would meet, must extinguish every hope of an equal spirit of accommodation."[30] Virginia's vote for ratification encouraged New York Federalists, who eked out a vote of approval on July 26. Had pro-Constitution forces failed in Virginia, the New York convention might well have turned against adoption of the Constitution and the battle for a truly united states would have been lost.

The struggle did not end there, however. Playing on the widespread concern over the absence of a bill of rights, Governor George Clinton pursued the matter by circulating a letter in which he picked up Edmund Randolph's earlier suggestion for a second national convention to consider amendments to the Constitution. Madison responded with letters to key leaders, saying, "The great danger is that if another Convention should be soon assembled, it would terminate in discord, or in alterations of the federal system which would throw back essential powers into the State Legislatures."[31] Clinton's efforts failed to interrupt the process of implementation, which began with the election of delegates to the Senate and House of Representatives and the choice of electors who were to choose the first president. This was accomplished during the winter of 1788–89; and the first administration of George Washington began on March 4, 1789, nine months before North Carolina agreed to ratification and fifteen months before the last approval came from Rhode Island.

The final stage of constitutional reform came only after the new Congress had convened. Concerned initially with organizing the executive department and raising revenue to support the federal government, Congress had to be prodded to take up the amendments demanded by so many states. Elected to the House of Representatives, Madison provided the spur that eventually led the national legislature to pass and send 12 amendments to the states for ratification. Of these, ten were quickly approved by the states and became part of the Constitution on November 3, 1791.

WHAT OF RELIGION?

When Congress rejected John Dickinson's proposal to include in the Articles of Confederation a section on freedom of religion, its action was understandable. After all, the Articles were not intended to permit intrusion by the central government into areas considered the exclusive province of the states, much less to exercise direct control over individuals within the states. That situation changed radically when proceedings at the Constitutional Convention in Philadelphia gave evidence that the Framers intended to establish a level of sovereignty above that of the states. By assigning regulatory and taxation powers to the federal government and making its law enforceable upon individuals everywhere in the United States, the Framers inevitably provoked questions as to the need for protection against federal encroachment on individual rights. Those convention delegates who warned of the need for some defense against unrestrained or capricious use of federal authority anticipated a similar reaction in the states by suggesting that the Constitution include a bill of rights. In doing so, they stressed the need for guarantees of trial by jury and freedom of the press, but no one referred specifically to freedom of religion.[32] Even John Dickinson did not reintroduce the subject that he had attempted to raise when the Articles of Confederation were drafted. Nor did he contribute to the brief discussion that followed a formal motion to prepare a bill of rights, a motion that was made and promptly rejected only a few days before the convention adjourned.[33]

When on August 20, 1787—three-quarters of the way through the convention's work—Charles Pinkney submitted a series of proposals, the few that concerned individual rights dealt with a free press and the writ of habeas corpus. The only item related to religion was one attached to a suggested oath of office. This included a declaration that "no religious test or qualification shall ever be annexed to any oath of office under the authority of the United States."[34] The committee to which Pinkney's long list was assigned for review returned the material to the convention stripped of the reference to a religious test. Pinkney immediately reintroduced that section of the oath, and the item was approved unanimously.[35]

In making this decision, it is unlikely that the convention was influenced by a letter sent to its president, George Washington, by a Pennsylvania Jew. The writer, Jonas Phillips, pointed out that state constitutions did not offer equal protection to all citizens; they omitted even some who had supported the Revolution "with their lives and fortunes." In Pennsylvania, he reminded the convention president, the requirement "to swear and believe that the new testament was given by divine inspiration is absolutely against the Relgious principle of a Jew and is against his Conscience to take any such oath. By the above law a Jew is deprived of holding any publick office or place of Government."[36] As convention members were fully aware, similar discriminatory provisions existed in the laws and constitutions of most states. Failure to address this problem reflects the reluctance of most delegates to face a charge by states-rights advocates that the Constitution would deprive the states of the power to deal independently with such matters.

Only one other reference to religion occurred in the federal convention. Three days before adjournment, Madison and Pinkney suggested that the enumerated powers of Congress include the right "to establish a University in which no preferences or distinctions should be allowed on account of religion." With almost no discussion, the motion was defeated, 6–4, with one state delegation divided.[37]

Postconvention criticisms aimed at the potential excesses of federal authority were countered by Madison, Hamilton, and others, who insisted that, because the centralized powers would be limited to those specifically enumerated in the Constitution, there could be no interference with the civil rights of any citizen. This did not still demands for a federal bill of rights; and, as the challenges multiplied, even defenders of the Constitution acknowledged the desirability, if not the necessity, of adding such protections. However, freedom of religion played only a small part in the bill of rights debate.

Six of the first seven states to ratify the Constitution did so without attaching proposals for a bill of rights, five without questioning either the ban on a religious qualification for office or the absence of a guarantee of religious freedom. Delaware was the "first state" in this group, as it now proudly advertises on every automobile license place.[38]

Massachusetts set a pattern for the rest by submitting along with its resolution of ratification, a statement that read: "It is the opinion of this Convention that certain amendments and alterations in the said Constitution would remove the fears & quiet the apprehensions of many of the good people of this Commonwealth & more effectually guard against an undue administration of the Federal Government." This appeal was followed by nine suggested amendments, most of which were designed to protect states' rights, rather than the rights of individuals. Only two dealt with personal protections, and these called for grand jury indictment for major crimes and trial by jury in civil actions between citizens of different states. None mentioned religious freedom—not an unnatural omission, in view of the fact that the Massachusetts state constitution, although it guaranteed freedom of conscience, authorized the use of public funds "for the support and maintenance of public Protestant teachers."[39] The subject of religion did not pass unnoticed, however. One delegate charged that, in the absence of a religious oath, "we may have in power unprincipled men, atheists and pagans." Another "shuddered at the idea that Roman Catholics, Papists and Pagans might be introduced into office, and that Popery and the Inquisition may be established in America." The latter opinion, offered by a Major Lusk, was rebutted by Reverend Backus, who declared that "religion is ever a matter between God and individuals, and therefore no man or men can impose any religious test without invading the essential prerogatives of our Lord Jesus Christ." Demonstrating an understanding of human experience remarkable for a clergyman raised in a Puritan environment, Reverend Backus reminded his audience that from "the history of all nations . . . it will appear that the imposing of religious tests hath been the greatest engine of tyranny in the world."[40]

In Maryland, Luther Martin's slashing attack on the Constitution, delivered to the legislature in November 1787, contained but one sarcastic reference to the clause forbidding a religious test as a qualification for office. Some members of the Philadelphia convention, Martin said, were "so unfashionable as to think that a belief in the existence of a Deity, and of a State of future rewards and punishments, would be some security for the good conduct of our rulers, and that in a Christian country it would be at least decent to hold out some distinction between the professors of Christianity and downright infidelity or paganism."[41] Notwithstanding Martin's caustic criticism and wide influence, Maryland accepted the Constitution without recommending any change in the oath.

A few months later, Patrick Henry raised a broader question at the Virginia convention, asking, "Wherefore is religious liberty not secured?" Yet, although at one point he referred to "the liberty of religion, liberty of the press, and trial by jury" as the "three great rights," Henry did not dwell on the matter of religion in his frequent prolonged lectures on the need for protection of the individual. Nevertheless, James Madison, who was also a delegate to the state ratifying convention, felt called upon to respond to Henry's question. He opened the defense with questions of his own: "Is a bill of rights a security for religion? Would the bill of rights, in this state, exempt the people from paying for the support of one particular sect if such sect were exclusively established by law?" His answer was that "if there were a majority of one sect, a bill of rights would be a poor protection for liberty." The religious freedom enjoyed by Americans, he said, "arises from that multiplicity of sects which pervades America, and which is the best and only security for religious liberty in any society." In conclusion, Madison reiterated the basic Federalist theme that "there is not a shadow of right in the general government to intermeddle with religion. Its least interference with it would be a most flagrant usurpation."[42] This spirited defense did not prevent Virginia from including, with its ratification message, a suggested bill of rights that contained an article on religious freedom as well as a variety of other protections for both individuals and states.[43]

When, after agonizing delay, New York finally agreed to ratify the Constitution, its message to Congress opened with a declaration of principles, followed by a 13-item bill of rights. The first stated "That the People have an equal, natural and unalienable right, freely and peaceably to Exercise their Religion according to the dictates of Conscience, and that no Religious Sect or Society ought to be favoured or established by Law in preference of others." Like Virginia's proposed bill of rights, New York's covered all of the protections that ultimately were to comprise the first ten amendments to the Constitution.[44]

If ratification by the remaining states was less critical to adoption of the Constitution, their actions on the subject of religion were as revealing as the conclusions drawn by the Massachusetts, Virginia, and New York conventions. New Hampshire's reservations were almost identical to those of Massachusetts, with the important addition that "Congress shall make no law touching Religion or to infringe the rights of conscience." This last recommendation was included despite the existence of a provision in the state constitution that, as in Massachusetts, authorized public support of Protestant ministers.[45]

South Carolina's first concern was for states' rights. Its ratification resolution repeated the Massachusetts injunction that states "retain every power not expressly released by them" to the federal government. The only reference to religion was a request that Article 6 of the Constitution be revised to stipulate that "no *other* religious test" would be required for public office, leaving the door open to the use of an oath tied to religious belief.[46]

Until North Carolina's convention opened in July 1788, bill of rights discussions in the various states reflected only moderate interest in the question of religious freedom. Delegates in North Carolina, however, attacked the problem early and often, several expressing greater concern and visualizing more menacing possibilities than were forecast in all previous conventions. One speaker reported the fear of some citizens that "should the Constitution be received, they would be deprived of the privilege of worshipping God according to their consciences, which would be taking from them a benefit they enjoy under the present [state] constitution." This same speaker found another threat in the treaty-making power of the central government, which, he conjectured, could be used to "make a treaty engaging with foreign powers to adopt the Roman Catholic religion in the United States." His final warning was that "if there be no religious test required, pagans, deists, and Mohametans might obtain offices among us, and the senators and representatives might all be pagans." In such circumstances, he said, if every person employed by either the federal or state government had to take an oath of loyalty, "some are desirous to know how and by whom they are to swear . . . by Jupiter, Juno, Minerva, Prosperine, or Pluto."

Another delegate, finding no humor in the situation, judged that, under the Constitution, Congress could establish ecclesiastical courts, suggesting a return to one of the darker periods of English history. Still another looked far into the future and forecast that "In the course of four or five hundred years . . . Papists may occupy that [presidential] chair, and Mohametans may take it." An equally nervous colleague expressed no fear of Mohammedans or Papists but believed that, in the absence of a religious requirement, "there was an invitation for Jews and pagans of every kind to come among us." He foresaw that "At some future time, this might endanger the character of the United States."[47]

The leading defender against this assault was James Iredell, soon to be named an associate justice of the first U.S. Supreme Court. Giving the impression of a mildly impatient professor before an undergraduate class in political science, Iredell reminded his audience that "Every person in the least conversant in the history of mankind knows what dreadful mischiefs have been committed by religious persecutions." Such intolerance, he said, had brought each church to "set itself up against every other, and persecutions and wars of the most implacable and bloody nature have taken place in every part of the world." With the help of a few other pro-constitutionalists—and a variety of historical anecdotes—he went on to rebut each of the criticisms that had been offered.[48]

The extent to which the religious issue contributed to the initial defeat of ratification in North Carolina is difficult to judge. Nevertheless, after little more than a week of debate, the North Carolina convention voted to withhold ratification until Congress or another convention of all the states will have amended the Constitution to include a bill of rights. Only after the new federal government had come into being and had begun to discuss amendments to the Constitution did North Carolina's legislature call for a new state convention. Dominated this time by Federalists, the second convention met in November 1789 and required less than a week to approve the Constitution.[49]

Rhode Island continued its boycott of strong central government until a year after George Washington had assumed the presidency and after the new House and Senate had approved and sent to the states the 12 amendments most frequently requested by the ratifying conventions. Recognizing that it could not survive economically or politically outside the new republic, Rhode Island finally called a convention, which drew up a lengthy ratification resolution after "having maturely considered the Constitution of the United States of America." Rhode Island's suggested amendment for religious freedom followed word for word a paragraph in the Declaration of Rights written by the Virginia convention. However, by that time, freedom of religion had been incorporated by Congress into a relatively brief provision that also covered freedom of speech, assembly, and the press.[50]

The statement of principle that finally became the First Amendment to the Constitution was far less specific than either the corresponding sections of some state constitutions or the declarations recommended by state conventions. The fact that Congress took any action at all on the problem of amendments during its first year of operation was due largely to Madison's repeated prodding and to his careful distillation of some 200 suggestions into a more digestible group of 20. One of these, which he designed himself, was aimed at the states rather than at the federal government: "No state shall violate the equal rights of conscience, or freedom of the press, or the trial by jury in criminal cases." Not unexpectedly, this curtailment of state authority was eliminated by Congress, which nevertheless adopted the abbreviated form that combined religion with other protected activities in the First Amendment.[51]

Contrary to modern popular notion, the First Amendment did *not* make all religious discrimination unconstitutional. Like amendments two through ten, it limited the power of Congress, but not that of the states. "*Congress* shall make no law respecting an establishment of religion, or prohibiting the free exercise thereof" is the exact wording used (with emphasis added). If the states chose to support either an established religion or one variety of Christian belief, they were free to do so, where their own constitutions permitted it. As indicated earlier, several state constitutions gave specific authorization for this kind of discrimination. In effect, the so-called protection of religion in the federal Constitution changed nothing. Rather, it simply confirmed what Federalists had said all along—that the central government had no right to concern itself with religion in any way. As Madison had pointed out, the best protection was the diversity of religious sects in the 13 states, which made establishment of a national church (on the style of the Church of England, for example) impossible. Any other interference "with the free exercise" of religion by the federal government would have been equally unthinkable. Thus, the practical effect of the religious clause was to leave the matter in the hands of the states, where it always had been. Until the Supreme Court asserted its jurisdiction some 60 years later, it was in the states that the battle over public support of religion continued to be fought.

In short, the faith that the Founding Fathers were defending was not a religious concept but the belief in the ability of the American people to decide for themselves how they wanted to shape their own society.

5

The Economics, Politics, and Ethics
of Slavery

Like religion, the practice of slavery evolved early in human history. Captives taken in tribal wars became the victors' possessions to keep, sell, or destroy, as the conquerors saw fit. Only when freed—at the whim of the owner—could a slave make any claim to the rights or privileges accorded society's accepted members.

Religion had little influence on the institution of slavery until after the concept of equal rights began to take hold. While Christians were still struggling to gain their own freedom from persecution by Roman emperors, "The Council of Elvira in Spain, c. 309, proclaimed worse penalties for adultery than for killing a slave." Moreover, even within Christian society, "slaves were taken for granted and so, too, were their masters' rights to inflict arbitrary punishment."[1] Biblical references to slavery show an awareness of the practice, but nowhere is it the subject of a clear moral judgment.

Islam, the only religion to challenge Christianity in lands shared by followers of both beliefs, took no exception to slavery. Like the Bible, the Koran does not address the problem directly, but Mohammed's "Recital" contains a number of passages that indicate acceptance of slavery as a normal part of Muslim life. There is no suggestion of an ethnic or racial basis for the practice, as is evident from allusions to Muslim slaves.[2] Moreover, not only are believers urged to treat their slaves well, they are permitted to marry them. In a chapter dealing with family life, these messages appear: "Take in marriage those among you who are single and those of your male and female slaves who are honest. . . . As for those of your slaves who wish to buy their liberty, free them if you find in them any promise and bestow on them a part of the riches which Allah has given you."[3]

In countries whose history and literature were more familiar to educated American colonists, slavery was an accepted institution. This included the so-called democratic state of ancient Athens, the militaristic kingdom of Sparta, and the Roman Empire. Talented slaves could rise to positions of eminence,[4] but rebels like Spartacus faced death by crucifixion.[5]

With the fall of Rome and the fragmenting of political power in Europe, the peasantry of that continent, controlled by feudal lords in largely agricultural pursuits, enjoyed no better than the semi-slave status of serfdom. As practiced by Europeans, however, true slavery was a product of the Age of Exploration. Following in the footsteps of Arab slave traders in North Africa, Portuguese explorers discovered the Dark Continent and its wealth of human resources early in the fifteenth century. Portuguese traders soon developed a thriving business from the capture and sale of relatively defenseless Africans. When Spanish, English, and Dutch adventurers entered the field, Portugal sought, and eventually received, the pope's confirmation of its ownership of Guinea, which was the major staging area on the west African coast for embarkation of slaves.[6]

Competition for a share of the slave market was sponsored by kings and clerics as well as merchants. The monarchs of Portugal, Spain, France, and England gave their royal assent to companies engaged in the trafficking of slave labor.[7] Church officials confirmed the legitimacy of this form of commerce and supplied monks and ministers to convert the heathen captives to Christianity. The question of ethics in the capture, purchase, and sale of human beings rarely arose. King Charles II of Spain initiated an investigation in 1684 after learning that ships owned by Dutch heretics (that is to say, Protestants) were being used to transport slaves to the Spanish West Indies. Responding to an order from the king, a committee of high officials, including a Franciscan father, considered what they called "the religious question" and "unanimously declared that they had no doubt with regard to this matter." Their concern was not with the rights of slaves, but with the danger of dealing with heretics in the course of procuring slaves. They supported the liaison, on the very practical grounds that "the Dutch own the factories whence the negroes are brought" and that, economically, "the Indies could not be maintained without negroes." Even the Council of the Inquisition, the committee reported, was satisfied with the care taken to preserve the "purity of our Holy Faith." Pressed by the king to answer the specific question of "whether the traffic in negroes was lawful," the Council of the Indies assured their sovereign that the writings of theologians and jurists proved conclusively that the practice was justified by "its long-lived and general custom in the Kingdoms of Castile, America, and Portugal, without any objection on the part of his holiness [the pope] or ecclesiastical state, but rather with the tolerance of all of them."[8]

SLAVERY COMES TO NORTH AMERICA

While Portuguese domination lasted, most African slaves were sold in Europe or in the Portuguese colony of Brazil. As exploration opened new territories in the western hemisphere, the principal market for slaves moved to that part of the world. The competition to supply the new market broadened to include every major maritime nation of Christian Europe: England, France, the Netherlands, and Spain contesting with Portugal for a share of the lucrative trade.[9]

Initially, demand in the western hemisphere was for farm labor in the Caribbean islands where sugar and tobacco plantations flourished. Jamaica's slave population in 1670 was less than 7,000; but within 20 years "slaves outnumbered the whites by four to one," and a century later the labor of 200,000 slaves made the island the world's leading sugar producer.[10]

The first slaves imported into the English colonies of North America were brought to Virginia only a dozen years after the first permanent settlement was established. A history written by an "inhabitant of the place" reports that in August of 1620 "a Dutch Man of War landed twenty Negroes for sale."[11] Whether this event occurred in 1620 or, as more recent studies conclude, in 1619, there is no dispute over the fact that a Dutch warship was the carrier.[12] Less than a decade later, American slave ships began to ply their trade from bases, not in the South, but in New England.[13]

During the following century of English colonization the slave population grew slowly; but, as settlers in the southern states cleared and developed more and more farming areas, awareness of the economic benefits of slave labor brought increasing demand, and slave traders—many operating out of Massachusetts and Rhode Island—responded with alacrity. Two crops in particular lent themselves to what was, for that era, large-scale farming: rice and cotton. By 1780, before Eli Whitney's invention of the cotton gin in 1793, the number of slaves in the thirteen colonies had risen to approximately 550,000, or one-fifth of the total population.[14] Whitney's device so speeded the processing of raw cotton that production skyrocketed, further stimulating the demand for slaves to plant and harvest the crop, and rooting the institution of slavery more firmly than ever.

This system of applying a seemingly simple economic solution to the agricultural needs of the South had a profound impact on the social and political values and customs of people in the slave states. A chronicler of South Carolina's early history describes the effects this way:

> The majority of the settlers of Carolina had had no previous acquaintance with slave labor; but they readily embraced an agrarian economy stemming from slave labor, which promised both pecuniary and social rewards. The Huguenots, for example, after wasting much time and effort in an attempt to produce silk, turned to stock raising and to the cultivation of Indian corn, indigo and rice with slave labor. In brief, they abandoned their Old World legacy for the mores and pursuits of the leading English families of Carolina. They intermarried with the English, gradually dropped the use of the mother tongue, joined the Anglican Church and, in general, became identified with the planting gentry.[15]

For have-not whites, the goal was expressed more succinctly in this three-line ditty:

> All I want in this creation
> Is a pretty little wife
> And a big plantation.[16]

The advantages of slave labor were appreciated in the North as well, particularly during the colonial period, although this category of worker was found to be more economical in nonagricultural pursuits. Northern attitudes toward blacks varied from state to state and community to community. In New York, which in 1780 had the largest Negro population of the area at 19,000, slavery "was primarily a labor system, but it was also a method of race control." According to one account, the citizens of that state "lived in fear and sometimes panic of their enslaved neighbors and servants." Oppressive legislation led to a minor revolt in 1712. Thirty years later, when rumors of a new uprising began to circulate, the system of justice gave way to hysteria and "judges sentenced eighteen Negroes to hanging, thirteen to burning, and seventy to exile."[17]

Regardless of whether slaves were used as plantation workers, household servants, or chore boys, their legal status throughout the colonies was that of personal property. Other elements in the social structure inherited by American settlers permitted varieties of bondage that were less onerous than slavery, but that nevertheless severely restricted both the freedom and the privileges of a significant portion of the population. Women comprised the greatest segment of the disenfranchised, having no voice whatever in political or religious matters and few legal rights that could stand against the word or will of a parent or husband. Bonded servants worked under contractual conditions that, for all practical purposes, made them "slaveys," an English term that appropriately described the servile condition of employees subject to their masters' every whim. Apprentices fared somewhat better, as they could contribute to the success of a business, but while they were so engaged they had little opportunity for independent decision making.[18]

Notwithstanding the lack of freedom and the paucity of privilege among these deprived groups, they had at least the advantage of being acknowledged human beings with recognizable legal rights and access—however limited—to the law for protection of those rights. If slaves were considered part of the human race, it was as a subspecies not entitled to any legal standing in society. Most of the laws passed to limit either the merchandising or holding of slaves were applicable to the owners and did not bestow any legal rights upon those held in bondage. One apparent exception was the Massachusetts Body of Liberties of 1641, which proclaimed: "There shall never be any bond slaverie, villinage or Captivitie amongst us unles it be lawfull Captives taken in just warres and such strangers as willingly selle themselves or are sold to us."[19] Two conditions made this guarantee illusory. One was its frame of reference, which was established by its place in a section applicable only to "Forreiners and Strangers." Further, the exception of "Captives taken in just warres" recognized the argument used by English slavers to justify their trade, namely, that the people they brought from Africa were prisoners of war turned over to them by embattled African tribesmen. The ineffectiveness of this pledge as a means of preventing slavery in Massachusetts is further demonstrated by subsequent accounts of the importation and sale of slaves within the colony.[20]

A more restrictive piece of legislation was an act of the General Court of Rhode Island, which in 1652 declared that "no blacke mankind or white being [be] forced by covenant bond, or otherwise, to serve any man or his assighnes longer than ten years, or untill they come to bee twentie four yeares of age.''[21] In the absence of similar legislation in the other colonies, the obvious escape route from this situation was for the slaveholder to transfer his property to an owner in another colony.

These early restrictions made little impact on either the slave trade or the growth of slave ownership in the American colonies. They were, in fact, more than offset by the actions of some colonies to increase, rather than inhibit, that commerce. Beginning in 1671, Maryland passed a succession of laws urging traders and shipowners to greater activity in bringing slaves to the colony. This purpose was set forth clearly in 1704 by ''An Act to encourage the Inhabitants of this Province to Adventure their shipps and Vessels more freely abroad to import Rum, Sugar, Negroes and other Commoditys.''[22] In 1714, South Carolina levied a tax on slaves imported from Africa, because its slave population had burgeoned to what whites considered threatening proportions. The receipts were to be used ''for the better Ordering and Governing Negroes and all other Slaves,'' who were multiplying so much faster than whites that ''the safety of the Province is greatly endangered.''[23] Georgia's James Oglethorpe pleaded in vain with the trustees of that colony to deny a ''Petition for Negroes which affirms that white men cannot work in this Province.'' Ignored was his warning that ''if the Petition is countenanced the Province is ruined.''[24]

Considering the almost universal sanction given the institution of slavery by the major powers, including England, it is little wonder that New England shipowners (principally in Massachusetts and Rhode Island) continued to vie with European entrepreneurs in the business of supplying slaves to the colonies. Most slaves went to settlements from Maryland to Georgia. The middle colonies offered only a limited market for slaves and took almost no part in the process of securing and transporting Africans to the Americas.

Throughout the colonial period, most of the opposition to slavery came from minority religious groups, principally Quakers, Mennonites, and Dunkers. Historian Anson Phelps Stokes reports that ''The first published protest against the institution in North America was by the monthly meeting of Friends in Germantown, Pennsylvania, in 1688.'' In this they were supported by Lutherans, who had prohibited the introduction of slavery into their early Swedish settlements along the Delaware River.[25] Although some Quakers were known to own slaves, the influential Philadelphia Yearly Meeting of Friends declared in 1693 that ''it should be the policy of Friends to buy no slaves 'except to set free.' '' They also agreed that the society's aim should be "to release their own slaves 'after a reasonable time of service.' "[26] Persistent efforts to eliminate slaveholding by Quakers culminated in resolutions to disown those who continued to buy, sell, or hold slaves.[27] Despite these actions, however, Pennsylvania never reached the point of legislating the gradual abolition of slavery until 1780, more than 20 years after the Quakers had lost control of the state assembly.[28]

Serious opposition to slavery did not begin to build until the 1770s, when notions of independence from Britain stirred the colonies. The subject of emancipation arose in the Massachusetts General Court in 1773 and was urged, unsuccessfully at that point, by some who saw human bondage as irreconcilable with the demands for freedom. As one writer to the Massachusetts *Spy* put it, "The patriots in every town throughout the province are weekly telling us how highly they value freedom . . . yet at the same time they are stopping their ears to the cries of their poor unhappy suffering brethern."[29] That same year, Pennsylvania physician Benjamin Rush wrote and published a masterful "Address to the Inhabitants of the British Settlements in America," attacking every major argument that had been offered in support of slavery.[30] Extraordinary in scope and perception, Rush's essay sought to demolish not only the economic justification for slavery, but the validity of biblical references to that practice. More boldly than that, Rush even challenged the purportedly superior intellect of whites over blacks and, in terms that anticipated Charles Darwin by almost a century, explained the Africans' physical characteristics as a natural adaptation to "that part of the Globe in which Providence has placed them."

Legally, the ice was broken—or at least cracked—when, in 1774, Rhode Island passed "An Act for Prohibiting the Importation of Negroes into this Colony." Except for "Servants of persons travelling through this colony" and those brought from other British colonies, all other slaves brought into the province were to be "rendered immediately free." This did not mean, of course, that the emancipated slave would assume all the rights of Rhode Island citizens. The limits of this new freedom were indicated by the act's concluding phrase that it was to apply "in the same manner as [to] the native Indians."[31]

Churchmen other than Quakers and Lutherans joined in the debate during this period. Congregational minister Levi Hart denounced slavery as "contrary to the law of nature, which is the law of God," and warned that such a system was an invitation to tyranny and oppression.[32] Thomas Jefferson, on the other hand, expressed serious doubts as to the capacity of blacks to assume a place of equality with whites in American society.[33] Still, Jefferson's original draft of the Declaration of Independence included a two-paragraph denunciation of slavery as "cruel war against human nature itself, violating its most sacred rights of life and liberty." However, Jefferson later reported that this entire statement "was struck out in complaisance to South Carolina and Georgia, who had never attempted to restrain the importation of slaves, and who on the contrary still wished to continue it." His comment goes on to confirm what the record of slave trading clearly reveals: "Our Northern brethren also I believe felt a little tender under those censures; for tho' their people have very few slaves themselves, yet they had been pretty considerable carriers of them to others."[34]

Although the assertion that "all men are created equal" found its way from the Declaration of Independence into many early state constitutions, none of those written in the original 13 states interpreted this basic principle as meaning the end of slavery. Delaware came closest, declaring that "No person *hereafter* imported into this State *from Africa* ought to be hald in slavery under any pretence whatever; and no negro, Indian, or mulatto slave ought be brought into this State, *for sale*, from any part of the world" [emphasis added].[35] It remained for Vermont, which was not admitted into the Union until 1791, to write into its constitution a prohibition against holding "any male person . . . as a servant, slave or apprentice, after he arrives to the age of twenty-one years, nor female, in like manner, after she arrives to the age of eighteen years, unless they are bound by their own consent, after they arrive to such age, or bound by law, for the payment of debts, damages, fines, costs, or the like."[36] The other New England states, plus New York, New Jersey, and Pennsylvania, brought slavery to an end by legislation or court action rather than by explicit constitutional provisions. A precedent-setting case in 1781 brought freedom to a Massachusetts slave named Quork Walker when the court decided in favor of his claim that the state's constitutional adoption of the concept that "all men are created equal" meant it could not tolerate enslavement of any person.[37] By similar reasoning, the rest of the northern states eliminated, if not all slavery, at least the slave trade, by the time the call came for a constitutional convention to revise the Articles of Confederation. Imports had also been stopped by Maryland and Virginia where natural reproduction satisfied the needs in those states; but in South Carolina and Georgia the trade still flourished.

One other advance was won by anti-slave forces prior to adoption of the Constitution. In 1784 Jefferson induced Congress to consider a law setting forth the basic principles for governing the western territories that had been relinquished to the nation by the 13 states. Included in his proposal was a provision that "after the year 1800 there shall be neither slavery nor involuntary servitude" in any of the states formed out of this territory. Voting by states, as usual, Congress rejected the plan, 7–6, Jefferson's own state joining the opposition. Two years later, before the constitutional convention completed its work, Congress passed the Northwest Ordinance which prohibited slavery in all territories northwest of the Ohio River.[38]

THE LINES ARE DRAWN

In terms of geography, the battle lines over slavery were drawn in Philadelphia in 1787. That is not to say that opinion was wholly pro-slavery in the South or wholly anti-slavery in the North. Many of the most outstanding southern leaders acknowledged the evil of that institution and the danger of allowing it to continue. Men like James Madison and George Mason, who were on opposite sides in the bitter debate over the Constitution, agreed, in Mason's words, that the trade in human beings "is diabolical in itself, and disgraceful to mankind." However, where Mason felt so deeply about slavery that he "would not admit the Southern States into the Union unless they agree to the discontinuance of this disgraceful trade," Madison saw it as a lesser evil than the threat of disunion.[39]

Given the importance of slavery in economic, social, and political life, it was inevitable that an accommodation be made if the confederation were to be replaced by a national government—as inevitable as the earlier acceptance of a one-state-one-vote arrangement had been to agreement on the Articles of Confederation. Evidence of the importance of this issue came early in the Philadelphia convention. As delegates discussed the question of equality of state voting power in the Senate, Madison remarked that "the states were divided into different interests, not by their difference of size, but by other circumstances ... principally from [the effects of] their having or not having slaves."[40] When it became clear that representation in the House must be based on population, Hugh Williamson of North Carolina proposed that a census for this purpose include "the free white inhabitants and 3/5ths of those of other descriptions." South Carolina argued for full slave representation; but, when Elbridge Gerry and Nathaniel Gorham of Massachusetts pointed out that the three-fifths rule had already been agreed upon for purposes of taxation, that formula was approved.[41]

Agreement on the treatment of slaves in the calculation of taxes and representation simply confirmed the obvious, namely, that the southern states would not enter a constititional union without recognition of their right to continue the use of slave labor. The question of unrestricted trade in support of that system raised more heated objections. Most states had, by 1787, prohibited further imports of slaves and had sought to end this aspect of the system entirely. After vigorous opposition, mainly from South Carolina and Georgia, agreement was reached on a clause that prevented interference with the slave trade until 1808.[42]

In the Philadelphia discussions of slavery, the matter was debated principally as a problem in practical economics and equally practical politics. Few delegates offered support or opposition on moral grounds. Gouverneur Morris of Pennsylvania was one of those few, terming slavery "the curse of heaven on the States where it prevailed" and denouncing its acceptance by others as "a sacrifice of every principle of right, of every impulse of humanity."[43] George Mason of Virginia voiced similar distaste for "this infernal traffic," asserting that "every master of slaves is born a petty tyrant" who will "bring the judgment of heaven" down upon the entire country.[44]

The only effect these criticisms might have had was to encourage the use of euphemisms in that section of the Constitution that gave temporary protection to the slave trade. Thus, as Luther Martin pointed out in a wide-ranging, postconvention analysis of the proposed system of government, the Framers deliberately avoided the use of the word "slaves" in denying Congress the right to restrict "the migration or importation of such persons," and so forth. In this way, he said, "they anxiously sought to avoid the admission of expressions which might be odious in the ears of Americans."[45]

The most vigorous criticisms of slavery were voiced after the constitutional convention had adjourned. Much of the adverse comment appeared in the newspapers and pamphlets of the day, but some was heard in the state ratifying conventions. As delegates to the Massachusetts convention considered the Constitution, one member asked, "Shall it be said that after we have established our own independence and freedom, we make slaves of others?" To make the point more graphically, he charged that George Washington had lost stature by holding "those in slavery who have as good a right to be free as he has." Another delegate queried, "Shall we do any thing by our act to hold the blacks in slavery, or shall we become partakers of other men's sins?" A third compared what he viewed as the idyllic existence of Africans in their native lands with "their wretched, miserable and unhappy condition in a state of slavery."[46]

At the convention in Virginia, John Tyler, like George Mason, "warmly enlarged on the impolicy, iniquity, and disgracefulness of this wicked traffic."[47] Even the staunchly pro-slavery convention in South Carolina produced a few dissenters. Acknowledging the need for a temporary compromise, James Iredell nevertheless characterized the continued importation of slaves as "a trade utterly inconsistent with the rights of humanity." Others denied the immorality of slavery, one member insisting that "this trade could be justified on the principles of religion, humanity and justice; for certainly to [transport] a set of human beings from a bad country to a better was fulfilling every part of these principles."[48]

One of the most emotional appeals for rejecting any extension of the slave trade was made at the New Hampshire convention. Echoing the view of a Massachusetts representative that, in approving the Constitution, "we become consenters to, and partakers in, the sin and guilt of this abominable traffic," Joshua Atherton challenged his fellow delegates to put themselves in the same position as that faced by the victims of slave raiders. He asked them to imagine this scene:

> A company of these mansteelers, well equipped for the enterprise, arrives on our coast. They seize and carry off the whole or a part of the inhabitants of the town of Exeter. Parents are taken, and children left; or possibly they may be so fortunate as to have a whole family taken and carried off together.... Dragged at once from every thing they held dear to them ... they are hurried on a loathsome and distressing voyage to the coast of Africa, or some other quarter of the globe, where the greatest price may await them; and here, if any thing can be added to their miseries, comes on the heart-breaking scene: A parent is sold to one, a son to another, and a daughter to a third!

Atherton's further imaginings of the horrors his neighbors would be exposed to so unnerved him that he confessed the scene was "too affecting" and concluded, "I have not the fortitude to pursue the subject!"[49] This moving presentation did not deter the convention from ratifying the Constitution, nor did it produce a suggested amendment that would require elimination of slavery.

Outside convention halls, the moral exchange followed a similar course. In public print, Madison acknowledged that it would have been better to settle the slavery issue once and for all, but he urged that it "be considered as a great point gained in favor of humanity that a period of twenty years may terminate forever within these States a traffic which has so long and so loudly upbraided the barbarism of modern policy."[50]

On a pro-slavery side, a South Carolina physician-politician asserted that "In the Southern Colonies, slavery nurtured a spirit of liberty among the free inhabitants," explaining that the Revolution had saved free Americans from "a degree of dependence . . . equally humiliating with that which existed between his slaves and himself."[51]

As the extension date of 1808 approached, pressure began to build for an end, not to slavery, but to the slave trade. Congress responded in 1807 by passing "An Act to Prohibit the importation of Slaves into any port or place within the jurisdiction of the United States, from and after the first day of January, in the year of our Lord one thousand eight hundred and eight."[52]

Important as this step was, it had little effect on the domestic institution of slavery, since, by this time, normal reproduction in the black population provided an ample labor supply for both old and new slave states. Additions to the latter category kept well ahead of new non-slave states: Until the 1840s and 1850s, when five new states from Wisconsin to California entered the Union, free-state additions were more than matched by admitting slave states from Florida westward to Texas and Arkansas. By 1860, eighteen states were committed to the principle that all men are born free—but not necessarily equal. Fifteen states permitted slavery; however, when it came to the critical question of secession, four of them (Delaware, Maryland, Kentucky, and Missouri) refused to take this drastic step.[53]

THE ROLE OF THE CHURCHES

One of the most striking contradictions in the development of the United States from 1800 to 1860 was the growing strength of slavery during a period in which the trend in politics was toward greater democratization. As the country's frontier moved farther and farther west, settlers in the new territories left the habits of the eastern aristocracies behind and took into their own hands the operation of town, county, and state politics—often with far fewer restrictions regarding the qualifications of electors. At the national level, the election of Andrew Jackson in 1828 signaled the start of a new era. Jackson announced his intention of introducing a system of rotation in public office, his purpose being "to destroy the idea of property in office, cut down an office-holding class, and give all citizens an equal opportunity to enjoy the privilege of participating in the task of self-government."[54]

Much of the enthusiasm for Jacksonian democracy came from the west. As settlers moved west, so did the churches, although not in the organized fashion of the priests who accompanied the Spanish conquest of Latin America. "Without societies or other means of organizing their scanty resources," one chronicler wrote, the churches nevertheless "kept step with the colonizing enterprise of the people."[55] This writer was speaking principally of Baptist preachers, who were among the more venturesome clerics in the movement westward. Methodist ministers were equally active in these migrations, and the story of that sect reveals the extent to which religion and politics were inextricably entangled in the half-century before the Civil War.

The Methodist Episcopal Church was relatively young at the close of the Revolution. At that time it was in the throes of organizational upheaval, occasioned by its adoption of an episcopate, with a bishop now overseeing what had been largely independent congregations. It was saved from dissolution, one historian believes, by the opening of trails across the Appalachians. "The men of the Methodist itinerancy had no time to sit down and fuss about the details of church order after the roads opened to the new settlements beyond the mountains. . . . There were Methodist preachers in almost every wagontrain of pioneers who took the trail to the wilderness."[56]

Like other church groups, Methodists experienced internal disruptions from time to time over purely ecclesiastical questions. Its most fundamental split, however, was over the issue of slavery. Almost all U.S. churches were similarly affected, but the shock was especially severe for the Methodists, whose first leader, John Wesley, had denounced slavery as "the sum of all villainies."[57] His principal representative in the United States was Dr. Thomas Coke, who brought "an equally unequivocal conviction as to the evil of the slave trade and never hesitated to proclaim his views when he was preaching in this country."[58]

At the church's first general conference in 1784, "Rules were adopted requiring members who owned slaves, and lived in States where emancipation was possible, to free them or withdraw from the church." That was not the last word, however. With the advent of the cotton gin and the impetus that invention gave to the demand for slaves, a retreat began and discussion of slavery was discouraged, even in the North.

Finally, abolitionist members withdrew and formed a separate Wesleyan Methodist Church. This did not prevent an even deeper split, which came with the demand that a southern bishop "desist from the exercise of this office" for as long as he insisted on retaining his slaves. At that point, in 1844, southern church members and ministers, who owned more than 200,000 slaves, left the mother church and formed the Methodist Episcopal Church, South.[59] When the Civil War broke out, seventeen years later, Methodists on both sides enlisted in the contending armies, supplied chaplains for the fighting forces, and held prayer meetings and revivals in support of their separate causes.[60]

The year 1844, when southern Methodists seceded from the national church, was a critical one for the country in other ways. National political parties had adopted the convention system for nominating presidential candidates; and, although their goals were not always set forth in official platforms, their statements of principle had begun to show the significance of the slavery question. Abolitionists unsatisfied with both major parties of that period (Democrats and Whigs) formed the Liberal Party and, in 1844, ran their first candidate for president. Their 44-point platform—an unusually lengthy document for that era—devoted half of its resolutions to the evils of slavery. The brief Whig platform avoided the subject altogether; but the Democrats met it head-on by repeating this denunciation of anti-slavery that they had issued four years earlier:

> That Congress has no power, under the Constitution, to interfere with or control the domestic institutions of the several States; and that such States are the sole and proper judges of everything pertaining to their own affairs, not prohibited by the Constitution; and that all efforts by abolitionists or others, made to induce Congress to interfere with questions of slavery . . . endanger the stability and permanency of the Union and ought not to be countenanced by any friend to our Political Institutions.[61]

Thus, the Democratic Party attempted to define the problem of slavery in legal terms—while the churches were attacking or defending that institution principally on moral grounds. Like it or not, practically all churches were involved, for their members made up a significant portion of the voters in the political parties that were soon to make the slavery issue one of life-and-death for the nation.

On the moral issue, no church could remain a disinterested party. A few tried, with varying degrees of success. The Catholic church and its nearest Protestant counterpart, the Episcopal church, stood above the conflict and in this way avoided the schisms that tore other sects apart. This posture was more easily assumed by the Catholic clergy, who were not free to take a position on slavery one way or another without instruction from Rome. Officially, the church was a neutral in this struggle as it had been in earlier years when, for example, South American liberator Simón Bolívar issued his 1816 edict against slavery, or when England decided to abolish slavery in 1833. Another 140 years were to pass before the crusading Pope John Paul II was to break tradition by asking "pardon from our African brothers" for the slave trade that had been carried on for so long by Christian nations.[62] By comparison, a history of Catholicism written less than a decade earlier devoted a chapter to the U.S. church without making any reference whatever to slavery or the Civil War.[63]

Among Protestant churches, those least affected by the slavery issue were the Quakers, who had abandoned slave owning before the close of the eighteenth century, and the Congregationalists, whose westward expansion was primarily from New England into the territories north of the Ohio River, where slavery was proscribed by federal law. Quaker participation in the Underground Railroad, a loosely organized system of aid to escaped slaves, carried on in direct defiance of the federal Fugitive Slave Law, is part of church history. On the other hand, although many Congregationalists were strong supporters of the abolitionist movement, an approved history of the Congregational church includes no coverage—or even an index reference—to either slavery or the Civil War.[64]

The Episcopal clergy tried to prevent disruption within that church by ignoring the problem, and they were very nearly successful. In a sense, this was consistent with the Episcopal tradition that "secular affairs were matters of no concern to the Church." In consequence, there was a "deep reluctance of the Church . . . to express itself on any subject which could possibly be described as 'political.' "[65] This did not prevent individual church members from having strong opinions about slavery, but it did avoid an open split until after the southern states had seceded from the Union. Then, in the Anglican tradition of a national (rather than international) church, Episcopalians in the new nation formed by the Confederacy drew up a constitution for the Protestant Episcopal Church of the Confederate States of America. Thus, "it was political secession which preceded and prompted ecclesiastical secession." By the same logic, the church became reunited, with no acknowledgment of separation ever having been made, after the war ended and the southern states had resumed their place in the Union.[66]

Lutheran and Presbyterian congregations were more severely affected by the rising conflict. As one church chronicler points out, "for most Lutheran people the question of slavery was theoretical." This was because they were concentrated in the farming areas of the North and West and only thinly scattered through the South. Like the members of other sects, however, they were inclined to follow the local trend, "opposed to slavery in the North, favoring it in the South, and divided in the West." Despite a long history of anti-slavery in Lutheran settlements (largely Swedish and German), the official church publication attempted to maintain a neutral position in the 1830s and 1840s. "Editorials rebuked the North for trying to force its ideas of right and wrong on the whole nation, and took the South to task for threatening a violent breach." This did not satisfy individual synods, some of which came out in flat rejection of slavery as "an evil which all Christians should deplore" or, more forcefully, "revolting to humanity and repugnant to the laws of Christ." Synods in southern states reacted by denouncing the "intermeddling . . . of affected patriots and more than rotten hearted benefactors" or by declaring abolitionism "a combination of ignorance, fanaticism, and dishonesty." Like the Episcopalians, Lutherans held out against a formal split until the very last moment. Then when southern groups refused to send delegates to the 1862 General Synod, that body "read the southern synods out of its fellowship," citing the "open sympathy and active cooperation which they have given to the cause of treason and insurrection."[67]

Presbyterians had a more significant membership in the South, which brought their differences over slavery to a head well before the Civil War. The 1845 General Assembly, under dominant Southern influence, approved a resolution "that the Assembly . . . was originally organized and has since continued . . . upon the conceded principle that the existence of domestic slavery, as found in the southern portion of this country, is no bar to Christian communion." When the ultimate test came, by way of South Carolina's secession from the Union, Presbyterians reacted in the same way as the members of other churches: they put political loyalty to their state or region ahead of either religious solidarity within the church or unity of the nation. Thus, when South Carolina seceded, that state's Presbyterian synod followed suit. For another three years, some of the most influential leaders attempted to hold the church together. The issue was finally decided in 1864, when the Assembly approved a compromise resolution that omitted any condemnation of slavery but affirmed its support for the Union. This purely political decision, which seemed to confirm the attitude expressed in a Philadelphia newspaper that "In times like these patriotism *is* Christianity," proved to be the last straw. The southern churches, many of which had already defected, joined together in forming the Presbyterian Church in the United States.[68]

Of more lasting significance to the nation as a whole was the struggle within the Baptist community, which had grown from a persecuted minority in early New England to a flourishing establishment in all parts of the country. Attempting to maintain a neutral position in the face of the increasingly vocal abolitionist movement led by William Lloyd Garrison and others, the General Convention in 1844 adopted the following resolution:

> Resolved, That in co-operating together as members in this Convention in the work of foreign missions, we disclaim all sanctions either expressed or implied, whether of slavery or anti-slavery; but as individuals we are free to express and to promote elsewhere our views on these subjects in a Christian manner and spirit.

This action merely postponed the inevitable. As one of the most active proselytizing organizations in the religious community, it had to face the question of missionary activity by slave owners. Here the executive committee drew the line, sending this reply to an inquiry from a southern church:

> If any one who should offer himself for a missionary, having slaves, should insist on retaining them as his property, we could not appoint him. One thing is certain, we can never be a party to an arrangement which would imply approbation of slavery.

The following year, delegates from the southern churches formed the Southern Baptist Convention, convinced that, as a later church historian put it, the executive committee had "misjudged their duties as Christian men" by departing from the policy laid down by the General Convention.[69]

The critical nature of the cleavage over slavery experienced by the religious community is revealed by the bitterness of the doctrinal debate and the animosities that persisted for almost a century after the Civil War, in some cases to this very day. Prewar wrangling, whether on the political level or between churchmen, was acrimonious and uncompromising. Abolitionist William Lloyd Garrison inflamed the South with his unrelenting campaign, castigating every aspect of slavery and demanding its immediate abolition.[70] His rage, in turn, was fed by attitudes like that of Governor Hammond of South Carolina, whose view was that "God created Negroes for no other purpose than to be subordinate 'hewers of wood and drawers of water'—that is, to be slaves of the white race." Against the abolitionist charge of immorality, a professor at William and Mary College in Virginia declared, in effect, that "slavery was so beneficial to both blacks and whites that it ought to be encouraged."[71] In Charleston, South Carolina, the local Baptist Association replied to abolitionists in political terms, essentially, when it charged that "the deluded and mischievous fanatics who interfere with the domestic institutions in the slaveholding states" were engaged in deliberate disruption that was "not only officious and unfriendly but incendiary and murderous in its tendency, highly injurious to the interests of the slaves and fatal to the feelings of a common brotherhood."[72]

Argued in religious terms, slavery was denounced as "a sin ... opposed to the spirit of the Gospel"[73] and defended on the ground that "if the new Testament nowhere condemns slaveholding ... then to pronounce slaveholding to be in itself sinful is contrary to Scriptures."[74] Within one Lutheran seminary, a professor pursued the debate after the war had begun, writing a series of articles chiding a colleague for charging that "the North had violated God's law in carrying on the Civil War, that Negro slavery in the United States was a 'divine institution,' and that those who did not agree were neither Lutheran nor Christian." The theologian who opposed this position declared in his own published articles that slavery was indefensible "from the point of view of Scripture."[75]

Pro-slavery sentiment was by no means limited to the South. One Northern sympathizer was a rector of the New York Church of the Annunciation (Episcopal). Denying that the problem of slavery should "be complicated with questions of morality, religion, and social reputation," he concluded, like Governor Hammond, that since "the Anglo-Saxon race is king, why should not the African race be subject?"[76] Thus, not for the first time in human experience, both sides offered the same holy scriptures as the basis for their opposing points of view. Neither was defending the Christian faith but, rather, a sociopolitical concept of the good society. The substitution of military force for verbal battle marked the culmination of a breakdown in the Founders' faith in the ability of the people of the United States to maintain a feeling of national unity through compromise and consensus.

When the guns around Fort Sumter signaled the opening of the Civil War, the event was observed by a western world that had eliminated slavery decades earlier without resorting to open warfare. In the midst of that world, a nation dedicated to freedom, and proud of its Christian heritage, found Christianity incapable of meeting its most serious challenge or of avoiding the bloodiest conflict in U.S. history. Moreover, the war's end did not bring about a reconciliation of attitudes, even in the churches, where healing might have been expected to occur first. Except for the Episcopal church, northern and southern branches of the major Protestant organizations remained divided, unmoved by the rapid erosion of the equal rights that were theoretically extended to the freed slave population by the Thirteenth, Fourteenth, and Fifteenth Amendments.

One response to that indifference was a rapid expansion of the Negro churches, which had formed under white guidance and control prior to the Civil War. Over the years, the growth of black churches has been most rapid in the two largest Protestant sects, Baptist and Methodist. Latest available membership figures show that the National Baptist Convention of America and the National Baptist Convention, U.S.A., both black, have a combined membership of more than 8 million, second only to the white Southern Baptist Convention's 14 million. Northern and southern Methodist Episcopal churches finally recombined in 1939 as the United Methodist church; and, by 1981, membership had passed the 9 million mark. However, this figure did not include parishioners of the African Methodist Episcopal church and the African Methodist Episcopal Zion church, which, together, recorded a membership exceeding 3 million.[77]

6

New Trends—New Problems

The Civil War marked the beginning of a new era in more ways than one. In the century preceding that conflict, the United States had been a land of farms and farmers. Agriculture had been the principal occupation of the 13 original colonies. It continued to provide a living for the over-whelming majority of the population throughout the decades of expansion into the Northwest Territory and the enormous tracts to the south and west that were secured by treaties with France, Spain, and Mexico.[1] From the first census, taken in 1790, to the eighth in 1860, the country's population leaped from just under 4 million to over 31 million. During that same period, despite rapid development of commerce, manufacturing, and other nonfarm pursuits, the enormous farming areas added by the country's physical growth kept this a largely rural nation. In 1790, over 99 percent of the population was recorded as rural, and only 24 cities could boast more than 2,500 persons. By 1860, almost 400 metropolitan centers existed, the largest exceeding 500,000 population, compared to the few in 1790 that contained from 25,000 to 50,000 souls. Nevertheless, in 1860, approximately 71 percent of the total labor force was still engaged in agriculture.[2]

Notwithstanding the enormous additions of western land converted from territories to states after the Civil War, the percentage of people employed in agriculture declined steadily, until, according to the first census after Arizona was admitted as the forty-eighth state, that figure was down to 27 percent. The simultaneous growth of nonagricultural activity was just as dramatic. In terms of employment, the fledgling manufacturing community of the early nineteenth century rose from 14 percent in 1860 to 20 percent in 1900. During the same period, the share of workers engaged in trade rose from 8 percent to 14 percent. Employment in transportation, mining, construction, and the service industries rose less sharply but, taken together, these increases reflected the declining importance of agriculture.[3]

Changes in the character of the economy were accompanied by a shift in the ethnic and religious mix of the population. Immigration, which had always been a significant factor in the country's growth, continued to add substantial numbers to the population, but with some notable differences. To begin with, less than 10 percent of the newcomers were farmers looking for open land. Most were attracted by the prospect of employment in the expanding commercial, industrial, and transportation centers, or in service opportunities created by the growth of cities.[4] Pre-Civil War immigration—even that spurred by the Irish famine during the 1840s—paled by comparison with the flood that followed the war. From 1865 to 1900, aliens seeking a better life streamed into the United States at an average rate of 450,000 a year. Until 1880, the great majority of these newcomers were from northern Europe, particularly Ireland and Germany, both of which had long since displaced Great Britain as the chief source of "new blood." During the last two decades of the century, increasing numbers came from central, eastern, and southern Europe, with much smaller contingents from Asia (primarily China), and, from the other American countries (mostly Canada). Except for the Asians, this influx was preponderantly Catholic. As a result, a traditionally Protestant country found that, by 1890, its Catholic population had grown to be the largest single denomination in the religious community. Protestants of all varieties still accounted for the majority of church memberships, but the 6¼ million Catholics numbered more than either of the two largest Protestant sects, the Methodists and the Baptists, even counting all the disunited branches.[5]

BY-PRODUCTS OF INDUSTRIAL GROWTH

The second half of the nineteenth century was notable also for the passing of the old frontier, which ended at the Pacific Ocean, and the opening of new frontiers in science, invention, and business organization. In the last category, railroads led the way, supported by federal and state grants of land and special tax and other concessions. Covering the nation in a network that mushroomed from 35,000 miles of track in 1865 to 200,000 miles in 1900, the enormous increase in available transportation not only invited but spurred the development of industry and trade. It also established a pattern of monopolistic enterprise; manipulation of markets, prices, and securities; control and bribery of public officials, and indifference to political and social ethics—a pattern that came to characterize much of the business community well into the twentieth century.

The moral chaos of the post-Civil War period was exhibited in its most degrading form during the administration of President Ulysses S. Grant. The problem continued long afterward, however, and involved far more than "rotten politicians." As commentators from the 1860s to the 1880s repeatedly complained, "the diminished value of character" was evident throughout the commercial world as well.[6] Writing for *Century Magazine* in 1884, one contributor expressed his despair in this fashion:

> No feature of the present age is more displeasing to the moralist than the dishonesty that so widely prevails in commerce and politics. In whatever direction we turn, this phenomenon meets our eye; and there is no branch of business, no department of government, and no class in society in which it does not appear. The forms of Commercial dishonesty are almost endless in variety.[7]

That summary followed two decades of public and private corruption highlighted by national scandals involving four of President Grant's cabinet officers; Internal Revenue tax collectors in the pay of the Whiskey Ring; politicians and railroad officials in the Credit Mobilier stock fraud; and U.S. marshals who "plundered the public treasury by fraudulent and fictitious charges."[8] During the Grant administration, officials were protected by the president, who refused to believe that his appointees could be guilty of more than carelessness or poor judgment. Some years were to pass before either Congress or the executive branch would consider regulatory legislation a proper method of protecting the public interest. It was assumed that, where private enterprise was concerned, the federal government had no jurisdiction beyond the very limited areas specified in the Constitution.

The concept of a public interest more important than private rights and freedoms had existed long before the United States was established as an independent nation. Two centuries earlier, Britain's Lord Chief Justice Hale had written that, when private property is "affected with a public interest," it ceases to be a purely private matter.[9] However, in the United States, such problems were handled on the state or local level; the national government participated only if a constitutional question brought the matter before a federal court.

The constitutionality of state regulation of private business rose as early as 1824, when New York State insisted that it could grant an exclusive license to navigate that state's waters, even to transport passengers to and from New Jersey. The U.S. Supreme Court disagreed, finding this an intrusion into federal control of interstate commerce.[10] In another case, Maryland tried to tax importers to control "articles which endanger public health." Although the Supreme Court acknowledged the importance of this factor, it insisted that a tax on imports intruded on the constitutional right of the federal government to control foreign and interstate commerce.[11] On the other hand, the court supported state control over construction of dams, bridges, and the licensing of ferries on navigable waters used for interstate transportation. State and local regulatory legislation was successfully challenged only when such laws were found to be in conflict with federal legislation or when they assumed a power (principally, commerce power) reserved to the national government. In the District of Columbia, federal statutes of 1820 and 1848 authorized the city of Washington to "regulate the rates of wharfage ... the sweeping of chimneys, ... the weight and quality of bread" and, further, "to make all necessary regulations respecting hackney carriages and the rates of hauling by cartmen, wagoners, carmen and draymen."[12]

Acceptance of a state's or city's right to guard against threats to the general health and welfare of the public opened the door to more far-reaching controls over a company's managerial judgments. This more stringent exercise of regulatory authority is precisely what a few major agricultural states of the Middle West undertook, attempting to protect farmers against unconscionable freight and storage rates levied by the completely unregulated and ruthless railroad system. There followed a series of confrontations in the country's courts, in what came to be known as the Granger Cases. The most famous of these reached the Supreme Court in 1877, indicating the depth and breadth of the philosophical debate, which has continued down to the present day.[13] The basic question was whether or not the Fourteenth Amendment to the Constitution prohibited a state from adopting a regulation that would "deprive any person of life, liberty, or property without due process of law." The majority of the Supreme Court found that "Common carriers exercise a sort of public office, and ... their business is, therefore, 'affected with a public interest.' " Because of this, an Illinois law affecting warehouse rates was declared to be "not repugnant to the Constitution of the United States."

The long-term implications of this decision were pointed out in a vigorous dissenting opinion by Justice Stephen J. Field, who called the majority view "subversive of the rights of private property, heretofore believed to be protected by constitutional guarantees against legislative interference." Field insisted that "the public has no greater interest in the use of buildings for the storage of grain than it has in the use of buildings for the residences of families." Citing public interest in a variety of manufactured products, he concluded that "there is hardly an enterprise or business engaging the attention and labor of any considerable portion of the community in which the public has not an interest in the sense in which that term is used by the court in its opinion." Justice Field was more farseeing than he knew—as late-twentieth-century controls over rents, prices, and working conditions in industry demonstrate.

Federal regulatory legislation was forced on the scene by economic problems stemming from concentrations of industrial power. Best known are the Interstate Commerce Act of 1887 and the Sherman Antitrust Act of 1890, both based on the constitutional grant of authority over foreign and interstate commerce, and introduced to control practices that the individual states were powerless to deal with. Hailed as important protectors of the public interest, the ICC and Sherman acts did little to curb the authority and excesses of the corporate giants they purported to challenge. Government victories in a few widely publicized cases made scarcely a dent in the economic power of major industrial concerns.[14] Moreover, where the rights of employees were concerned, federal power over interstate commerce was more likely to be applied against labor than against business. When Congress enacted legislation to forbid interstate commerce in the products of child labor, or to deny the use of an injunction against labor unions, the Supreme Court declared these statutes to be unconstitutional.[15]

In relations between government and the individual, one element of the post-Civil War settlement had far-reaching consequences of a sort unsuspected at the time. During the decades when guarantees of freedom and equal rights for black citizens were being eroded by violence, intimidation, and manipulation of voting procedures in most southern states and many northern communities, the Fourteenth Amendment was used to defend economic interests rather than civil and political rights.

THE STRANGE STORY
OF THE FOURTEENTH AMENDMENT

Ten months before the close of the Civil War, the Republican Party, nominating Abraham Lincoln for a second presidential term, included in its 1864 platform this goal for legitimizing Lincoln's 1863 Emancipation Proclamation:

> Resolved, That as slavery was the cause, and now constitutes the strength of this Rebellion, and as it must be ... hostile to the principles of Republican Government ... we are in favor of such an amendment to the Constitution ... as shall terminate and forever prohibit the existence of Slavery within the limits of the jurisdiction of the United States.[16]

The immediate objective of this pledge was accomplished by the Thirteenth Amendment, which was passed by Congress and ratified by the states in 1865.[17] Immediately thereafter, Congress, which included no representatives from the Confederate states, drew up a further amendment, conferring citizenship on the freed slaves and stipulating that, when the right to vote in a presidential election is denied to any male citizen of the United States, "except for participation in rebellion or other crime," the basis for that state's representation is to be reduced accordingly. The more radical of the Republicans, unwilling to wait for the amendment process to run its course, attempted to grant the rights of citizenship to all freedmen, by pushing the Civil Rights Act of 1866 through Congress, passing it over the veto of President Andrew Johnson.[18] Debate over the legality of this measure ended two years later, when the Fourteenth Amendment became part of the Constitution.

That modification of constitutional law was not accomplished easily, however. The major sticking point was the implication (not specifically stated) that the former slave population would have the right to vote. This was resisted as bitterly by northern Democrats and conservative Republicans as by southerners.[19] The compromise version reached after long debate and negotiation was designed to resolve the problems that remained after the Thirteenth Amendment had eliminated slavery, but to do so in a way that would coax—rather than bludgeon—the southern states into resuming their place in the Union. In the critical area of suffrage for black citizens, still another amendment was necessary, the Fifteenth, which was not ratified until March 30, 1870, two years after acceptance of the Fourteenth.

The Fourteenth Amendment began life under conditions whose repercussions are still being felt today. Realizing the strength of the opposition, its sponsors sought to gain southern approval by giving the impression that readmission of representatives from secessionist states would be the reward for ratification. In the end, and with the help of military governors in what constituted occupied territories, this tactic succeeded, but not before Ohio and New Jersey legislatures had passed resolutions rescinding their earlier ratifications. When Secretary of State Seward finally reported that three-quarters of the states had ratified the amendment, he included Ohio and New Jersey in his tally as well as some southern states "not yet reinstated by Congress."[20] As one historian summarized the procedure, "the ratification process was most unusual, if not contrary to constitutional principles."[21]

Adoption of the Fourteenth Amendment may have closed the book on the bloody conflict over slavery, but it created a new battleground on which opposing philosophies of government and economics would contend far into the future. Political intrigue and judicial bias played no small part in this contest.

Of all the provisions designed by the Fourteenth Amendment to protect the country's black citizens, the one having the greatest impact was a single sentence that read:

> No state shall make or enforce any law which shall abridge the privileges or immunities of citizens of the United States; nor shall any State deprive any person of life, liberty, or property, without due process of law; nor deny to any person within its jurisdiction the equal protection of the laws.

Ostensibly a link in the armor woven to protect the newly freed slaves, this section was used by the legal and political arms of the nation to extend constitutional rights and safeguards from people to "artificial persons," that is, corporations. This interpretation was first offered by Roscoe Conkling, a lawyer representing the Southern Pacific Railroad in an 1882 case before the U.S. Supreme Court.[22] Conkling explained that when the Fourteenth Amendment was drafted, the word "citizen" was used to designate human beings, while "person" was introduced specifically to include both humans and artificial beings such as corporations. Conkling had been a member of the congressional committee that drew up the amendment. After leaving Congress, he had achieved sufficient fame as an attorney to win him a recommendation for appointment to the Supreme Court. Impressed by his reputation as well as his personal participation in the design of the Fourteenth Amendment, the court accepted his view that the intent of that amendment was to include corporations among the "persons" given the protection of not only due process but of the equal protection clause as well.[23]

Many historians of a later era concluded that, because Conkling's argument was based on inference and innuendo, the intention to include corporations under Fourteenth Amendment protection was cleverly masked from the outset, in what amounted to a conspiracy to accomplish an end not related to the basic purpose of the amendment.[24] What is more likely is that no such intent was present in 1866, but that Conkling, following standard legal practice, put winning the case ahead of presentation of "the whole truth and nothing but the truth" and twisted the facts to attain that end. As a more recent researcher has revealed, the words "citizen" and "person" were used interchangeably during the drafting of the Fourteenth Amendment, and at no time was the word "corporation" mentioned in support of that amendment in either the conversations of the congressional committee or the later speeches of Conkling. On the contrary, explanations given for use of the word "person" by Representative John Bingham, who claimed to have written every word of the amendment, indicated that the committee's purpose in using the word "person" instead of "citizen" was to extend the due process and equal protection clauses to aliens as well as citizens.[25] Nevertheless, the interpretation that Conkling conned the court into accepting became rooted in constitutional law, notwithstanding the evidence that had led an earlier Supreme Court to declare that the equal protection clause was "so clearly intended as a protection for the Negro race" that it was doubtful whether "any action of a state not directed by way of discrimination against the negroes . . . will ever be held to come within the purview of this provision."[26]

Even more far-reaching in its effect upon the nation's social and economic development was the interpretation given the due process clause of the Fourteenth Amendment. Taken directly from the Fifth Amendment, which was aimed at the federal government, the post-Civil War enactment stipulated that no state may "deprive any person of life, liberty, or property, without due process of law." No taint of conspiracy touched this section, but its application to social and labor legislation proved devastating to reform efforts that today would be regarded as enlightened by all but the most politically reactionary elements of the population. As a leading analyst of constitutional history has said, the

Supreme Court's assumption of "supervisory power over state legislation" evolved in a tidal wave of appeals "for adequate protection of property rights against the remedial social legislation which the states were
increasingly enacting in the wake of industrial expansion."[27] As these
challenges reached the court, it proceeded to dismantle the framework of
state authority established in the Slaughterhouse Cases and Munn v.
Illinois. The minority opinions in those Supreme Court cases, which had
rejected the notion that government could regulate business activity in
any area not directly associated with the health, morals, or safety of the
entire community, became the majority view of the 1880s court.

From 1887, when this new approach was adopted,[28] until the Depression of the 1930s, the theory of laissez-faire economics dominated the
court's thinking and led it to substitute its judgment for that of elected
federal and state legislatures in determining where to draw the line between the individual's freedom of activity and the welfare of the community. In this capacity it permitted Kansas to maintain an anti-liquor
law on the grounds that the "deleterious social effects of the excessive
use of alcoholic liquors" justified the state's action.[29] Similarly, the court
upheld an Oregon law forbidding the employment of women in factories
for more than ten hours a day in deference to "woman's physical structure and the functions she performs in consequence thereof," a polite
reference to the problems of pregnancy and child-rearing.[30]

In subsequent cases, protective legislation for women and children
continued to be upheld, but no such permissiveness was shown most laws
involving business regulation where, routinely, the court took the position
that government-imposed limits were an unconstitutional invasion of the
Fourteenth Amendment right to "life, liberty, or property." These decisions were particularly damaging to the efforts of industrial workers attempting to organize and negotiate labor contracts that would ensure
better wages and working conditions. In this area the court went so far as
to assume a protective attitude toward employees when it declared that a
New York law restricting employment in bakeries to 10 hours a day and
60 hours a week was an unconstitutional interference with "the freedom
of master and employee to contract with each other in relation to their
employment."[31] Adopting the attitude of Justice Field in the 1877 case
cited earlier, the court in 1905 justified its defense of the individual
employee in these terms:

> It is unfortunately true that labor, even in any department, may
> possibly carry with it the seeds of unhealthiness. But are we all, on

that account, at the mercy of legislative majorities? No trade, no occupation, no mode of earning one's living, could escape this all-pervading power, and the acts of the legislature in limiting the hours of labor in all employments would be valid, although such limitations might seriously cripple the ability of the laborer to support himself and his family.

Federal regulations met a similar fate. When Washington attempted to prosecute a railroad company for discharging an employee merely "because of his membership in a labor organization," the Supreme Court found such federal interference unconstitutional.[32] Again, the decision was offered as a defense of the rights of employees as well as employers:

> It was the legal right of the defendant Adair ... to discharge Coppage because of his being a member of a labor organization, as it was the legal right of Coppage ... to quit the service in which he was engaged because the defendant employed some persons who were not members of a labor organization.

This principle, the court said, maintained the *"equality of right"* between employer and employee, "and any legislation that disturbs the equality is an arbitrary interference with the liberty of contract which no government can legally justify in a free land" (emphasis added).

For the next quarter-century, protests against such decisions were to no avail. The majority position in Lochner v. New York (1905) was criticized by four Supreme Court justices for judicial intrusion into matters of legislative judgment and, as Justice Holmes pointed out, for legally enshrining "an economic theory which a large part of the country does not entertain." In effect, the faith that the court was defending in the seventy years following the Civil War was the conviction that uninhibited economic freedom was the natural, God-given right of every man, and any interference with that right was contrary to the basic precepts of U.S. society. Not until the country had been devastated by the worst depression in its history did the notion of government responsibility for general welfare beyond the court's narrow limits of "health, morals, and safety" take hold.

RELIGION AND GENERAL WELFARE

Prior to the Civil War, both clerical and lay members of most churches took an active part in debating the most critical political issue of that era: slavery. In the decades following the war, the little that was heard from the churches on matters of public policy concerned much narrower, less explosive issues—such as prohibition, education, and, in many Protestant circles, the threat of Catholicism.

The more fundamental problems arising out of industrialization the churches approached much more gingerly, as the testimony of their own historians reveals. Individual Congregational ministers, for example, expressed themselves on the subject of "the church's responsibility for community life—the welfare of the state," but in matters of social policy "the leaders hesitated to enter so complicated a situation" until near the end of the nineteenth century. When they did acknowledge the existence of a problem in this area, by formation in 1895 of a Committee of Five on Capital and Labor, the result was a report that disavowed the need for the church "to take either side" of the quarrel between employees and employers. Rather, it suggested that "the solution of the labor problem . . . consists, fundamentally, in the recognition of the Christian law as the law of business, and the regulation of all our industrial life by Christian principles."[33] Subsequent sermons, books, and articles by individual clergymen were more pointed in their condemnation of "unbridled individualism" and their calls for replacing "this principle of selfishness and strife with the principle of good-will and service." However, appeals for a greater sense of brotherhood had little impact on public policy.[34]

In similar fashion, the Episcopal and Presbyterian churches recognized the difference between philanthropy and reform, the latter noting in 1893 "the spirit of uneasiness that pervades the masses."[35] An Episcopal chronicler acknowledged that "because the church and its leaders are characteristically conservative" the kind of radical reconstruction required to accomplish social reform "enlisted only a handful of church members."[36] Subsequently, that handful were responsible for establishing organizations like the Church Association for the Advancement of the Interests of Labor and the Society of Christian Socialists. However, the Association's support for legislation dealing with sweatshops, slum tenements, and strikes was limited to New York, while the Society's principal effort was educational. On a national level, resolutions promoting "the ideal of social justice" and urging industry to consider "the service of the community and the welfare of the workers, not primarily private profit," had little impact on either industry or legislation. Even prohibition—a subject that excited most churches—was of little interest to the Episcopal church.[37]

The General Assembly of the Presbyterian Church was more forceful in its 1934 condemnation "as godless, any system of economics which requires war for its support and maintenance," and in its suggestion that "competition as the major controlling principle of our economic life must be reexamined, and an attempt made to secure rational planning in our economic life."[38] Again, these statements of principle were guides to church members rather than slogans in support of statutory reform.

Other churches, including the dominant Baptist and Methodist organizations, were no more involved than the smaller sects, concentrating principally on charitable works and avoiding political issues. As a Baptist historian put it, the church's early history "taught American Baptists to be chary of interfering through church discipline with questions not strictly religious." Thus, even on the subject of prohibition, Baptist policy was to leave the matter entirely in the hands of individual worshipers.[39] On this score, at least, Methodists as a group acted more forcefully. Departing from its attitude in the early 1800s, when a level of tolerance was evident from the fact that "the second and third Methodist churches in New York City had rooms for storing liquor in the basement," the church in 1848 readopted John Wesley's rule "forbidding the buying and selling of spiritous liquors." Thereafter, support for prohibition was unrelenting. Following the formation of the Prohibition Party in 1869, "many Methodists were among [that party's] candidates for both the presidency and governorship of various states."[40]

Catholic clergy faced (then and now) a different kind of reality, in that their views of social problems must take into account the stance of the Vatican. That, in turn, has always been affected by conditions in Europe, where industrialization bred a far more radical labor movement than in the United States. The influence of Karl Marx and other nineteenth-century revolutionaries, which had only minimal impact on organized labor in the United States, ignited the fires of class consciousness and revolution in Europe. In recognizing the problems created by industrialization, Pope Leo XIII warned against the evils of class hostility and, in his 1891 encyclical, *Rerum Novarum*, called for a cooperative attitude between capital and labor in which "the moral value of man and the dignity of human labor are cardinal points."[41] More important, however, was the same pope's earlier encyclical, which "had explicitly affirmed the right of the papacy to judge when the affairs of the civil order must yield to the superior authority of the Roman Church."[42]

In Europe, pressure for reform led to the establishment of church-oriented unions and political parties, but no such development was possible in the United States, where separation of church and state had been adopted as a basic constitutional principle. The presumed threat to this principle led to periodic anti-Catholic campaigns that made Catholicism itself a political issue. This had much to do with the church's reluctance to support reforms that appeared to challenge the authority of those in command of the country's economic and political structure. Not until the Depression of the 1930s did Catholic clergy become widely involved in the labor movement, and even this involvement did not constitute a major influence on public policy.[43]

Despite the general conservatism of most churches in their approach to the problems of industrialization, extraordinary efforts were made by a few exceptional Catholic and Protestant churchmen in the battle for social reform. Congregationalist minister Charles M. Sheldon reached millions of readers with his book *In His Steps: Or, What Would Jesus Do?*, an 1897 novel that presented the problems of industrialization from a religious point of view. Episcopal Bishop Frederic Dan Huntington did the same in his writings for *The Church Review*. Baptist Walter Rauschenbusch castigated the attitude and talk of men "as if they were horse-powers or volts" and the tendency to "measure our national prosperity by pig-iron and steel instead of by the welfare of the people." James Cardinal Gibbons risked Vatican censure by arguing the validity of union organization, even if it meant exposing Catholic union members to the "evil influence" of Protestants, atheists and communists. Monsignor John Ryan began writing in defense of labor in 1905 and, 30 years later, "joined with enthusiasm" the efforts of President Franklin D. Roosevelt at social reform. Leaders of the much smaller minority of Jewish clergy were equally active. In fact, the Central Conference of American Rabbis acted as a body in 1928 to brand as unjust a policy "which would make the fundamental goal of industry the exploitation of the material world on the basis of unbridled competition and the unlimited and unrestricted accretion of goods in the hands of a few while millions are in want."[44]

Traditional churches, having their origins in Europe, were not the only sources of religious influence during the transitional period in which the United States evolved from a predominantly agricultural country to a world industrial power. Christian organizations that originated in the United States added to the social ferment with activities that gave rise to some of the most important legal questions considered by the federal courts. Among the homegrown doctrines that came into being during the last century are the Church of Jesus Christ of Latter-Day Saints (Mormon), Jehovah's Witnesses, and the Church of Christ, Scientist. The last two will bear mention in the next chapter. Joseph Smith's Mormon church deserves comment here as one that created—and overcame—a special problem, and went on to become the dominant political power in the state of Utah.

Like other Protestant sects, Mormons accept the Old Testament version of the world's origin and man's early development. Unlike others, they rely on the revelations of a nineteenth-century American prophet, Joseph Smith, and his Latter-Day Saints for an understanding of God's will. Evidence of Smith's credentials as the receiver of the Lord's word is a latter-day bible, the Book of Mormon, purportedly translated by Smith from plates of gold that were written in "Reformed Egyptian" and discovered by him in 1823 with the help of an angel.[45]

The made-in-America quality of Mormon beliefs did not prevent its adherents from being subjected to attacks that ranged from ridicule to lynching. Smith and his brother Hyrum were murdered by a lynch mob in 1844, but not before they had converted "possibly as many as 35,000 persons," including Brigham Young, who led the faithful from Illinois to Utah following Smith's death. Once firmly established in that sparsely populated area, the church came into conflict with the federal government through its practice of polygamy. Justified by sympathetic church members as a continuation of a tradition "that God chose to introduce," and one followed by "Abraham, Jacob, Solomon, David and indeed all the old prophets," polygamy was in fact forbidden by the Book of Mormon as "abominable."[46] Plural marriage was not announced as official church doctrine until 1852, by which time Mormons so dominated life in Utah that Brigham Young had been named territorial governor. Although during this period the proportion of all married Mormon men who took more than one wife probably did not exceed five percent, "all the central church leaders were polygamists."[47] Nevertheless, this one aspect of Mormon belief was the principal barrier to acceptance of statehood for Utah. What was initially an enormous region including most of the Rocky Mountain area was subdivided into four separate territories. Applications for statehood were accepted from Nevada in 1864, Colorado in 1876, and Wyoming in 1890. Statehood for Utah was deferred until the Mormon hierarchy had formally disavowed polygamy as church doctrine. This was done in 1890, and six years later Utah became the forty-fifth state of the Union.

Statehood did not end the controversy over polygamy, as Mormon fundamentalists continued to resist the restrictions imposed by federal law and the Utah constitution. Nevertheless, when Republican Mormon apostle Reed Smoot was elected to the U.S. Senate in 1902 (and seated by that body after a grueling investigation of his credentials), the church's position in both politics and religious practice was secured. At the same time, church leaders were assuming control of a variety of business and industrial firms, which, together with tithing by church members, contributed to the financial success of what soon became an extremely wealthy organization. As subsequent events were to demonstrate, the conservative character of Mormon leadership would be felt in national as well as state politics.[48]

During the years when polygamy was a public issue, the U.S. Supreme Court ruled upon the legal aspect of the matter long before it was settled politically. When the right of Congress to pass a law making a specific religious practice (in this case, polygamy) illegal was challenged, the court was unanimous in its opinion that the First Amendment left the federal legislature "free to reach actions which were in violation of social duties or subversive of good order."[49] This was neither the first nor the last contest over the meaning of the constitutional provision that "Congress shall make no law respecting an establishment of religion, or prohibiting the free exercise thereof." Other religious groups were testing this concept in ways that opened up questions ranging far beyond the relatively simple matter of polygamy. Many of these contests began as challenges to state authority, but those that were of more than local significance ended up in the U.S. Supreme Court. Books have been written on this subject.[50] Here the purpose is to demonstrate the extent to which religious questions have influenced, or been influenced by, politics in the United States.

Religion, Politics,
and
the Law

7

Religious Freedom Reconsidered

Today's concept of religious freedom as the right of every person to adopt any faith—or no faith—would have been incomprehensible to most of colonial America. In many of the colonies an individual advancing such a notion would have been arrested and tried for the foulest kind of heresy—tried, that is, in a court of law. In the early settlements it was the law that dictated the rules of religious practice and the penalties for non-comformance. The price paid by religious dissidents ranged from a modest fine for failure to attend church on the Sabbath to death for professing a belief in the tenets of an outlawed sect.

By the time of the Revolution, most of these legal controls over religious belief and practice had been abandoned. Prejudice dies hard, however, and remnants of the old system found their way into most state constitutions. Frequently the guarantees of civil rights were tied to Christian belief, some states limiting those protections to Protestant Christians. Membership in a Protestant church was frequently a requirement for public office.[1]

For the most part, these restrictions were eliminated during the next half-century, one state at a time. South Carolina's religious distinctions, including its established church, were abandoned in its 1790 constitution, while in neighboring North Carolina the Protestant-only rule for public officers was continued until 1868 when the disqualification was reduced to "persons who shall deny the being of Almighty God."[2] Until 1851, Maryland retained its constitutional protection for "all persons professing the Christian religion" and its legislative authority to "lay a general and equal tax for the support of the Christian religion." Officeholders were still required to make "a declaration of belief in the Christian religion" or, "if the party professes to be a Jew, the declaration shall be of his belief in a future state of rewards and punishments."[3]

In Puritan New England, Connecticut clung most tenaciously to its standing order in which the Congregational church continued to dominate state politics until 1818, when it lost its majority in the legislature. A constitutional convention called in that year to replace the colonial charter of 1662 saw to it that equal rights were accorded to "each and every society or denomination of Christians."[4] Until 1833, Massachusetts resisted eliminating public support of Protestant churches, at which point it established equal protection for "every denomination of Christians."[5]

Among the middle states, Delaware revised its revolutionary constitution in 1792, when it deleted the requirement that officeholders must "profess belief in God the Father, and in Jesus Christ His only Son, and in the Holy Ghost."[6] Pennsylvania abandoned its one discriminatory provision in 1838 when it dropped the civil rights reference to "all who acknowledge the being of a God" and the legislators' oath to swear belief in God "and the Old and New Testaments."[7] New Jersey's only restriction, which limited officeholding to Protestants, was deleted from the constitution in 1844.[8]

All of these changes were accomplished by state legislatures or conventions. Despite repeated efforts by outraged individuals to invoke the federal Bill of Rights against state authority, the courts rejected every suggestion that the protection of the first ten amendments was applicable to state actions. The U.S. Supreme Court made this clear in general terms in 1833.[9] The court addressed the question of religious freedom more directly in 1845 in the following declaration:

> The Constitution of 1789 makes no provision for protecting the citizens of the respective states in their religious liberties; this is left to the state constitutions and laws; nor is there any inhibition imposed by the Constitution of the United States in this respect on the states.[10]

Although the First Amendment did not permit the federal government to challenge discriminatory treatment by the states, Congress was still the judge of the acceptability of each constitution submitted with a territorial application for the formation of a new state. Given the certain knowledge that Congress would not accept an application for statehood that did not contain guarantees of personal liberty including religious freedom, the constitutions designed by prospective new states invariably included such provisions. A further stimulus for such guarantees was the preponderance of Baptist and Methodist preachers among the westward-moving pioneers.[11]

Typically, constitutions prepared by states entering the Union after the Revolution opened with an acknowledgment of the favor of Almighty God, followed by a bill of rights that prohibited any interference with the rights of conscience or profession of religious belief. Occasionally, a restriction would be included to keep out of public office any person "who denies the being of a God," but most states incorporated the federal ban on any religious test for officeholders. When, in 1796, Tennessee adopted both that restriction and a ban on officeholding by anyone "who denies the being of God," it seemed to suggest that the two were not considered contradictory at that point in the nation's development.[12]

In this one area, independence can be said to have brought (after much foot-dragging) a social, as well as a political, revolution. Under the bills of rights ultimately adopted by state constitutional conventions, state courts became the guardians of religious liberty, where once they had been instruments for the prosecution of nonconformists. Rarely, however, was Jefferson's "wall of separation" between church and state as firmly constructed as that statesman might have wished. As a result, appeals for protection beyond that offered by state constitutions were directed to the federal courts.

REENTER THE FOURTEENTH AMENDMENT

Professor James' companion studies (*The Framing* and *The Ratification of the Fourteenth Amendment*) devote considerable space to the origin of the notion that the amendment's authors intended the equal protection clause to cover corporations as well as individuals. However, nothing in those volumes will prepare the reader for a later interpretation that was even more significant, namely, that the amendment extends the protection of the federal Bill of Rights to individuals discriminated against by state law or action. When the court's first acknowledgment of that view occurred in 1897, it came in defense of property rights rather than personal freedom. At that point the justices decided that, although the Fourteenth Amendment made no reference to the taking of private property without just compensation, the due process clause included this Fifth Amendment protection.[13]

Another quarter-century was to pass before First Amendment guarantees were to be declared applicable against invasion by state authorities. The circumstances had nothing to do with the plaintiff's religion. In fact, almost the opposite was the case, involving a left-wing member of the Socialist Party who had been found guilty of criminal anarchy under New York law for having published a manifesto that advocated the revolutionary overthrow of government.[14] The U.S. Supreme Court upheld the constitutionality of the statute and the conviction of the accused, Benjamin Gitlow. Buried in the majority opinion was this startling reversal of all previous decisions:

> For present purposes we may and do assume that freedom of speech and of the press—which are protected by the First Amendment from abridgement by Congress—are among the fundamental personal rights and "liberties" protected by the due process clause of the Fourteenth Amendment from impairment by the States.

Included almost as an aside in the majority opinion, the point was picked up by Justices Oliver Wendell Holmes and Louis Dembitz Brandeis; their dissent focused directly on the proposition that the protection of free speech "must be . . . included in the Fourteenth Amendment."

This happened in 1925. Six years later, a Minnesota publisher appealed his conviction under a public nuisance statute and won a Supreme Court decision that clearly and specifically extended the protection of the Fourteenth Amendment to freedom of the press.[15] After six more years, another liberty was added to the protected list, when the conviction of an Oregon resident for criminal syndicalism was overturned by the Supreme Court on the ground that state laws interfering with the right of peaceable assembly were "repugnant to the due process clause of the Fourteenth Amendment."[16]

None of these decisions had any direct relation to religious belief, but all had implications for religious questions that arose subsequently. Beliefs of any kind are evidenced by speaking, publishing, and assembling, the very actions that the court had passed upon before the matter of religious freedom became a Fourteenth Amendment case in 1940. When the test came, it followed an age-old tradition: the unpopular minority challenge to the establishment concept of justice.

Newton Cantwell and his two sons, Jesse and Russell, belonged to a sect whose members call themselves Jehovah's Witnesses. Interpreting the Bible to deny such commonly accepted Christian doctrines as the

Trinity of Father, Son, and Holy Spirit, Witnesses preach the Second Coming of Christ who, after the final battle of Armageddon, will rule the earth in peace and joy with the assistance of his earthly agent, the Watchtower Bible and Tract Society.[17]

In their proselytizing efforts, Witnesses have used not only material from their leaders' books and their principal periodical, *The Watchtower*, but also recordings played to anyone who will listen. Frequently, these recordings include direct attacks on the beliefs of other religious groups. The record used by the Cantwells described a book entitled *Enemies* and entertained its listeners with a verbal assault on organized religion in general and Catholicism in particular. Those exposed to this message were the residents of a heavily Catholic section of New Haven, Connecticut. Inevitably, so direct an affront brought threats of physical reprisal and complaints to the local police. New Haven authorities responded by arresting the Cantwells and charging them with inciting a breach of the peace and soliciting without a license.[18]

As with all of the cases referred to earlier, the highest state court had upheld the constitutionality of the statute and the conviction of the accused. The U.S. Supreme Court acknowledged the state's right to interfere when there was a "clear and present danger of riot, disorder, interference with traffic upon public streets, or other immediate threat to public safety, peace, or order." However, it found no evidence of such danger or interference by the Cantwells. Moreover, it denied the state's right to use a licensing system to prevent any group from expressing its religious views in public. On both counts the court determined that the Cantwells had threatened no one and had interfered with no other person's rights or with any public function. Recognizing that religious persuasion often involves exaggeration, vilification of other church leaders, and even direct falsehood, the court observed that "the people of this nation have ordained in the light of history, that, in spite of the probability of excesses and abuses, these liberties are, in the long view, essential to enlightened opinion and right conduct on the part of citizens of a democracy." On this basis, the court held that the Connecticut law, as applied to the Cantwells, "deprives them of their liberty without due process of law and in contravention of the Fourteenth Amendment."

In essence, the issue in the Cantwell case was as much freedom of speech as freedom of religion. In fact, it demonstrated the inseparable nature of these two basic rights. Once free speech had been declared a right protected by the Fourteenth Amendment, it was inevitable that speaking as a way of propagating religion would be afforded the same protection.

A more severe test of principle involved a rabble-rousing speech by a suspended Catholic priest. Although no question of religious freedom was raised, the situation reviewed by the court in 1949 revealed the depth of religious animosity that permeated one element of the country's political right wing. Invited to speak by the Christian Veterans of America and the U.S. fascist leader Gerald K. Smith, Father Arthur Terminiello appealed to his *"Fellow Christians"* to beware the *"slimy scum,"* which he identified as "atheistic, communistic, Zionist Jews" who, he said, were "trying to *destroy America by revolution.*"[19] Convicted of disorderly conduct for "misbehavior which violates the public peace and decorum," Terminiello appealed this judgment on the ground that it violated his right of free speech under the federal Constitution.

The several opinions handed down by members of the U.S. Supreme Court reflect the range of heated public reaction to this event. A bare majority of the court held that the trial judge's definition of a breach of the peace went too far in including speech that "stirs the public to anger, invites dispute, brings about a condition of unrest, or creates a disturbance." Speaking for a majority of five of the nine justices, William O. Douglas pronounced what is probably the most liberal interpretation of the protection offered by the First Amendment, saying:

> A function of free speech under our system of government is to invite dispute. It may indeed best serve its high purpose when it induces a condition of unrest, creates dissatisfaction with conditions as they are, or even stirs people to anger. Speech is often provocative and challenging. It may strike at prejudices and preconceptions and have profound unsettling effects as it presses for acceptance of an idea. This is why freedom of speech, though not absolute . . . is nevertheless protected against censorship or punishment, unless shown likely to produce a clear and present danger of a serious substantive evil that rises far above public inconvenience, annoyance, or unrest.

Dissenting opinions by the four remaining justices were vigorous, if not bitter. Justice Robert H. Jackson directed a blistering attack on the majority for "indulging in theory" rather than facing the ugly facts of Terminiello's speech and the near-riot it created. He cited an earlier decision in which a unanimous Supreme Court had upheld the right of local authorities to punish as a breach of the peace the use of language far less provocative than that used by Terminiello.[20] Picturing this new confrontation as a contest between right-wing and left-wing radicals for "mastery of the streets," he stressed the danger to the country in these words:

This drive by totalitarian groups to undermine the prestige and effectiveness of local democratic governments is advanced whenever either of them can win from this Court a ruling which paralyzes the power of these officials... if they can do nothing to him [Terminiello] they are equally powerless as to rival totalitarian groups. Terminiello's victory today certainly fulfills the most extravagant hopes of both right and left totalitarian groups, who want nothing so much as to paralyze and discredit the only democratic authority that can curb them in their battle for the streets.

Within two years the court had retreated to a position closer to that expressed by Justice Jackson.[21] Still, the same court denied New York City's right to require a license for holding public worship meetings on the streets, even if denial of a license to Baptist minister Carl Jacob Kunz was based on evidence that he had previously "caused some disorder" and had ridiculed and denounced other religious beliefs in his meetings.[22] In this case Justice Jackson again dissented, viewing the problem in terms that were emerging, even then, as Washington's rationale for the defense of democracy around the world.

Other aspects of religious activity were not so directly associated with the protections provided by the federal Bill of Rights. However, this has not discouraged challenges based on the First Amendment clause "respecting an establishment of religion, or prohibiting the free exercise thereof." Indeed, throughout the first half of the twentieth century, the country witnessed a bewildering series of legal contests over state laws that some believed injected government authority into areas prohibited by the two restrictions in the First Amendment. Cases reaching the U.S. Supreme Court ranged in subject matter from tax-free property and public funding of church-school expenses to military service and, in public schools, Bible reading, prayer, flag salutes, and the teaching of evolutionary science. Viewed another way, the two major battlegrounds have been, first, the limits on "free exercise" of religion by individuals and, second, the limits on government to prevent "an establishment of religion."

THE LIMITS OF PERSONAL FREEDOM

As the previous discussion has demonstrated, religious freedom for the individual and the right of government authorities to intervene in religious matters cannot be treated as separate and distinct problems.

The principal reason for considering them separately is to recognize the difference in emphasis implied in the two First Amendment references to "an establishment of religion" and "prohibiting the free exercise thereof." In the latter clause, the accent is on freedom, which is the point of departure here.

During the colonial period, government efforts to contain personal freedom often were dictated by church concepts of what constituted acceptable behavior. With the gradual elimination of church–state ties, the debate over the distinction between liberty and license involved relatively few questions of religious practice. The outstanding exception was the issue of polygamy, which both Congress and the courts condemned as contrary to the country's accepted code of social and moral values. In similar fashion, the courts have declared that "Whilst legislation for the establishment of a religion is forbidden, and its free exercise permitted, it does not follow that everything which may be so-called can be tolerated. Crime is not the less odious because sanctioned by what any particular sect may designate as religion."[23] This 1890 pronouncement was further strengthened in 1919 by a Supreme Court decision on obstruction of military recruitment by people who professed no religious connection or objective.[24] The oft-cited doctrine announced by Justice Holmes defined the limits of free speech in these terms:

> The question in every case is whether the words used are used in such circumstances and are of such a nature as to create a clear and present danger that they will bring about the substantive evils that Congress has a right to prevent.

Never applied to the propagation of religious doctrine, this test would nevertheless be appropriate if a religious group such as Islamic Jihad should attempt to incite or engage in acts of force or terrorism in the United States.

One particular problem that has concerned the nation throughout its history is the anti-war position of some sects. During the Revolutionary War, some of the more intense patriots regarded Quakers and other pacifists as little better than traitors. However, except for a group of Quakers who were temporarily exiled from Pennsylvania to Virginia, pacifists suffered more from ostracism than from criminal prosecution.[25] In every subsequent war this nation has fought, an accommodation has been made to exempt, at least from combat service, people whose religious convictions forbid their participation in activities that involve the taking of human life.[26] This does not mean that draftees need not register when required by law to do so. Nor may a draftee claim exemption on the basis of objection to a particular war, rather than to war in general.[27]

Acceptance of the general principle that religious pacifism justifies exemption from military service has not resolved the problem of balancing national security and religious liberty. In the aftermath of the Civil War, a Missouri court tried and convicted a Catholic priest for the crime of "teaching and preaching as a priest and minister" without having first taken an oath "that included thirty distinct affirmations or tests" of loyalty to the state and nation.[28] Both the wording and application of this section of Missouri's constitution indicated that it was aimed at anyone even remotely associated with, or sympathetic to, what was called "the Rebellion." A prime example of the effect that smoldering hatred can have on basic concepts of justice, the oath was declared invalid by a bare 5–4 majority of the U.S. Supreme Court. The minority, which included Chief Justice Salmon P. Chase, disputed the majority conclusion that the Missouri oath made the enjoyment of a right "dependent upon an impossible condition" and was, "for its severity, without any precedent that we can discover." The same four justices dissented from a similar decision that invalidated a federal statute requiring a Missouri-like oath of all attorneys practicing in federal courts.[29]

More recent loyalty-oath cases have been directed principally at communists. Still, as religious zealotry intrudes further and further into politics, both at home and abroad, the possibility of more sweeping application of loyalty tests becomes ever more real.

Symbols of loyalty can be as important as the spoken word. In every country, the flag is the nation's foremost symbol, and disrespect for the flag is taken as direct evidence of disloyalty. In Nazi Germany and Fascist Italy, failure to salute the flag in a passing parade meant, at a minimum, an immediate beating by watchful brown- or black-shirted bullies. Officials in the present-day theocracy of Iran view disrespect for the flag as not only treasonable but sacrilegious as well.

The right of an American to abstain from the standard salute and pledge of allegiance came into national prominence when Lillian and William Gobitis, 12- and 10-year-old children of parents affiliated with Jehovah's Witnesses, were expelled from the public schools of Minersville, Pennsylvania, for refusing to salute the national flag as part of a daily school exercise.[30] Coming just before World War II and on the heels of widely publicized committee hearings on un-American activities (conducted by Congressman Martin Dies), the Gobitis challenge to the authority of the Minersville Board of Education was not sympathetically received by a public saturated with flag-waving publicity.[31] Despite the superpatriotic atmosphere fostered by Dies, the Gobitis family defended their children's right to a public school education without being obliged to participate in a ritual that they believed to be scripturally forbidden.

Members of the Supreme Court were certainly aware of the political situation. Whether or not they were influenced by the fervor of the patriotic campaign, they had little difficulty reaching an 8–1 decision that all school authorities had "the right to awaken in the child's mind considerations as to the significance of the flag contrary to those implanted by the parent." The only member of the court to register a dissent was Justice Harlan Stone, who went to the heart of the matter in this one sentence:

> The Constitution may well elicit expressions of loyalty to it and to the government which it created, but it does not command such expressions or otherwise give any indication that compulsory expressions of loyalty play any such part in our scheme of government as to override the constitutional protection of freedom of speech and religion.

Three years later, with only two new faces on the bench, Stone's dissenting view became the basis for a 6–3 majority opinion that flatly overturned the Gobitis decision.[32] This shift was made possible by a reversal in the stand taken by Justices Hugo Black and William O. Douglas, who were soon to assume leadership in the protection of First Amendment rights.

THE LIMITS OF GOVERNMENT INTERVENTION

As highly charged as the question of religious freedom has been, it has provoked no greater controversy than the recurring debates over what constitutes "an establishment of religion." Unlike the situation during colonial times and in the early years of the republic, few later problems involved direct ties between church and state. After states discontinued direct support of churches by public funding, the principal remaining preference shown to all religious institutions was in the nationwide practice of exempting them from taxes, which have long been levied on individuals and commercial organizations. When even this was challenged

in 1970, the Supreme Court upheld the exemption as one that had traditionally been extended to all nonprofit organizations regarded as
"beneficial and stabilizing influences in community life."[33] Once public
funding of churches had been abandoned, the overwhelming majority of
disputes over the meaning of the establishment clause were triggered by
state or local laws providing specific public assistance to students,
parents, or schools of religious organizations.

There is nothing strange in the fact that the educational system has
become the battleground for conflicting concepts of church–state relations. The earliest schools in this country were organized and operated, if
not by churches themselves, then by clergymen whose main concern was
to instill the principles of Christianity in the student body. The first formal system of public education was designed by the Massachusetts
legislature in 1647. The explicit purpose of this law being to impart a
knowledge of the Scriptures, and thus to frustrate "ye ould deluder,
Satan," it was inevitable that "the governing authorities for church and
civil affairs were much the same. When acting as church officers they
were known as Elders and Deacons; when acting as civil or town officers
they were known as Selectmen."[34]

The earliest colleges in the United States were also church oriented.
Harvard University, founded in 1636, was supported by a grant from the
Massachusetts Bay Colony and was run by a board of overseers, who saw
the institution as a means of serving the Congregational church by
producing a highly educated clergy. Yale University, established in 1701,
was equally Puritan in character, and for many years was dominated by
hard-line Congregationalists. Other churches undertook similar ventures,
but with varying degrees of strictness in their administration of religious
instruction. In Virginia a charter for the College of William and Mary was
granted in 1693 to an Anglican clergyman. Princeton University was
originally established by the Presbyterian church as the College of New
Jersey. Rutgers, first named Queen's College, was chartered in 1756 by
King George III at the request of the Dutch Reformed church.

At primary and secondary levels, many private academies were established by Protestant denominations. This trend continued well into the
nineteenth century when, following the Civil War, the demand for public
education brought a rapid growth in the public school system. Even as little red schoolhouses were springing up in communities all over the country, the Catholic church was opening its own teaching centers, in greater
numbers than any other sect. Many of the subsequent tests of
church–state relations stemmed from this proliferation of parochial

schools and the view of their supporters that, because they were sharing the burden of educating the country's youth, they were entitled to some kind of public assistance.

Other problems evolved from remnants of religious education that remained in the public school system. These included the recitation of prayers, Bible reading, and "released time" for students to take religious instruction during school hours.

Suggestions of an impending conflict emerged shortly after the Civil War. In 1866 the Supreme Court rejected a protest from Catholic parents against the enforced participation of their children in religious exercises conducted in Protestant fashion in public schools.[35] This situation was not materially affected by an 1872 Ohio state court decision that declared religious freedom in the United States to mean "absolute equality before the law of all religious opinions and sects," which, in turn, means that "the government is neutral and, while protecting all, it prefers none and disparages none."[36]

As the country's Catholic population continued to grow, so did the number of parochial schools. The right of the church, or of any private organization, to provide educational facilities as an alternative to public schools became a legal issue in 1925, when Oregon passed a law that required "every parent, guardian, or other person having control or charge or custody of a child between 8 and 16 years to send him to a public school for the period of time a public school shall be held during the current year."[37] The wording of the statute made it clear that parents who failed to enroll their children in a public school would be guilty of a misdemeanor. State courts found that the act would put every private school out of business, for all practical purposes. When the matter reached the U.S. Supreme Court, that body agreed that, although a state may regulate all schools to assure that "studies plainly essential to good citizenship" are taught by qualified teachers, the statute in question "unreasonably interferes with the liberty of parents and guardians to direct the upbringing and education of children under their control."[38] Subsequent contests involved legislation aimed at providing (at public expense) transportation, physical facilities, and teachers for church-operated schools. Each of these services was bitterly opposed by individual taxpayers as well as by organizations having a particular interest in First Amendment problems.

Student busing became a public issue long before it had anything to do with racial integration. In the early 1940s a number of communities undertook to provide student transportation from distant points to all schools, public or private, in some cases excepting schools operated for profit. A New Jersey law authorizing its towns to institute such a service was challenged by one taxpayer as a violation of both state and federal constitutions. The chief complaint was that the town's action forced its residents to pay taxes to help support and maintain schools "which are dedicated to, and regularly teach, the Catholic Faith." The statute permitting this arrangement was cited as "a law respecting the establishment of religion."[39]

In its consideration of the problem, a bare majority of five justices of the U.S. Supreme Court arrived at what is the most definitive available statement on the establishment clause of the First Amendment. Speaking through Justice Hugo Black, who wrote the majority opinion, the court said:

> The "establishment of religion" clause of the First Amendment means at least this: Neither a state nor the Federal Government can set up a church. Neither can pass laws which aid one religion, aid all religions, or prefer one religion over another. Neither can force nor influence a person to go to or remain away from church against his will, or force him to profess a belief or disbelief in any religion. No person can be punished for entertaining or professing religious beliefs or disbeliefs, for church attendance or non-attendance. No tax in any amount, large or small, can be levied to support any religious activities or institutions, whatever they may be called, or whatever form they may adopt to teach or practice religion. Neither a state nor the Federal Government can, openly or secretly, participate in the affairs of any religious organizations or groups and vice versa. In the words of Jefferson, the clause against establishment of religion by law was intended to erect "a wall of separation between Church and State."

None of these restrictions, the court said, was violated by providing a general program to help parents get their children to school safely and expeditiously, "regardless of their religion."

In a lengthy dissent, Justice Wiley B. Rutledge insisted that the First Amendment prohibited "not simply an established church, but any law respecting an establishment of religion." He also found that by refusing transportation to students of private schools operated for profit, the law gave preferred treatment to Catholic school children only. Notwithstanding the slim margin by which the court decided this case, states thereafter felt free to adopt transportation systems that would serve all elementary and secondary school students, public or parochial.

The following year, a very different attitude was expressed by the court, when it considered a complaint by a Champaign, Illinois, parent against the use of public school buildings by "religious teachers employed by private religious groups . . . to come weekly into the school buldings during the regular hours set apart for secular teaching, and . . . for a period of thirty minutes substitute their religious teaching for the secular education provided under the compulsory education law."[40] Only one justice disagreed with the court's verdict that, when a state's tax-supported buildings are used to disseminate religious doctrine, "this is not separation of Church and State." The dissenting justice insisted that the system in question merely permitted children to be released from the regular program to attend religious classes, a view that raised a new dispute only a few years later.

Released time, as a means of permitting students to interrupt their normal public school studies to attend religious classes, was introduced in New York State in 1940. On the basis of the McCollum decision just discussed, the parents of children unwillingly involved in the released time program challenged that system as a violation of the First Amendment.[41] As the arguments were rehashed, new divisions appeared in the Supreme Court. The majority saw a distinction between the McCollum situation, in which religious classes were held in public school buildings, and the new case, in which they were taught in religious institutions unconnected with the public school system. The latter arrangement, they felt, could not be challenged. This position was supported by three members (Justices Frederick M. Vinson, William O. Douglas, and Harold H. Burton) who had joined in the earlier opinion that the program McCollum complained of was unconstitutional.

The difference in teaching locations did not impress Justices Felix Frankfurter, Robert H. Jackson, and Hugo L. Black. Acknowledging the state's right to close the doors of public schools so that all students might be released for such religious or nonreligious activities as they chose to follow, those dissenters pointed to "the pith of the case . . . that formalized religious instruction is substituted for other school activity which those who do not participate in the released-time program are compelled to attend." However, notwithstanding Associate Justice Jackson's disdainful comment that "My evangelical brethren confuse an objection to compulsion with an objection to religion," the majority view opened the door to released-time programs across the nation.

Public funding of facilities used to educate parochial school children continues to be the subject of litigation, as proponents of such aid seek new ways of achieving their goal. One innovation was devised by the New York City Board of Education, whose members are strongly supportive of the city's large Irish, Italian, and Puerto Rican Catholic population. Intent on providing remedial education to all students requiring this assistance, but aware of court decisions that prohibit assigning public school teachers to parochial schools, the board voted unanimously to install, on the streets in front of parochial schools, classroom trailers in which public school teachers would provide remedial instruction for parochial school children. Protests against this "extension of parochial schoolrooms" from the main building to the street were rejected by both the board and Mayor Edward Koch, paving the way for still another legal challenge.[42]

Less critical issues, such as supplying (at public expense) nonsectarian textbooks and incidental services to students in religious institutions, have generally received court approval. On the other hand, when Pennsylvania and Rhode Island adopted legislation authorizing the use of public funds for partial reimbursement of salaries paid to teachers in nonpublic, largely church-related schools, the Supreme Court found this to be "excessive entanglement between government and religion" and, therefore, a violation of the establishment clause.[43] However, these were minor matters compared to the bitter disputes soon to arise over decisions by local boards of education affecting the teaching content in public school classrooms and libraries. As new "defenders of the faith" organized to bring morality and religion back to its "rightful place" in American life, the stage was set for a series of major confrontations.

8

Religion Returns
to the Political Arena

Supreme Court Justice Robert H. Jackson, in suggesting that an evangelistic attitude lay behind the court's decision in the Zorach case, may not have been wholly serious, but he certainly was aware of the nation's religious history. On several occasions, a surge of evangelistic fervor has swept the country, and multitudes of people have responded eagerly to the call to "return to Christ." The Great Awakening of the 1730s was followed by a similar revival a century later, which may well have influenced Adventist William Miller, Mormon prophet Joseph Smith, Disciples of Christ leader Thomas Campbell, and Christian Scientist Mary Baker Eddy in their search for a more satisfying interpretation of the Scriptures.

Widespread as the general reawakening movements were, they had little impact on the nation's political life, being concerned with the saving of souls rather than with laws and elections. Revivalism in the late twentieth century has followed a very different road. The message of modern fundamentalists is that the higher law of God must be made the law of the land, and true believers must use all available political tools to reach this goal.

THE PUBLIC SCHOOL BATTLEGROUND

Twentieth-century educators have debated, sometimes passionately, how best to educate the youth of the United States. For the most part, these disputes have focused on the problem of providing the individual with a foundation of knowledge and understanding necessary to cope with the demands of modern living. While this approach does not ignore moral concepts, it does not rest its case on the religious foundation of society's needs and moral codes. Modern revivalists have a more simplistic view, stemming from biblical injunction. In the case of education, the mandate reads: "Train up a child in the way he should go; and when he is old he will not depart from it."[1] Because education at public expense has assumed so great a part of a child's training, the evangelist has chosen the classroom as the battleground for determining "the way he should go." Specific issues over which repeated skirmishes have been—and are being—fought include prayer in public schools, Bible reading, and the teaching of evolutionary theory.

Prayer in public institutions has been a common practice throughout most of this country's history. As justices William O. Douglas and Potter Stewart pointed out in a landmark case, described below, the Supreme Court and Congress open each session asking God's blessing, and the assertion "In God we Trust" appears on all U.S. coins and in the national anthem. The pledge of allegiance to the flag, Stewart added, was amended by Congress from "one nation, indivisible" to "one nation under God, indivisible." If, in his pointed examples, Stewart did not venture into the procedure followed by the Constitutional Convention of 1787, it may have been because, despite Benjamin Franklin's suggestion that "prayers imploring the assistance of Heaven ... be held in this assembly every morning," the proposal was not accepted by his colleagues, who were sharply divided on this question.[2]

The event that led to Supreme Court consideration of this matter in 1962 was an action filed by five New York parents protesting classroom use of a prayer adopted by the State Board of Regents. These nonconformists included two Jewish parents, one Unitarian, a member of the Ethical Culture Society, and one nonbeliever. According to the Regents' instructions, the following prayer was to be recited by the students in every class at the beginning of each day: "Almighty God, we acknowledge our dependence upon Thee and we beg They blessings upon us, our parents, our teachers, and our country."

The five parents challenged the constitutionality of both the authorizing statute and the procedure mandated by the Regents, claiming them to be violations of the First Amendment ban on any law "respecting an establishment of religion" and the Fourteenth Amendment, which made this ban applicable to state governments. More specifically, they insisted that the prayer was "composed by governmental officials as part of a governmental program to further religious beliefs." New York trial and appeals courts rejected this interpretation of the federal Constitution, which left the final decision up to the U.S. Supreme Court.

There was no disagreement on the facts as to the origin of the prayer, its mandated use in the classroom, and the ability of any student to be excused from joining in the recitation. After a lengthy review of the history of church–state relations in England and the United States, six of the seven justices summarized the experience in this fashion:

> The history of governmentally-established religion, both in England and in this country, showed that whenever government had allied itself with one particular form of religion, the inevitable result had been that it had incurred the hatred, disrespect and even contempt of those who held contrary beliefs. That same history showed that many people had lost their respect for any religion that had relied upon the support of Government to spread its faith.

Citing the unavoidable stigma that follows from nonconformance, and the ultimate danger of persecution for disbelief when a law respecting religion is flouted, the court quoted James Madison's warning "to take alarm at the first experiment on our liberties" lest the first step lead to ever-increasing intrusions by government into the sphere of religion.

One dissenting justice, Potter Stewart, found the history of established churches irrelevant. He also noted that the phrase "wall of separation" cannot be found in the Constitution. The key question, Stewart said, was "whether school children who want to begin their day by joining in prayer must be prohibited from doing so." Neither the majority opinion nor Justice Douglas's concurring opinion picked up this assumption that the choice was up to the children in each class rather than the State Board of Regents.[3]

If either the court or the public thought the matter settled in 1962, opponents of the Regents prayer decision came to no such conclusion. In communities where objections were not likely to be raised, school prayers, Bible reading, or religious studies went on as usual. Pennsylvania, for example, continued to enforce a statute requiring daily reading of Bible verses, until the Supreme Court invalidated that law in 1963.[4] To this day, public schools in Mercer County, West Virginia, offer optional Bible classes taught by uncertified teachers from the Bluefield Bible Study Association.[5]

On the legislative front, attacks on the Supreme Court's position were mounted by way of state and federal laws that would authorize voluntary prayer or a moment of silence. In Congress, constitutional amendments offered in 1962, 1966, and 1971 failed to receive the required two-thirds majority vote. During the same period, some state legislatures petitioned Congress to either initiate an amendment to the Constitution that would permit public school prayer or submit the question to a constitutional convention.[6] Members of Congress sympathetic to this movement responded by introducing the desired constitutional amendment. In 1973, seven such resolutions were proposed by senators and thirty-four by representatives in the House.[7] When no action was taken on any of these proposals, a new effort in 1975 produced seven more resolutions in the Senate and fifty-two in the House.[8] All met the same fate as their predecessors, being referred to committee, where they died.

Despite the apparent rise in strength of pro-prayer forces, they were unable to muster enough support in state legislatures to approach the goal of 34 petitions, the number required by Article V of the Constitution before obliging Congress to call a national convention to consider amendments to the Constitution. Lacking sufficient power to force the issue on an amendment basis, congressional supporters of school prayer tried another approach: A favorite tactic of Senator Jesse Helms of North Carolina was to propose an amendment to a bill already under consideration, in the hope that the Senate would approve the modified measure rather than risk defeat of the bill's principal objective. What came to be known as the "Helms amendment" raised a bitter debate when it was added to a bill on the federal judiciary in such a way as to remove the subject of voluntary school prayer from the jurisdiction of all federal courts. This method of altering the Constitution by ordinary legislation actually passed the Senate in 1979, but failed to win approval in the House. The following year, school prayer became an issue in the presidential election.

Indications of what was to come appeared in a joint statement of intent made by Helms and Representative Philip M. Crane of Illinois on January 28, 1980.[9] The following day Senator Helms inserted into the record a Declaration of Voluntary School Prayer, issued by the Association of National Religious Broadcasters, an organization representing principally evangelical sects.[10] At the same time, new proposals for a constitutional amendment on prayer were submitted in the House.[11] As discussion of the subject heated up, expressions of concern, particularly about the Helms tactic, came from the National Council of Churches, the Baptist Joint Committee on Public Affairs, and the Anti-Defamation League of B'nai B'rith.[12]

When the presidential nominating conventions met in the summer of 1980, the Democrats were content to let the prayer matter rest. The Republicans were not; and their platform committee, strongly influenced by Senator Helms, inserted the following resolution into the 1980 Republican platform: "We support Republican initiatives in the Congress to restore the right of individuals to participate in voluntary, nondenominational prayer in schools and other public facilities."

Despite the clear language of this pledge, in the first year of his presidency, Reagan did little to encourage either legislation or constitutional change relating to public prayer. On the contrary, his chief supporters were asked to defer action on moral issues and concentrate on backing for his economic program.[13] Nevertheless, toward the end of 1981, Senate Republicans pushed through a type of Helms amendment by attaching to a Justice Department appropriation bill a proviso that would prevent the use of federal funds to interfere with "programs of voluntary prayer and meditation in the public schools."[14] Successful in the Senate, the amendment failed to get House approval.

Public debate on this issue saw the full force of Christian activist groups brought to bear on a much wider program that included not only school prayer but abortion and exemption of church schools from taxation. In March 1982 the chairman of Christian Voice announced the opening of a crusade to broadcast its message to the nation using free time made available by the hundreds of Christian radio and television stations, which by 1982 dotted the country from coast to coast. Claiming an evangelical audience in excess of 50 million, the crusaders opened their campaign with television commercials by professional actors Buddy Ebsen and Efrem Zimbalist, Jr., warning that to forbid "freedom of religious expression" in the classroom undermines children's faith in God and accounts for the spread of "violence, illiteracy, narcotics and illegitimate births."[15]

Rebuttals offered on the air and in the press pointed to the danger of imposing prayer on children rather than leaving them free to pray when, where, and how they wished. This view came from laymen and clerics alike. Presidents A. Bartlett Giamatti of Yale University and Donald W. Shriver, Jr., of Union Theological Seminary cautioned against state-mandated prayer as a return to the kind of forced ritualism that existed before the country acknowledged the need for a separation of church and state.[16] When the Southern Baptist Convention reversed its previous stand against mandated school prayer and voted 9-1 to support a constitutional amendment permitting organized voluntary school prayer, the Union of American Hebrew Congregations condemned the action and announced that it would undertake a campaign to counter the effects of what it believed were attempts to undermine the Bill of Rights.[17]

The divisive effect of the school prayer issue was felt within denominational groups as well as in political circles. A nationally televised discussion of the subject revealed that, while Baptist preacher Jerry Falwell applauded the move for a constitutional amendment, the Baptist Joint Committee on Public Affairs denounced it as "despicable demagoguery."[18] If the discussion brought out nothing new, the nature of the opposing forces was clear from the participants on the panel. On one side were Edward McAteer of the conservative Religious Roundtable and Richard Viguerie, publisher of the *Conservative Digest*. On the other side were Victor Kamber, political consultant to the Democratic National Committee, and United Methodist minister Dean Kelley representing the National Council of Churches.

One of the points made during the televised exchange was that a 1982 Gallup Poll showed 53 percent of the people in the United States favoring prayer in public schools. No member of the panel commented on the fact that this was a poll of adult opinon and that no similar canvass of student opinion had been made. Subsequently, a newspaper columnist, thinking that the views of students would be equally significant, reported the actual responses that one public school teacher received when she asked her 122 Virginia eighth-graders to write their opinions on the subject. A summary of the results showed startling departures from the picture of adult attitudes gathered by Gallup's interviewers:

> Specifically, the students were against voluntary school prayer by a figure of 96 to 26. In many of the essays, the kids stated their religion. They were Methodists and Catholics and Jews and Southern Baptists and even one Moslem who felt obliged to point out that he prays "in a totally different way."

Individual responses were equally revealing:

> One student was opposed to school prayer because "the teacher might pray in Catholic" and another, solicitous of his classmates, wrote that "some students are Jewish and they don't believe in God." Several of the students wrote they were very religious, but felt no need to pray in school and some declared themselves to be either atheists or agnostics and vowed, as one put it, that he would not pray "even if beaten with a stick."[19]

As contention continued, Congress, although it had backed away from a constitutional amendment on school prayer, agreed to a joint resolution acknowledging the Bible's "unique contribution in shaping the United States as a distinctive and blessed nation and people," and authorizing the president to designate 1983 as a national Year of the Bible.[20] Meanwhile, at the state level, advocates of public prayer continued to defy Supreme Court rulings. Alabama's legislature, in a deliberate attempt to challenge the court's 1962 ruling, passed a law to permit public school teachers to lead willing students in prayers.[21] Side by side with this new surge of pressure to "return God to the classroom," was a fundamentalist drive to establish "creation science" as a required course of instruction in public schools.

RELIGION CHALLENGES SCIENCE

The United States was born in a period known alternatively as the Age of Enlightenment or the Age of Reason. Stimulated by the discoveries and scientific reasoning of English physicist Isaac Newton, French mathematician Renè Descartes, and others, many Americans turned to logic and the test of experience for answers to political, social, and economic questions. The reaction of religious conservatives was to brand as atheists Christians like Thomas Jefferson, who believed that each individual's relation with God was a purely personal matter.

During the nineteenth century, church influence in politics waned, although an undercurrent of anti-Catholicism persisted and occasionally intruded by way of political action groups like the Know-Nothing Party of the 1850s and the post-Civil War Ku Klux Klan. Education, however, continued to feel the effects of a long tradition of religious training. In the U.S. public schools of the twentieth century, the question of science versus religion flared again into controversy.

The renewed struggle was sparked by John T. Scopes, a teacher who introduced his students to Charles Darwin's theory of the evolution of human beings from lower forms of animal life. Darwin's *Origin of Species* had created an international stir in both scientific and religious communities when it was published in 1859. In the United States, Darwin's heresy became the target of religious fundamentalists again when, in 1925, Tennessee enacted a statute that prohibited teaching any evolutionary theory contrary to the biblical conception of man's origin. On the basis of this law, Scopes was charged and convicted in one of the most famous and emotional trials in U.S. history. Scopes appealed, but his case never reached the U.S. Supreme Court, because Tennessee's appellate judges reversed the lower court's judgment on a technicality. The reversal had no effect on the law, which remained on the books. Nor did it discourage efforts to reintroduce similar legislation when fundamentalist leaders returned to the political arena more than 50 years later.

A new test of strength followed the recognition that fundamentalists received by their contribution to Reagan's election in 1980. Riding the crest of that wave, fundamentalists in Arkansas and Louisiana won passage of state laws mandating that "creation science" be taught in public schools along with the traditional course in what was called "evolution science." The declared purpose of this legislation was to bring the biblical story of creation to all students.

When the Arkansas law was challenged in a federal district court, the judge examined that statutory definition of creation science, which was stated to be based on "scientific evidences and related inferences that indicate: (1) sudden creation of the universe, energy and life from nothing ... (5) explanation of the earth's geology by catastrophism, including the occurence of a worldwide flood; and (6) a relatively recent inception of the earth and living kinds."[22] The state's argument—that creation from nothing does not involve a supernatural deity and that teaching the existence of God is not religious unless the teaching seeks a commitment—was found by the court to be without rational support or common understanding. What the state called "creation science," Judge William Overton held, failed to meet the essential characteristics of a science, which must be explained in terms of natural law and tested against the empirical world. Pointing out that the statute was taken almost verbatim from the writings of the fundamentalist Institute for Creation Research, the judge declared that such an approach to creation required one to "accept the literal interpretation of Genesis or else believe in the godless system of evolution." His finding was that "since creation science is not a science, the conclusion is inescapable that the only real effect of [the law] is the advancement of religion," which is unconstitutional. In passing, the judge also noted that the unalterable and unchallengeable character of fundamentalist beliefs precludes all scientific inquiry into the subject of evolution and that the law, if upheld, would influence both teaching methods and textbook selection.

The implications of the textbook problem had already been felt nationwide. For those who believe that control of the classroom is a battle for the human mind, textbook selection is one of the chief battlegrounds.

The godless element in this contest is seen as the secular humanist, according to one of the most ardent "defenders of the faith."[23]

Not all investigators of suspect books purport to represent religious organizations. Mel and Norma Gabler are leaders in this field. Their Texas-based Educational Research Analysts has established itself as the country's chief censorship organization. Despite the absence of any specific church connection, the Gablers have joined hands with fundamentalists in condemning secular humanist influence on textbooks, library books, and teachers. Similar attacks have been carried out by evangelists Jerry Falwell, Pat Robertson, and others, who charge the public schools with contributing to a general breakdown of character, morality, and patriotism.[24]

By 1982 the American Library Association estimated that book banning had spread across the country, with local school boards from Arizona to Maine pulling off the shelves or removing from class reading lists books by Ernest Hemingway, Mark Twain, John Steinbeck, and even the ancient Greek Homer. While most such actions were instigated by conservative religious organizations like Falwell's Moral Majority or the equally conservative lay organization, Eagle Forum, others were encouraged by the trend, as when black parents in a Virginia town complained of the racism expressed in Mark Twain's *Huckleberry Finn*.[25]

Many book publishers, cowed by the threat of sharply reduced sales, adjusted their authors' presentation of material to take account of the views of purported defenders of Christian morality. These modifications were especially noticeable in textbooks intended for classes in the social and physical sciences.[26] The first important break in the trend came in 1985, when the California Board of Education announced that it had refused to accept any of some 30 science texts offered by a dozen major publishers for use in the seventh and eighth grades of junior high schools throughout the state. This decision, the chairman said, was based on the finding that the publishers had "watered down" sections on evolution in an obvious effort to avoid controversy. The Board's conclusion was that the books failed to explain scientific principles in a meaningful way.[27]

A less dramatic but equally significant step was taken by the Texas Board of Education, which eliminated its earlier rule against textbook treatment of the theory of evolution. As a result, according to one researcher, "Not a single biology textbook reviewed by the committee last year [1984] was defeated or changed to conform to fundamentalists' objections."[28] However, a broader study of high school biology textbooks revealed inadequate coverage of evolution in half of those examined, and no reference to the subject whatever in one-sixth of the texts.[29]

Book banning became a legal issue of national importance when five high school students in New York challenged the action of the school board in removing from the library a number of books that board members found objectionable "based on their personal values, morals, tastes and concepts of educational suitability."[30] When the school board's lawyer denied the validity of charges that the board "follows its own social, moral and political values in making curricular decisions," Justice Sandra O'Connor asked, "Did I hear you say political values?" The lawyer's response was that he meant "politics in its loose sense—the study of government." He did acknowledge that, in the sanitizing process, "if the board members disapproved the word 'ain't,' their decision to remove all books containing that word should withstand a constitutional challenge."[31]

The court's reaction to both the facts and implications of this case reveal the nature and depth of the struggle over control of the classroom. Four members of the judicial panel (Chief Justice Warren Burger and Associate Justices Sandra D. O'Connor, Lewis F. Powell, and William H. Rehnquist) supported the school board's right to remove books that it found to be "irrelevant, vulgar, immoral, and in bad taste." Chief Justice Burger insisted that, if the final judgment announced by Justice William Brennen were to become law, "this Court would come perilously close to becoming a 'super censor' of school library decisions." This view failed to convince the majority, which found the board's action prompted by more than a sense of decency and relevancy. The opinion written by Brennan noted, first, that the banned books were taken directly from a list compiled by Parents of New York United, "a politically conservative organization of parents concerned about education legislation in the State of New York." Further, despite the board's denial of any religious or political intent, the news release it issued to justify its removal of the books characterized them as "anti-American, anti-Christian, anti-Semitic, and just plain filthy." The board also ignored its own Book Review Committee's recommendation that 5 of the 11 questioned volumes be retained: all 11 were removed from the library and from use in the curriculum. In light of these facts, the majority summed up its position in this paragraph:

> [N]othing in our decision today affects in any way the discretion of a local school board to choose books to *add* to the libraries of their schools. Because we are concerned in this case with the suppression of ideas, our holding today affects only the discretion to *remove*

books. In brief, we hold that local school boards may not remove
books from school library shelves simply because they dislike the
ideas contained in those books and seek by their removal to
"prescribe what shall be orthodox in politics, nationalism, religion or
other matters of opinion."[32]

Not all of the religion-based conflicts experienced in schools and colleges found their way to the courtroom. In 1982 an earth science teacher
in a St. Louis suburban high school was prevented by his principal from
using the film *Inherit the Wind* to illustrate the differences in attitude
toward creationism and evolution. This movie version of the Scopes trial
was held by school officials to be inaccurate historically as well as derisive
in its treatment of the religious side of the question. The local teachers'
association was still pressing for a reversal of this decision two years later.
That same year, a play about a German Mormon's opposition to Adolph
Hitler in the 1930s became the second production to be suppressed by
Mormon officials, whose belief in submission to whatever ruler is in
power had led them to urge their German members not to resist Hitler's
government. Farther west, the valedictory address written by a U.S.-born
student of Latin American parentage was censored by her San Jose high
school principal because it contained a reference to the suffering of
friends in her parents' native land of El Salvador. In Greenwich, Connecticut, when three nonconformist citizens did go to court to prevent the
local firefighters from erecting a cross over the firehouse, they were subjected to hundreds of telephone calls from fellow townspeople, who expressed regret that these Jews had not died in Auschwitz, or that America
did not have an Auschwitz with ovens to consume them.[33]

THE POLITICIZING OF RELIGION

In most communities, candidates for board of education posts run
for office in the same fashion as candidates for mayor, councilman, and so
forth. Inevitably, then, the choice of board members becomes a political
one, swayed by the preferences and prejudices that accompany all such
contests. Board members who yearn for a return to what they conceive to
be the fundamentals of education—reading, writing, and arithmetic—are
usually the strongest advocates of textbook, library book, and curriculum
control under "community standards" that they themselves determine.
Frequently this attitude is paired with a concept of morality that calls

upon higher levels of authority to "return God to the classroom." When supported by members of the national legislative and executive branches, who are influenced by the same preferences and prejudices as local board members, these religious principles become matters of state.

What marks the 1980s as this century's decade of "awakening" is the strength of the call to reestablish the Bible as the ultimate source of authority and, more specifically, to incorporate the fundamentalist concept of Christianity into the basic law of the land, the U.S. Constitution. This movement did not begin in 1980. Nor did it start as a politically oriented crusade.

When Presbyterian minister William Ashley Sunday made the name Billy Sunday famous by his rousing revivalist meetings before and after World War I, he was following in the footsteps of evangelists who led the eighteenth and nineteenth century "awakenings" mentioned earlier. His appeal was for a personal commitment to Christ and involved no effort to restore church dominance in the design of public policy. This nonpolitical tradition was continued by most twentieth-century evangelists until after World War II. Moreover, revivalist efforts of that period were largely those of individual preachers and, although most were Baptists, there was no central direction to the movement by that church or by voluntary association. An effort at coordination began in 1941 with the formation of an American Council of Christian Churches under the leadership of a strict fundamentalist, Reverend Carl McIntire, and the National Association of Evangelicals led by the more liberal Reverend Harold J. Ockenga. A decade later, McIntire's followers prepared the ground for political action with a Christian Anti-Communist Crusade (ACC). Coming on the heels of Senator Joseph McCarthy's wide-ranging attack on every real or imagined source of communist influence, the McIntire crusade established a common goal with that of conservative Republicans. Involvement of the ACC with like-minded political factions increased to the point that "during the Goldwater campaign in 1964 the work of the two groups became almost indistinguishable."[34]

The incorporation of political goals into sermons, speeches, and religious publications brought a radical change in the nature of evangelism. Where, formerly, most churches shied away from involvement in political questions, the new trend has been quite the reverse. This about-face was summarized in the words of a California fundamentalist minister, who recalled, "When I was growing up, . . . I always heard that churches should stay out of politics." Now, he added, "it seems almost a sin *not* to get involved."[35]

Among those most active in the effort to reintroduce religion into politics are Jerry Falwell, Pat Robertson, James Robison, W.A. Criswell, and Tim LaHaye. Most of these crusaders seek to accomplish their political ends by influencing voters to choose elected officials who will support pro-prayer, anti-abortion, and other types of moral or patriotic legislation. One self-styled prophet of God is not content to stop there. Marion B. (Pat) Robertson has let it be known that he is considering running for president in 1988.[36]

The messages of modern evangelists vary from one to another, but there is unity in the goal of making the nation's laws conform to their conception of the will of God. Tim LaHaye, a Baptist pastor and prolific writer, has assumed the role of philosopher of strict fundamentalism. Upholding the inerrancy of the Bible—the Protestant equivalent of papal infallibility—LaHaye devotes an entire volume to the dangers of humanism, which he describes as "not only the world's greatest evil but, until recently, the most deceptive of all religious philosphies." The most recent contender for this title is the "socialist one-world view," LaHaye says, but this is just one of five tenets of humanism. The other four, are atheism, Darwin's theory of evolution, amorality, and the concept of autonomous man. All of these add up to overt hostility to Christianity and a plot aimed at the purposeful destruction of "almost all biblical moral standards."[37] This "degeneracy by design," LaHaye finds, is being accomplished by 275,000 hard-core humanists in organizations like the American Civil Liberties Union, the National Education Association, the National Organization for Women (NOW), and the labor unions. Together, they control the news networks, the educational system and the major organs of government. As evidence that the United States is really a humanist-controlled state "in all its atheistic, amoral depravity," LaHaye cites these decisions taken contrary to the will of the people: "the giveaway of the Panama Canal ... abortion-on-demand, legalization of homosexual rights, government deficit spending, the size and power of big government, elimination of capital punishment, national disarmament, increased taxes, women in combat, passage of ERA, unncecessary busing, *ad infinitum*."[38]

As to the original purpose of the doctrine of separation of church and state, LaHaye says, "Our forefathers were simply preventing the establishment of a state religion." This view prevailed until 1979, when "under the guidance of a well-publicized born-again president, the federal government established a Department of Education with a \$40 billion budget. Since the educational system has been taken over by humanism, and since humanism is an officially declared religion, we find the government establishing a religion and giving the high priest a position on the president's cabinet."[39]

LaHaye concludes with a plan of action in which every true Christian is urged to aid "pro-moral candidates for public office" and to "expose amoral candidates and incumbents." His 21-point candidate questionnaire features yes-or-no questions regarding the moral principles of the Bible, abortion, ERA, and voluntary prayer in public school.[40]

Although LaHaye boasts that the public annually purchases 300,000 copies of his many books on the threat to Christianity, the impact of his writings hardly begins to match that of the spoken word as expounded by another political activist, Jerry Falwell. A Baptist advocate of toughness in both religion and politics, Falwell wades into both subjects with a macho spirit he developed in his brawling, something-less-than-Christian youth. Early in his career, Falwell attracted a following with sideshow performances that featured ice-breaking karate experts, ventriloquists, and "the world's tallest Christian." He attempted to finance his ministry by methods that the U.S. Securities and Exchange Commission labeled as "fraud and deceit."[41] Similar practices characterize his political activity. During the 1980 presidential campaign, Falwell claimed to have had a conversation with President Carter in which the president indicated sympathy for homosexuals. Documenting this incident with a verbatim quotation from the conversation, Falwell got what he wanted, nationwide press coverage. In a subsequent interview aired by only one television network, he admitted what a tape of his conversation with Carter had already shown, that the quoted exchange was a deliberate fabrication.[42]

Other verbal corrections made by Falwell have not disguised his true feelings. Openly supporting segregation in his church, and denouncing the Supreme Court's 1954 decision declaring racial separation in public schools unconstitutional, Falwell later backed away from that position. However, in 1985 he traveled to South Africa to personally assure President P. W. Botha of his support for that repressive government's apartheid policy. Conferring only with blacks who had not taken a stand against apartheid, he characterized African Bishop Desmond M. Tutu as "a phony" for presuming to represent South African blacks who do oppose that policy.[43]

What many see as the most worrisome feature of religious politics is not the simple appeal for faith in God, but the undercurrent of anti-democratic thought that often accompanies such appeals. One organization actively opposing religion in politics, People for the American Way, offers evidence of the character of right-wing fundamentalist leadership in such statements as these:

> The idea that religion and politics don't mix was invented by the Devil to keep Christians from running their own country. (Reverend Jerry Falwell).

> If necessary, God would raise up a tyrant, a man who might not have the best ethics, to protect the freedom interests of the ethical and the godly. (Reverend James Robison).

> Freedom of Speech has never been right. We never have had freedom of speech in this country and we never should have. (Reverend Rich Angwin).

> We do not want a democracy in this land because if we have a democracy a majority rules. (Reverend Charles Stanley).[44]

Taken in context, most statements like these relate to proposed limits on the publishing of pornographic material, on birth control or abortion, or on sex education in public school curricula. Nevertheless, the end product is evident in the political preferences shown by such speakers—as when Jerry Falwell urged the U.S. public to support South Africa, even to the extent of illegally buying gold Krugerrands (which had been banned by President Reagan), and to support what he called the "paradise" created by Philippine President Marcos, without regard for that leader's violent and indiscriminate suppression of all opposition elements, democratic as well as communist.[45] Along with the appeal of authoritarian rule, the vengefully puritanical tendencies promoted by fundamentalism are evident in the prayers of ministers like Bob Jones, Jr., of South Carolina, Greg Dixon of Indiana, Everett Sileven of Nebraska, and Robert L. Hymers and J. Richard Olivas of California, who call on God to eliminate evil in the United States by killing those they consider enemies—such as the five Supreme Court justices who upheld legalized abortion in Roe v. Wade.[46]

The power of political evangelism stems not only from righteous indignation against immorality, but from the facilities developed to carry that message to the nation. By 1980, the first presidential election year in which the political activity of religious groups played an important part, radio and television programs aired by evangelist leaders had grown to significant proportions. As one study notes, "of the 8,000 radio stations in the United States, 1,400 are religious; 30 of the nation's 800 television stations and 66 of the 800 cable systems are religious. Including the small local ministries, radio and television evangelists probably take in over one billion dollars each year."[47] Among the leading attractions was Jerry

Falwell's *Old Time Gospel Hour*, carried by "over 324 television outlets to an estimated audience of fifty million viewers,"[48] and Pat Robertson's *700 Club*, said to reach 4.4 million people every month. A 1985 study by the A.C. Nielson Company, commissioned by the Christian Broadcasting Network, reported that "40.2 percent of all homes in the United States watched at least one of 10 television preachers for at least six minutes once a month." This was said to be as good as the rating achieved by the most popular commercial prime-time programs.[49]

Measuring the effect of evangelists on the outcome of an election cannot be done with any degree of precision. Both proponents and opponents of their political activity have overstated its significance. However, one analyst finds that, whereas most white evangelicals had supported Carter in 1976, some 60 percent switched to Reagan in 1980; and by 1984 exit polls indicated that Reagan's majority among white evangelicals had risen to 80 percent. Another measure of influence is suggested by the fact that, in the 1980 election, six out of nine U.S. senators targeted for defeat by groups supporting the Moral Majority and the National Conservative Political Action Committee (NCPAC) lost their bids for reelection.[50] On the other hand, 1982 was typical of congressional races that follow two years after a presidential election. Despite continued efforts by religious conservatives, the Democrats held their own in the Senate and increased their majority in the House by 26 seats. In the more meaningful presidential election of 1984, religious activists again supported conservative republicans across the country; but, nothwithstanding the landslide vote for President Reagan, Republicans gained only 13 seats in the House while losing 2 in the Senate.

As a gauge of religious influence on public policy, the end product of all political action is far more accurate—that is, the enactment and implementation of laws by which the nation is governed. In this area, presidential leadership is all important, both in the design of legislation and in the manner in which the country's laws are administered.

9

Ronald Reagan:
Defender of the Faith

From that autumn day in 1964 when Ronald Reagan rose to national prominence with his televised speech in support of Barry Goldwater's campaign for the presidency, the actor-turned-politician has been known as a crusader against evil. On that occasion, and repeatedly thereafter, he identified the enemy variously as big government, socialism, communism, or Marxism. Only once did he introduce what was later to become a companion theme, the threat to religion. In the course of a blistering attack on the Social Security system he remarked that one of the products of the trend toward socialism in the United States was an attitude that "a child's prayer in a school cafeteria endangers religious freedom."[1]

Reagan was not always a crusader. Nor did he, prior to his conversion to Republican politics, show any special concern for the problem of religious freedom. In his autobiography he suggests a strong religious influence in his upbringing, but there is little to support that suggestion beyond such brief statements as "my father was a Catholic, my mother a Protestant." Nothing is added to indicate the influence that these bare facts might have had on the religious training his parents provided for their children. Nor is any information given as to the nature or extent of his parents' activities in church affairs, other than a brief reference to his mother's involvement in "various ladies' societies" and charitable causes.[2] The most common experience of Christian youngsters of that era, which was attendance at Sunday school and participation in the various sporting and other activities associated with Sunday school, receives only passing mention:[3] this despite the later assertion of a friend, Herbert E. Ellingwood, that Reagan not only attended Sunday school regularly but subsequently became a Sunday school teacher.[4] Even the fact that he finally joined his mother's church, the Disciples of Christ, Reagan did not feel worth mentioning. Reagan does recall that Eureka, the college of his choice, "was a Christian Church college," but that is the closest he comes to a discussion of church affiliation.[5] Athough, since 1963, he has regularly attended the Bel Air Presbyterian Church in Los Angeles, and considers himself a born-again Christian, both of these shifts in association and belief went unnoticed at the time that they occurred. He neither confirmed nor denied his reported acknowledgment of having been born again when questioned by the moderator of his 1984 debate with Walter Mondale. At that point, Reagan seemed to refer to the Church of Christ when he said, "In our particular church we didn't use that term born again, so I don't know whether I would fit that particular term."[6]

The extent to which his early association with the Disciples of Christ and later adoption of Presbyterianism influenced Reagan's view of life may be revealed when a definitive biography of the man is written. However, it is interesting to note the character of the church he elected to follow in his early years. One religious historian offers this description of the origin of the sect:

> No religious body is more definitely an American product than the Disciples of Christ (sometimes known as Churches of Christ or Christian Churches), and it is therefore natural that the denomination should have been committed to the ideal of religious freedom. It developed on the frontier, and was an attempt to restore primitive Christianity.[7]

The character of the church may account for Reagan's frequent appeals to all believers in God. It does not square, however, with his present-day preference for organizations and leaders whose view of Christian faith is reminiscent of the uncompromising doctrine of early New England Puritans. Nor does it accord with his insistence on putting in the hands of state legislatures and public administrators decisions about prayer in public schools.

Other aspects of Reagan's youth reflect a similar blend of good intentions and confused means for arriving at the goal of a truly democratic society. His emphasis on the importance of the family is a recurring theme in his public statements. Reagan's own family relationships were, in fact, unusual. As he recalls in his autobiography, "For as long as I can remember we were on a first-name basis with each other."[8] Mother wasn't Ma or Mom to her two sons, she was Nelle; and father wasn't Pa or Pop, but Jack. Even in today's more permissive atmosphere, which Reagan frequently deplores, this is hardly a common practice except in families with one natural parent and one stepparent.

Reagan's further assertion that "Ours was a free family that loved each other up to the point where the independence of each member began" contrasts sharply with his later disparagement of modern notions as to where the independence of wives and children begin and end.[9] The question of equal rights for women, for example, which Reagan insists he has always supported, is not mentioned in the memoirs he wrote in 1964. Although recently he has criticized the "misplaced liberalism" of the Democratic party, in 1980 he joined other Republican leaders in a turnabout on the subject of an ERA, when they adopted a platform that reversed earlier Republican pledges to support an equal rights amendment.

Youthful associations outside the family also brought Reagan face to face with many of the ethical problems that continue to plague the nation today. He often speaks of the lessons he learned from his father, who rejected the anti-negro theme of *Birth of a Nation* and refused to take accommodations at a hotel where Jews were not admitted. He points to his own camaraderie with "our two colored boys" on the Eureka College football team as evidence that he "was no stranger to the color problem."[10] However, none of these experiences has led Reagan to support legislation such as anti-discrimination housing laws, tighter federal control over state election procedures, and affirmative action programs, which were developed as measures to reduce the kinds of discrimination Reagan says he deplores. On the contrary, a review of his adult political life clearly reveals that he consistently opposes such remedies.

In short, freedom—and the guarantee of equal treatment—is not freedom if it entails government interference with the individual's right to make choices in life, regardless of how those choices might affect the freedom of choice available to others. This concept of freedom leads Reagan to see U.S. politics as a contest between the advocates of government domination over the individual and those who stand for protection of individual choice as the fundamental basis of democratic society.

THE ENEMY IS IDENTIFIED

Long before Reagan changed his political affiliation from Democrat to Republican, he had come to the conclusion that the threat to "family, work, neighborhood, peace and freedom" lay in the Marxist influence that was responsible for the trend toward totalitarian "big government." His suspicions on this score, which ultimately hardened into conviction, were aroused by his experience with labor unions in the film industry. The importance of this aspect of his acting career is indicated by the ten (of eighteen) chapters in his autobiography devoted to his Hollywood days, with more than half of that space given over to a running account of his battles with either corrupt or communist-led unions.

Reagan first experienced disillusionment with big government during the Depression, when his father rebelled at referring to those on relief as nameless cases, and then later, when he returned from military service in the summer of 1945. A few months earlier, he had learned of a strike by a coalition of Hollywood unions, not including the Screen Actors Guild. At that point, Reagan says, "I knew little and cared less about the rumors about Communists. I was truly so naive I thought the nearest Communists were fighting in Stalingrad." In this period of postwar naivete, Reagan reports that he "was blindly and busily joining every organization I could find that would guarantee to save the world."[11] Only three of these organizations appear worthy of mention in his memoirs, although an independent biographer discovered that Reagan also had "a brief fling with the World Federalists."[12] Reagan's own recollection is that he was deeply involved with the Screen Actors Guild, the American Veterans Committee, and the Hollywood Independent Citizens Committee of Arts, Sciences, and Professions (HICCASP). The objectives of the first two were hardly so broad as to classify them as world-savers. HICCASP, on the other hand, was very much a political group—one fronting for the communist cause, in fact, as Reagan was dismayed to discover.

As the nature of the HICCASP leadership and purpose became clear, a picture of America's enemies began to form in Reagan's mind. Underneath were hard-core communists dedicated to carrying out the commands of Russia's rulers; on the surface were U.S. liberals, whose adoration of Russian heroism during the war had blinded them to the dangers of the imported ideology they were urging upon their own government. He himself having been "used" by being featured as a speaker at HICCASP rallies, Reagan reacted bitterly to every evidence of collaboration by those who failed to see the truth as he now saw it.

His anger at communist duplicity and at gullible acceptance of the party line by some liberals did not immediately drive Reagan from the Democratic Party. He supported Hubert Humphrey in 1948 and Helen Gahagan Douglas in her California contest with Richard Nixon for a seat in the U.S. Senate. On Humphrey's behalf, he told Minnesota voters:

"While [Republican Senator] Ball is the banner-carrier for Wall Street, Mayor [of Minneapolis] Humphrey is fighting for all the principles advocated by President Truman, for adequate low-cost housing, for civil rights, for prices people can afford to pay and for a labor movement free of the Taft-Hartley Law."[13] However, by 1952, although he still professed to be a Democrat, Reagan voted for Eisenhower, whose position on domestic legislation was quite the opposite of Truman's.

Like Reagan, many registered Democrats voted for Eisenhower, but most returned to the fold when the smiling World War II hero gave way to the deviously cold Richard Nixon in 1960. Not so, Ronald Reagan. Having shifted his allegiance, he remained a Republican voter even though he retained his Democratic Party membership until 1962. In fact, when approached by Republican leaders to utilize his well-known General Electric oratory on behalf of Nixon's 1960 campaign for president, Reagan indicated a willingness to change parties. However, the professionals in Nixon's entourage recognized that Reagan's speeches would be more effective coming from a Democrat and urged him not to alter his registration. Reagan complied, and campaigned as a "Democrat for Nixon."[14] Two years later he again supported Nixon, this time in the race for governorship of California. By that time his membership in the Democratic Party was so obviously out of tune with that party's program that he decided to sever the relationship and register formally as a Republican.[15]

Neither in his autobiography nor in his later reminiscenses did Reagan discuss the rationale for supporting a candidate he had denounced in 1950, when Nixon ran against Helen Gahagan Douglas and conducted a vicious campaign that showed little regard for the principles of truth and honesty so ardently advocated by Reagan. One of his biographers feels that Reagan's conversion from liberal Democrat to conservative Republican was a slow, evolutionary process, influenced principally by his eight-year employment with General Electric. As Lou Cannon sees it, "in the process of answering questions in a manner pleasing to the questioners" in his business audiences, "Reagan became a defender of corporations and a critic of government." Because "Reagan believes in what he says, . . . he wound up believing what he was saying."[16] One of Reagan's earliest backers attributed Reagan's conversion to a combination of "his bitter experience with communists and his job with GE."[17]

Reagan's own contribution to an understanding of his political awakening is of little help. The last nine chapters of his autobiography are devoted to the years from 1948, when Reagan last supported a Democratic candidate for president, to 1962 when he joined the Republican Party; but they deal largely with his professional career in Hollywood and his employment with General Electric. The Hollywood-era anecdotes focus on his many battles with communists in the entertainment industry, in unions, and in civic organizations. However, Reagan's own account of these events offers no cause-and-effect analysis of the impact of postwar events on his political thinking. Key figures in the political and ideological contests of the 1950s—Truman, Eisenhower, Nixon, Stevenson, Humphrey—are mentioned only in passing, if at all.

To gain some understanding of Reagan's changed views on national policy, it is necessary to piece together the autobiographical comments and anecdotes as a background for the overtly political speeches by which he entered the national arena as a major player. The most significant entries deal with three things: the threat of communism in the United States, the idyllic character of business, large or small; and the evils of big government, which he associates directly with liberalism and indirectly with communism.

Reagan's preoccupation with communism is understandable if one considers the time and place of his experiences. The attention given this problem in Hollywood, both in the entertainment industry and its unions, made the threat of a communist takeover seem very real to Reagan. That Hollywood was hardly representative of the United States as a whole, and that communist doctrine had never gained any acceptance in the U.S. labor movement or in public support for political candidates, did not affect Reagan's evaluation of the threat. Moreover, he seemed unaware of the broader and deeper impact of such defenders of democracy as Wisconsin's Senator Joseph McCarthy, whose reckless charges of communist influence were leveled at targets ranging from Eisenhower's State Department to General George C. Marshall and Eleanor Roosevelt.

In Reagan's account of the era, McCarthy—and his ultimate censure after hearings by a Senate Committee—were not worth mentioning. The only investigations reported in his memoirs were those held by the congressional and California un-American activities committees. He dismissed people who protested the excesses of the committees as either "suckers" or communist conspirators, whose criticisms would, in wartime, be "treason, and the name for such is traitor."[18] As for his personal participation in investigations of un-Americanism, Reagan impressed both the public and his biographers by the moderate tone of his testimony and by his refusal to name those he suspected of communist leanings.

What neither the public nor historians of the period knew until 1985 was that long before he appeared before the House un-American Activities Committee, Reagan had acted as a secret informant for the FBI, transmitting to that agency the charges and suspicions he so bravely refused to offer in public.[19]

Reagan's claim to a "changing philosophy" based on nonpartisan analysis of the country's condition in the 1950s lacks credibility, not only for the questionable interpretations he puts on events of the period, but because of his omission of any mention of the most critical developments of the decade. His so-called analysis takes no account whatever of the McCarthy hearings, the often violent resistance to the Supreme Court's order to desegregate public schools, and the equally fierce resistance to enforcement of the first federal law since the post-Civil War period to protect the voting rights of black citizens. Instead, he focuses on the "quickening tempo in our government's race toward the controlled society" and the "miracle of American industry at work." Government interference with private enterprise, he decides, threatened the very basis of freedom in the United States. Reagan's symbol of a free society was that "vast corporation," General Electric, which he found "as human as the corner grocer." Notwithstanding his own experience as a union member in the battle between Hollywood actors and their big studio employers, he convinces himself that GE's 250,000 employees were "concerned, not with security as some would have us believe, but with their very firm personal liberties."[20] He does not define the personal liberties whose importance made the problem of economic security of little or no consequence to the wage earner at General Electric. However, with this interpretation of freedom, and this selection of evidence as to what was important in the 1950s, Reagan laid the foundation for his later political career as defender of the faith, the first stage of which was defense of uninhibited freedom of economic enterprise against any kind of government interference or restraint.

IN DEFENSE OF FREE ENTERPRISE.

Reagan entered the political lists as defender of the faith of Milton Friedman, whose thesis was, and is, that freedom of economic endeavor is the most fundamental of all human freedoms. With this as starting point, Reagan opened his crusade on the theme that liberalism is the first step on the road to communism. He has summarized the contest between liberals and conservatives (whom he came to represent) in these words:

The classic liberal used to be the man who believed the individual was, and should be forever, the master of his destiny. That is now the conservative position. The liberal used to believe in freedom under law. He now takes the ancient feudal position that power is everything. He believes in a stronger and stronger central government, in the philosophy that control is better than freedom. . . .

The conservatives believe the collective responsibility of the *qualified men* in a commuity should decide its course. The liberals believe in remote and massive strongarming from afar, usually in Washington, D.C. The conservatives believe in the unique powers of the individual and his personal opinions. The liberals lean increasingly toward bureaucracy, operation by computer minds and forced fiat, the submergence of man in statistics [emphasis added].[21]

Having defined and classified liberals and conservatives in this fashion, Reagan concludes by comparing his role in the defense of freedom with that of Moses leading the Israelites out of slavery, of Christ accepting crucifixion to save all mankind, of "those men of Concord" who resisted British tyranny, and of the World War II Allies in their resolve to defeat Hitler.

If the record compiled for Reagan's memoirs generally avoids mention of particular political figures as communist oriented, his off-the-record remarks showed no such reluctance. A 1960 letter to Republican presidential candidate Richard Nixon, written when Reagan was still a registered Democrat, suggested that Democratic candidate John F. Kennedy be publicly identified as a communist at heart. "Under the tousled boyish haircut," Reagan wrote, "is still old Karl Marx."[22] The same charge was leveled at high-ranking officials in the administration of Franklin D. Roosevelt, although, even as late as 1981, Reagan seemed uncertain as to whether the New Dealers were communists or fascists. In one interview, he stated both that "many New Dealers" espoused fascism and that F.D.R.'s Interior Secretary Harold Ickes had admitted that their goal was "a kind of modified form of communism." In characteristic Reagan style, no documentation was offered for either accusation. The charge that Ickes' statement appears in his writings was patently false, as any search of Ickes papers will reveal.[23]

In his grand entrance into national politics, Reagan exhibited publicly the same sentiments he was recording simultaneously for his autobiography. In a nationally televised speech on October 27, 1964, campaigning for Barry Goldwater, Reagan warned of the totalitarian trend in Democratic programs such as the Depression-born farm subsidies, the

TVA, Social Security, public housing, youth aid plans, the UN, foreign aid programs, and "the immorality and discrimination of the progressive surtax." On this last point he allied himself with economist Sumner Schlicter, whom he quoted as saying: "If a visitor from Mars looked at our tax policy, he would conclude it has been designed by a Communist spy to make free enterprise unworkable."[24] He concluded by ascribing to Republicans those same qualities of sacrifice (à la Moses, Christ, and the American revolutionary patriots) that were recounted at the end of his memoirs.

The enthusiasm with which this speech was greeted by many Republicans failed to impress the majority of voters, who emphatically rejected Goldwater's bid for the presidency by a margin of 43–27 million in favor of Lyndon Johnson. This neither discouraged Reagan nor altered his view of the threat to U.S. society. What it did do was to convince conservative Republicans that Reagan would make a more effective party leader than Goldwater. The first test of that belief came two years later, when a group of California millionaires persuaded Reagan to run for the governorship of that state. The result was a resounding victory over Democratic incumbent Edmund G. (Pat) Brown. The strength of public support for his candidacy convinced him that most people approved of his concept of America.

Reagan's California administration set the tone that would characterize his later political life. His belief that the country's major objective was to combat the liberal trend toward socialism (or communism—he used the terms interchangeably) never changed. However, his style of delivering this message to the public, along with his carefully honed acting talent, helped him to camouflage many of the policy reversals he was obliged to endure. Where once he decried Social Security as "a welfare program" demeaning to the individual, he accepted a 1980 presidential platform that guaranteed continuation of that system while still criticizing the welfare concept generally. Similarly, his gubernatorial campaign for tax reduction was compromised when he accepted California's largest-ever tax increase as a means of eliminating the deficit he had inherited from a Democratic administration. Later, as president, he successfully promoted an equally startling reduction in federal taxes, but at the expense of the goal he could boast of having achieved as governor: elimination of the deficit. The fact that the federal deficit ballooned to more than three times its 1980 level during the first Reagan administration was the direct result of Reagan's insistence that the Soviet threat required sharp increases in the military budget, whether or not those increases were matched by reductions in other programs.

More than any other aspect of the Reagan program, the battle against Soviet communism took on the character of a crusade of good against evil. Reagan's view of the Soviet threat, and of foreign policy problems generally, was not based on any purposeful study of that aspect of presidential responsibility. His experience with the country's external affairs consisted largely of two trips abroad, made at the request of President Nixon. The impact of his exposure to life and politics in other lands is indicated by Reagan's comparison of South Vietnamese President Nguyen Van Thieu's election on a single-candidate ballot with George Washington's uncontested election in 1788.[25] To mask Reagan's abysmal ignorance of world history, his staff saw to it that he never lacked appropriate quotations from both friends and enemies of democracy, to drive home the point that the Kremlin was the instigator of most of the world's troubles and was therefore the major threat to U.S. security and free-enterprise democracy. "Most" became "all" as Reagan took aim at the presidency. In 1968 he warned that every Russian ruler since the Bolshevik Revolution "has stated that they will not retreat one inch from the Marxian concept of a one-world socialist state."[26] Twelve years later, with wars against colonialism, poverty, and a variety of dictatorships raging throughout the world, Reagan asserted that "the Soviet Union underlies all the unrest that is going on. If they weren't engaged in this game of dominoes, there wouldn't be any hot spots in the world."[27]

In terms of domestic politics, Reagan has always associated the threat of Marxism with godless atheism. However, religion *per se* did not emerge as an issue in any of Reagan's campaigns for public office, although it did lie in the background of platform pledges to seek constitutional approval for pro-prayer and anti-abortion laws. By 1980, however, the religious influence appeared as an identifiable factor in national politics.

THE ALLIANCE WITH GOD

Although all U.S. presidents, without exception, have demonstrated their attachment to the God of the Christian Bible, none has presumed to associate God with his political philosophy as persistently as has President Reagan, who repeatedly offers the simple declarations of faith by Presidents Washington, Jefferson, and Lincoln as evidence of the inseparability of religion and politics. Our early presidents did not, however, attempt to link religious and political goals, as Reagan does.

When the Founding Fathers declared that "God is on our side," it was a rallying cry in time of war, representing the entire nation's interest rather than that of Federalist or Anti-Federalist political doctrine. This is not the sense in which Reagan uses his frequent quotations from the men who designed the Constitution. Nor does he seem to be aware of the historical inaccuracy of some of the selections his staff feeds him for his speeches. One of his favorites, which he has used time and again, is an appeal by Benjamin Franklin to the delegates of the Constitutional convention of 1787, asking that "prayers imploring the assistance of Heaven, and its blessing on our deliberations, be held in this assembly every morning before we proceed to business." From that day on, Reagan often assures his listeners, "they opened all the constitutional meetings with prayer."[28]

Although Franklin is correctly quoted, both the implication of his remarks and Reagan's conclusion are false. The proposal for daily prayers was *not* accepted, for the very good reason that the members were sharply divided on the question. To begin with, Franklin's suggestion was offered in an attempt to cool the rising tempers of convention delegates who seemed to have reached an impasse on some of the most basic problems of constitutional design. Franklin achieved his purpose, even though his formal motion was rejected, its author acknowledging later that "the convention, except for three or four persons, thought prayers unnecessary."[29] Taken in the context of the debates that were raging in the convention, Franklin's remarks cannot reasonably be interpreted as intended to incorporate religious doctrine into political decisions. Yet Reagan's suggestion to that effect has been picked up and reinforced by his supporters, one of whom took a full-page advertisement in the *Washington Post* on the day before the 1984 election, to repeat part of Franklin's statement under the heading: "Some People Say We Should Not Mix Religion With Politics. Benjamin Franklin Said We Should."[30]

Selective quotations from the writings and speeches of early American leaders, like isolated phrases from the Bible, can be used to support almost any point of view. In making his selections, Reagan ignores the basic philosophy of each individual he quotes. Like Thomas Jefferson, Benjamin Franklin was a deist who believed that the individual's relation with God was a purely personal one. He wrote profusely of the need for virtue in both private and public life, but without associating this question with any reference to the Bible or to any sectarian concept of God's word. Similarly, Reagan's references to Tom Paine's call to arms, "We have it in our power to begin the world over again," ignore the fact that Paine's goal for American society was as remote from Reagan's as is that of today's most left-wing Democrat.[31] Abraham Lincoln, the president Reagan calls "my favorite," was equally devout, but not one of the many quotations Reagan selects from this extraordinary man's life suggests that Lincoln's policies were closer to God's than were those of his political opponents. In this respect, the most pertinent of Lincoln's comments is one that Reagan never uses. As noted by President Eisenhower (whom Reagan rarely cites), Lincoln once remarked that "deputations and platoons came to him daily to define for him God's will, which led him to wonder why God never revealed His will directly to the President."[32] Even George Washington, whose appeals to heaven for guidance Reagan quotes on many occasions, was not one to propose laws or constitutional amendments relating to religious beliefs, or to boast the higher morality of his Federalist backers as against that of his Anti-Federalist opponents. On the contrary, the advice he gave the nation in his farewell address, while pointing to religion and morality as "indispensable supports" of "political prosperity," dissociated this subject from organized politics by a powerful attack on what he viewed as the greatest danger to the American system of government: "the baneful effects" of political parties.[33]

Finally, Reagan's frequent references to early American history reveal a profound ignorance of the variety of beliefs and practices that made the ultimate formation of a united republic such a remarkable achievement. He sees the brutally intolerant Puritans as seekers after religious freedom and initiators of the traditional holidays of Thanksgiving and Christmas. The fact is that no formal thanksgiving day was established, and Christmas was not observed at all. The latter holiday was made illegal by a Massachusetts law of 1659, which decreed that "Whosoever shall be found observing any such day as Christmas . . . shall pay for every offense five shillings." Since the Bible made no mention of a Christmas celebration, the literal-minded Pilgrims would have no part of such frivolity.[34]

Memorizing favorite phrases by famous men rather than studying the history of their times, Reagan seems unaware of the serious differences of opinion that divided members of the Constitutional Convention of 1787. He refers to the Founding Fathers as if they were of one mind as to the nature of the government and the social compact that was hammered out after the Revolution. The reality was, as Franklin explained in his reason for suggesting a moment of prayer, that these leaders were bitterly divided on such basic issues as the system of representation, slavery, strong versus weak central authority, and the need for a federal bill of rights. If there was a common understanding on any one point, it was that the new government would *not* be associated with religion in any way. This is clear from the very wording of the Constitution. Whereas state constitutions, written both before and after 1787, commonly refer to God as the source of man's right to liberty and a freely elected government, the federal Constitution cites only "We the People" as the source of authority for securing "the blessings of liberty." Indeed, the nonreligious Preamble to the Constitution excited no discussion whatever in the Philadelphia convention and was approved routinely without ever being challenged as lacking any acknowledgment of divine origin or blessing. Thus, Reagan's frequent plea for a return to the religious precepts of the Founding Fathers reflects a child's view of American history—sincere, reverent, and patriotic, but with little understanding of the forces and ideas that have shaped U.S. society.

Reagan's view of the place of religion in politics began to form in 1967 with the unexceptional generalization that "Belief in the dependence on God is essential to our state and nation." In what a friend described as "the beginning of the Jesus movement" in California, Governor Reagan went on to assert, "This will be an integral part of our state as long as I have anything to do with it." As president, he moved on to the purely fundamentalist position that "the Bible contains an answer to just about everything and every problem that confronts us."[35] Presuming to follow in the footsteps of the Founding Fathers, Reagan is obviously ignorant of the fact that, in their references to the Deity, the Founders never resorted to appeals in the name of Jesus. Nor would his heros have condoned Reagan's use of religion in election campaigns. On the contrary, Benjamin Franklin, George Washington, and Abraham Lincoln would have been horrified that Reagan applauds fundamentalist preacher James Robison, who in 1980 urged true Christians to organize bloc voting to ensure the election of candidates who supported Reagan's political programs.[36] The following year, Reagan called for a return to both "that old time religion and that old time Constitution," setting the stage for his later charge that "the first amendment has been twisted to the point that freedom of religion is in danger of becoming freedom from religion." His belief that recent Supreme Court decisions show the government to be "waging war against God and religion" justified a drive for constitutional amendments to prevent abortion and permit school prayer, as well as legislation to allow tuition tax credits for parents of children in private schools.[37]

Putting social issues aside in favor of reduced taxes during his first presidential year, Reagan in 1982 renewed the campaign for a constitutional amendment that would "restore the right to pray" in the classroom, a right no court had ever denied except when prayers were government sponsored.[38] Making this a political issue, he advised voters on the eve of the 1982 congressional elections that Democratic "big spenders" had not only brought on inflation but "even drove prayer out of our nation's classrooms."[39]

Consistently aligning himself with the nation's religious conservatives, Reagan has addressed cheering multitudes of fundamentalist ministers, Moral Majority enthusiasts, and their allies with a frequency and fervency unmatched by any previous president. Even nontraditional fundamentalists are drawn by his concept of "traditional" biblical values, which he has associated with patriotic pride in reference to "the splendor of this vast continent which God has granted as our portion of His creation" and such Churchillian prose as "There are no words to express the extraordinary strength and character of this breed of people we call Americans."[40] This brings into the alliance most of the leadership of the Mormon Church, many Catholic clergymen, and some Orthodox Jews. However, his most enthusiastic supporters are fundamentalist Protestants, who respond with delight to his attacks on "modern-day secularism" and his pledge to work with them on "social issues of common concern."[41]

Reagan's appeals to these groups have been repaid, not only with votes and organized pressure for his legislative program, but with publicity of a sort rarely seen in U.S. politics. As a Washington journalist reported shortly before the 1984 presidential election, bookstores specializing in religious literature have begun to feature books and pamphlets by or about Ronald Reagan. Moreover, all the Reaganabilia in one Maryland store's "most prominent single display" were found to have been "written with the cooperation of the White House."[42]

Republican acceptance of fundamentalist and electronic evangelists as full partners in the 1984 campaign contrasted sharply with the relatively minor role played by clergy in 1980. As reported by one member of the 1984 convention's human resources and opportunities committee, no moderates offered platform recommendations; but ministers Jerry Falwell, James Robison, Jimmy Swaggart, and Greg Dixon joined Phyllis Schlafly in pressing for sections on abortion, classroom prayer, homosexuality, tax credits for private schools, welfare, the ERA, and tests for federal judges—all adopted with little opposition.[43] Even in the selection of ministers for the opening and closing prayers, convention officials departed from the normal practice of alternating among different churches. Fundamentalist Baptists received both assignments: James Robison gave the opening prayer, and the closing benediction was performed by W.A. Criswell, whose religious intolerance had long since been demonstrated when he opposed John Kennedy simply because he was a Catholic.

If the general public seemed unaware of the significance of Reagan's alliance with the least tolerant of all religious groups, the implications of his campaign were not lost on other members of the clergy, who refused to accept either his view of church–state relations or his conclusions as to how God's will was to be effected in the design of legislation and constitutional principles. Episcopal Bishop Paul Moore, though not favoring abortion, declared this to be a "decision of conscience," and held that the first obligation of all public officials was to uphold the Constitution and laws of the land regardless of their religious beliefs.[44] Leadership of the 3 million member African Methodist Episcopal church came out flatly for Reagan's defeat, in a convention that was concerned with more than religious issues and that added to the general involvement of churches in the political process.[45]

Within the Catholic church, differences of opinion erupted into public debates as Catholic Democratic vice-presidential candidate Geraldine Ferraro and Catholic Bishop John J. O'Connor engaged in a widely publicized exchange over the question of abortion. At the same time, the Administrative Board of the United States Catholic Conference issued a formal statement asserting, "we do not take positions for or against particular parties or individual candidates." However, the Board added that "teachers in the Catholic Church entrusted with the responsibility of communicating the content of Catholic moral teaching" must encourage voters to "examine the positions of candidates on issues and decide who will best contribute to the common good of society."[46]

This was followed by a Pastoral Letter on Catholic Social Teaching and the U.S. Economy, whose specified objectives were "to provide guidance for members of our own church" and "to add our voice to the public debate about U.S. economic policies."[47] Opposing "collectivist and statist economic approaches," the letter "also resists the notion that an unimpeded market automatically produces justice." Even more challenging to Reagan's economic views was this statement: "We believe that the level of inequality in income and wealth in our society ... today must be judged morally unacceptable." This view was, in turn, contested by the Lay Commission on Catholic Social Teaching and the U.S. Economy, which extolled the U.S. economic system as one that "responds to the legitimate demands of the political system, is concerned for the welfare of all, including those who, for whatever reason, are not working and need assistance."[48]

Jewish groups did not diplay their differences publicly, but in some areas both pro- and anti-semitic appeals were made on behalf of Republican candidates. In New York and California, votes were solicited by telephone calls to people with Jewish-sounding names, the callers identifying themselves only as members of the National Jewish Coalition, not adding that this was a branch of the Republican National Committee. In Michigan, David Stockman's successor as representative of the fourth district joined two other Republican candidates seeking the ouster of the third district's Jewish congressman, Howard Wolpe, asking the ministers in Wolpe's district to "send another Christian to Congress."[49] The appeal failed, and Wolpe was reelected by a clear majority.

Members of the press also recognized the religious tone of Reagan's campaign. In September 1984, a reporter raised a question about the religious issue, asking the president, "Are you all overplaying it?" The answer was, "No, but I think some people in your profession here are."[50] A few days later, another reporter asked whether Reagan really thought religion and politics were as closely tied as he had said in Dallas. Reagan's answer was yes, "In the sense that I said it in Dallas," adding, "which none of you have correctly reported." Contrary to the president's charge of press inaccuracy, both the *New York Times* and the *Washington Post* carried the same report as the official White House publication, which printed his August 23 remark at a Dallas prayer breakfast as follows:

> The truth is, politics and morality are inseparable. And as morality's foundation is religion, religion and politics are necessarily related. We need religion as a guide. We need it because we are imperfect, and our government needs the church because only those humble enough to admit they're sinners can bring to democracy the tolerance it requires in order to survive.[51]

Unpublicized by the White House, although common knowledge among Washington reporters, were the occasions on which Reagan gave his personal blessing to fundamentalist efforts to reshape U.S. society. Tim LaHaye's American Coalition for Traditional Values, for example, was launched at a White House reception featuring a welcome by President

Reagan. This event was not recorded in the *Weekly Compilation of Presidential Documents*, which purports to report all presidential events not concerned with security. Neither did that official publication mention the president's letter lauding the Coalition for its efforts to reach "millions of committed Christians" and praising its chairman for his "faithful patriotism."[52] The Coalition's goal is revealed by Chairman LaHaye's comment that the problem with the United States is that "we do not have enough of God's ministers running the country."[53]

The religious issue did not end with Reagan's reelection. On the contrary, such an overwhelming vote of approval seemed to confirm all his views, religious and otherwise. Thus, it was not surprising that, in the private inauguration preceding the public ceremony, his Presbyterian pastor, Donn Moomaw, appealed to God to "fill Mr. Reagan and Mr. Bush with a new sense of their divine appointment," as though the election had been ordained by the Almighty.[54]

Moomaw's invocation was not entirely inappropriate. President Reagan makes a habit of depicting the ideal community in terms of what he conceives to be God's intent. In doing so, he invariably lectures as though he were God's spokesman, bringing His message to the people of the United States. At a 1984 Spirit of America Festival in Decatur, Alabama, he called on his listeners to recognize that "God has granted us the challenge to change our own country and to make it better by moving it closer to the intentions of the men who invented it." One of his favorite inventors of America is the Puritan preacher, John Winthrop, who envisioned New England as a holy commonwealth established under a covenant with God. Reagan considers this to have been accomplished, but subject to improvement. After describing the improvement process as a mixture of freedom of thought and religion with "greater freedom of the marketplace," he used Winthrop's most quoted phrase to round out the theme that all the basic elements of democracy are to be found in the society envisioned by this seventeenth-century cleric. In Reagan's words:

> You don't have to travel too far in the world to realize that we stand as a beacon, that America is today what it was two centuries ago, a place that dreamers dream of, that it is what Winthrop . . . with a little group of Pilgrims gathered around him, . . . said, "We shall be as a shining city for all the world upon the hill."[55]

Supporting Reagan's views in this area is Secretary of Education William J. Bennet, who repeatedly makes charges of religious intolerance on the part of the Supreme Court and the president's political opponents.

Bennet's speeches before sympathetic audiences like the Supreme Council of the Knights of Columbus and the fundamentalist Association of Christian Schools International reveal the administration's intent to reintroduce religious training in schools, by "legislation . . . judicial reconsideration and constitutional amendment," in order to correct what Bennet refers to as "the current situation of disdain for religious belief."[56] His use of the word "disdain" to describe the attitude of those who feel religious belief to be a purely personal matter (exempt from government intrusion) is typical of administration efforts to label the opposition in terms that are inaccurate but effective in eliciting an emotional response from the public.

Bennet's reference to "judicial reconsideration" is an equally significant sign of the administration's goal of selecting, for every federal court vacancy, a justice who will reflect Reagan's views on church–state relations. In the president's words, the objective is to establish "the independence of the courts from improper political influence" by appointing "individuals who understand the danger of short-circuiting the electoral process and disenfranchising the people through judicial activism."[57] Both critics and supporters of the president acknowledge that "judicial activism" is merely a label for decisions that do not square with Reagan ideology.[58] How well he has chosen is suggested by the timely assault on judicial activism by one of his appointees, Judge Robert H. Bork, who used not only Reagan's expressions but those of Attorney General Edwin Meese in his call for a return to the "original intent" of the men who drew up the Constitution.[59]

To explain the administration's legal philosophy in greater detail, Attorney General Meese, the president's principal advisor on court appointments, spoke at length in a series of speeches delivered during the summer and fall of 1985. Addressing the American Bar Association, Meese attacked Supreme Court decisions in three areas: federalism, criminal law, and freedom of religion.[60] To illustrate the court's failings in the third category, Meese selected only those decisions that ran contrary to administration views concerning acceptable government participation in the operations of religious institutions. With this as his takeoff point, Meese proceeded to blast all interpretations of the Fourteenth Amendment that apply Bill of Rights protection against the states. Borrowing a phrase from a 1959 case, he labeled the theory on which such interpretations were based "the doctrine of incorporation," a concept he derided as a johnny-come-lately device designed in 1925 by such judicial activists as Chief Justice William Howard Taft and Associate Justices

Pierce Butler, James C. McReynolds, Edward T. Sanford, George Sutherland, and Willis Van Devanter.[61] What the courts should follow, he said, is a "jurisprudence of original intention," which would reflect the Founders' "commitment to the ideal of democracy" and "would not be tainted by ideological predilection."

Like his president, Meese not only generalizes about the Founders' belief in democracy (a concept that many members of the Constitutional Convention rejected), he assumes that they were of one mind on all aspects of the final agreement. Nowhere in his speeches is there any reference to the deep divisions of opinion: What he calls a "commitment to democracy" allowed for both slavery and direct financial support of favored churches in some states. Condemning the Supreme Court for departing *in 1925* from the original intent of the Framers, which was to apply Bill of Rights protections only against the federal government, he overlooks the fact that the architects of the Fourteenth Amendment, Senator Jacob M. Howard and Representative John A. Bingham, stated *in 1866* that the purpose of that amendment was to make the federal Bill of Rights applicable to the states.[62]

On the particular point of religion, Supreme Court Justice John Paul Stevens has pointed out that Meese's "founding generation" included "apostles of intolerance as well as tolerance, advocates of differing points of view in religion as well as politics."[63]

In passing, it is appropriate to observe that Edwin Meese's attachment to Constitutional principles is demonstrated less by his public speeches than by these informal remarks on the conditions of his own time: a participant killed by police in the 1969 People's Park demonstrations at Berkeley "deserved to die"; the American Civil Liberties Union is a "criminal lobby"; the Supreme Court's decision to allow suspects in criminal cases to have an attorney present during police interrogation was "infamous"; and, in U.S. criminal practice, "if a person is innocent of a crime, then he is not a suspect."[64]

Meese's standards for the selection of supporting staff are also revealing. After successfully appointing to senior positions in the Justice Department individuals, such as William Bradford Reynolds, who are dedicated to the same limited application of civil rights protections as Meese, the Attorney General attempted to promote Herbert E. Ellingwood from chairman of the federal Merit Systems Protection Board to head of the Justice Department Office of Legal Policy. This would have placed in charge of the office that screens candidates for the federal judiciary an acknowledged Christian activist, of whom Representative

Patricia Schroeder said: "He seems to think Christians have a corner on decency. You really have the feeling he thinks he's answering to a higher law."[65] Ellingwood's record on the integration of church and state, which, by his own admission, included recommending that LaHaye's American Coalition for Traditional Values assist in recruiting selected Christians for upper-level federal posts, was too much for even the Republican-dominated Senate to swallow, and the nomination was withdrawn before formal hearings could be held.[66]

Taken in the context of constitutional debate, the church–state issue would appear to be a purely domestic problem. Unfortunately, it has assumed international significance, not only through the anti-religious stance of Marxist governments but by Reagan's association of religious freedom with his anti-communist campaign and by the actions of U.S. churches that have voluntarily and directly entered the arena of foreign policy.

Morality
and
World Politics

10

Religion and Foreign Policy

Religious fervor as a significant influence on a nation's foreign policy is no novelty in world history. Where Muslims, Christians, and Jews now engage in unending warfare, Hebrews and other semitic tribes battled more than 3,000 years ago, each appealing to its own god to bring victory over the others. Later on, the spread of Christianity proved to be a greater threat to the Roman Empire than rebellious Hebrew tribes or any of the nations that had contested Roman authority by force of arms.

To the east, the doctrines of India's Siddhartha Guatama (Buddha), China's Lao-Tse and Kung Fu-Tse (Confucius), who were more concerned with ethical patterns of human conduct than establishing the divinity of one almighty god, made little impression on countries from the Mediterranean to the Americas. Rather, the principal challenge to Christianity in the land of its origin was conceived early in the seventh century A.D. when Mohammed raised the flag of Islam. Arab armies carried that banner through Spain into southern France in the seventh and eighth centuries; and, after the defeat of the Christian Crusaders, Turkish forces dominated southeastern Europe, until their defeat in Hungary in 1442 signaled a withdrawal of Muslim armies to more secure positions in Turkey and North Africa. The eastward progress of Islam never ceased, however, and by the twentieth century it had attracted millions of followers all across southern Asia and the islands of Indonesia.

COMMUNISM AND U.S. FOREIGN POLICY

In the twentieth century, another ethical concept arose known as communism, which held organized religion of any sort to be an opiate used by the ruling class to help keep the mass of people in subjection. Even without its atheistic character, communism would have been considered an enemy by the United States for its overt dedication to the destruction of capitalism. The fact that Soviet spokesmen were equally blunt in their condemnation of religion reinforced the conviction of most people in the United States that the objectives of Moscow's leaders were inimical to this country's way of life.

In 1917, official U.S. reaction to the seizure of power by the Bolshevik faction of the Russian revolutionary movement was one of distrust, if not open hostility, toward a regime that had pledged to end the war with Germany on almost any terms. When Allied armies failed to overthrow the Bolshevik government that did indeed make peace with Germany in March 1918, the United States retreated to a policy of nonrecognition and official nonintercourse, which lasted until 1933, when diplomatic and trade relations were restored by President Franklin D. Roosevelt. Allies of the United States had long since accepted the fact of a communist government in eastern Europe, and the trade they had built up with the Soviet Union led U.S. businessmen to support Roosevelt's proposed recognition as a move that would allow them to share in the benefits of that commerce.[1]

Despite the enthusiasm with which some U.S. liberals viewed the Soviet effort to create a new society, the country as a whole showed little appreciation for either communist principles or the brutal totalitarian regime of Josef Stalin. Unlike the labor unions of western Europe, which were (and continue to be) vigorous participants in a variety of socialist-oriented political parties, the overwhelming majority of U.S. labor leaders and their union members remained adamantly opposed to any such commitment.

World War II produced a temporary alliance with the Soviet Union, which dissolved almost as soon as the conflict had ended. Soviet efforts to dominate the lands around its borders and to gain an ideological foothold elsewhere raised in Washington the spectre of a new worldwide menace. The resulting cold war, in which the United States sought to prevent the spread of communism everywhere, turned hot periodically as U.S. forces entered the battles for Korea, Vietnam, and Cambodia. Subsequent U.S. adventures—covert in Chile and Angola, overt in Grenada, and a combination of undercover and open engagements against Nicaragua—were applauded by those to whom aid was given, but were either ignored or roundly criticized by friends as well as foes throughout the rest of the world.

Ironically, in reviewing the 40 years since the close of World War II, England's Prime Minister Margaret Thatcher ignored the succession of major and minor military conflicts in which the United States had been involved, boasting that those 40 years marked for Europe "one of the longest periods without war in all our history." For this period of grace she paid tribute to the "shield of the United States," crediting this country with having been "the principal architect of peace in Europe." In this address to the U.S. Congress, Mrs. Thatcher politely omitted any references to Britain's 1982 war with Argentina over the Falkland Islands or to her own protest over the U.S. invasion of the British island of Grenada.[2]

President Reagan, in his use of armed forces and CIA operatives, has been influenced little by foreign opinion. This penchant for "doing it my way" has been made possible by Reagan's personal popularity in the United States, by uncritical public acceptance of his statements as to the facts in other parts of the world, and by enthusiastic public response to his use of the most consistently successful appeal in any land and any language—patriotism—which Reagan arouses by frequent perorations on the extraordinary strength, resolution, and courage of the American people.

For his entire first term in the White House, Reagan's foreign policy focused on the threat of international communism. That threat provided the rationale for unlimited military expenditures and denial of the validity of previous arms limitation treaties. It also conditioned acceptance of new proposals on Soviet agreement with the principles of the START (Strategic Arms Reduction Talks) program. A further condition was added after the Strategic Defense Initiative (Star Wars) program was announced.

Reagan's anti-treaty stance appears to have been borrowed from one of the few serious, nongovernmental studies that he claims to have read, a work that disparages political pacts because they are always broken.[3] Disinclined to be constrained by treaty obligations, his repeated charge that the Soviet Union has committed many violations of existing treaties has been challenged by his own intelligence services, most recently by the CIA.[4]

Departing from the harsh rhetoric of his first four years in the White House, Reagan opened his second term expressing a willingness to become personally involved in the peace process. His readiness to meet with the Soviet General Secretary was announced in a joint statement by the president and his guest, West German Chancellor Kohl, on November 30, 1984, two months after Reagan had met with Soviet Deputy Premier Gromyko without suggesting such a conference.[5] He later claimed that

"As long ago as last June 1, I said that I was willing to meet at any time." However, the only statement on Soviet–American relations published on June 1, 1984, appeared in the president's responses to questions from the editor of the Italian newspaper, *Il Giornale*, and no reference to a summit meeting was made in that exchange.[6] When the summit was finally held in November of 1985, the only areas of agreement reached by Reagan and Gorbachev after five hours of private discussions were on the "principle of 50 percent reductions in nuclear arms," a cultural exchange program, and further meetings between themselves as well as between staff members working on specific weapons reduction problems.[7]

More significant than anything in the postsummit joint statement was Reagan's retreat from 20 years of forecasting the Soviet government's demise "on the ash heap of history." Reporting to Congress on his Geneva meeting with Gorbachev, he quite accurately characterized the summit as the product of "a new realism." Although his address included standard references to the rebuilding of U.S. defenses achieved by his administration, the need for his Strategic Defense Initiative, and other policies that "we must not now abandon," he acknowledged the need for continuing cooperation with the Soviet Union in "a long-term effort to build a more stable relationship."[8]

Reagan's approach to the problem of more stable Soviet–American relations reflected the assumption that his reelection indicated public support for his foreign, as well as domestic, policies. However, as many of the elected members of Congress had demonstrated by their resistance to his persistent requests for a free hand in foreign affairs, the country was far from unanimous in its support of some major Reagan objectives. Nowhere was opinion on these matters more sharply divided than in the religious community.

RELIGION IN THE INTERNATIONAL CONFLICT

Routinely, the Reagan administration's verbal attacks on communist governments included references to discrimination against religious groups or suppression of religious expression. Supporting evidence was not hard to find, especially in the Soviet Union, where, notwithstanding a constitutional guarantee of "religious worship or atheistic propaganda," the practice of religion is inhibited by the government's conversion of many churches to museums or other public facilities, and its refusal to permit new construction or to protect clerics and religious meetings from harassment. Jews, in particular, have suffered from discrimination resulting in part from an age-old anti-semitism, most pronounced in the Ukraine, and, more recently, from the establishment of Israel, a nation regarded by the USSR as church-dominated and not entitled to diplomatic recognition.

In countries either dominated by the Soviet Union or tied to the Soviet bloc by their Marxist orientation, the practice of religion is less tightly controlled. Still, the more the general population demonstrates its attachment to religious beliefs, the greater is the likelihood of conflict with government policy. Poland and Nicaragua are cases in point. These two countries also provide examples of the different ways in which Washington reacts to communist governments. The Catholic church in Poland, allying itself openly with labor's Solidarity movement, has come under increased police surveillance and harassment. However, the traditional strength of the church in a country that, for centuries, has been overwhelmingly Catholic protects it from the kind of suppression exercised in the USSR. Indeed, when a priest was murdered by overzealous Polish police officers, public outcry forced the government to bring the murderers to trial. In this atmosphere, U.S. criticism of the Polish dictatorship has focused more on the oppressive treatment of Solidarity members than on the government's anti-religious stance.

Nicaragua offers a more fruitful opportunity for U.S. criticism of the latter type. The Sandinista government has not closed any churches or prohibited church attendance or religious ceremonies. It even allowed Pope John Paul II to visit and preach to thousands of the country's largely Catholic population. However, it has shown its antipathy to the church in the same way that it reacts to nonreligious opposition, by jeering and hooting public speakers—including the pope—and curtailing publication of opposition newspapers and the operation of radio and television stations. In October 1985, a Sandinista decree suspended the constitutional rights of free speech, assembly, travel, and other freedoms that President Ortega said were being used by some groups, including the church, to undermine the government. President Reagan cited this suspension of civil liberties in his November 14 message on Central America to the House and Senate. The report sent with this message was one of a series intended to support his request for greater aid to the contras.[9]

One of the most serious challenges to the Reagan concept of communism as the source of all the world's troubles is what has come to be known as "liberation theology." Equally disturbing to both Washington and the Vatican, this movement reflects the belief of some biblical scholars and clerics that "Christ said at the last judgment men would be judged solely on the basis of how they treated others" rather than by their religious beliefs.[10] Catholic priests in Latin American countries beset by grinding poverty have adopted this concept in their efforts to achieve social justice for the economically and politically downtrodden. Inevitably, this has led to a doctrinal conflict, which Pope John Paul has attempted to resolve, first by declarations of general principle.

The failure of some Catholic clergy to follow the pope's lead brought a more direct statement of policy in 1984. A formal instruction, while stressing the church's concern for the poor, had this as its declared purpose:

> To draw the attention of pastors, theologians and all the faithful to the deviations, and risks of deviation, damaging to the faith and to Christian living, that are brought about by certain forms of liberation theology which use, in an insufficiently critical manner, concepts borrowed from various currents of Marxist thought.[11]

Notwithstanding this clear exposition of church policy, sympathy for the social justice viewpoint continued in evidence, supported by as influential a church official as Superior General Peter-Hans Kolvenbach of the Society of Jesus (Jesuits).[12] When a friar in Brazil persisted in publishing and preaching what the church regarded as dangerous doctrines, he was ordered to maintain a "year of silence" by refraining from writing or speaking about these matters.[13]

Prior to his election in 1980, Reagan offered none of the praise that, as president, he has since lavished on Catholic leaders. Nor, at that time, was there any suggestion that he planned, if elected, to establish diplomatic relations with the Vatican. Only once in U.S. history has such a step been taken, and that was prior to the Civil War when the Papal States occupied a substantial area in the central part of a still disunited Italy. In 1848, after election of the liberal Pope Pius IX had aroused enthusiasm even among Protestant leaders, diplomatic relations were opened. However, the association was soured by the Vatican's virtual recognition of the Confederate States of America during the Civil War, after which an 1867 act of Congress made illegal the use of funds for a diplomatic mission in Rome.[14]

Not until World War II did the subject of U.S.-Vatican relations again become a significant public issue. Just before Christmas 1939, President Franklin Roosevelt wrote to the pope and to the presidents of the [Protestant] Federal Council of Churches (F.C.C.) and the Jewish Theological

Seminary, calling for "parallel endeavors for peace and the alleviation of suffering" by the three major western churches. Simultaneously he announced his intention to send Episcopalian Myron C. Taylor as his personal representative to the pope.[15]

The majority of Protestant churches in the United States opposed the Taylor appointment. F.C.C. President Buttrick wrote to President Roosevelt, expressing "a growing disillusionment" over the Vatican's view of Taylor as "just as much an ambassador to the Holy See as the representatives of other nations." Roosevelt replied that " this appointment does not constitute the inauguration of formal diplomatic relations with the Vatican."[16] In fact, Taylor was never commissioned by the Department of State or put through the constitutional process of Senate approval required for diplomatic appointments.

In the postwar period, only President Truman suggested elevating the personal representative to ambassador, and that proposal met such bitter opposition that his nominee for the position requested his name be withdrawn. Even the informal association was dropped by President Eisenhower and was not restored until Richard Nixon took office. Then, in 1983, Congress was prevailed upon to repeal the 1867 ban on funding a diplomatic office at the Vatican.[17]

Who or what prompted this step may not be known for some time, but the timing of the move was faultless. For three years the president had made a point of appealing to all churches for support of his campaigns against communism and abortion and in favor of "returning God to the classroom." After the pope's visit to Nicaragua in 1983, Reagan was quick to associate the pontiff's views with his own, even claiming to have received papal approval of U.S. policy in Nicaragua. Despite a prompt denial by the Vatican, Reagan continued to refer to the unity of the pope's and his own views on religious freedom[18] On May 2, 1984 (just six months before the 1984 presidential election), the implications of this association were clarified by the following White House announcement: "In his meeting today with Pope John Paul II, the President discussed his trip to China and the Holy Father's forthcoming visit to Korea. The two engaged in an exchange of views on arms control, East-West relations, regional and humanitarian issues."[19]

Given the global atmosphere of tension created not only by the Soviet-American arms race but by what were essentially religious wars in the Middle East, Reagan had little reason to fear the kind of opposition F.D.R. faced in 1939 over the prospect of political association with a pope. Besides, John Paul had aroused the enthusiasm of millions in his visits to countries in North America, Latin America, Europe, and Africa. Thus, when Reagan's plan for diplomatic relations with the Vatican was put to its first test in a 1983 congressional bill to repeal the 1867 statute forbidding such action, the uproar that might have resulted in less tumultuous times did not materialize: The action made no headlines able to compete with those occasioned by wars and rumors of war around the world. Moreover, the diplomatic authorization came by way of a 10-line amendment inserted by Senator Richard Lugar into a 47-page law intended principally to provide appropriations for the Department of State and other international agencies.[20] In the excitement generated by such events as the first space travel by a U.S. woman, the shooting down of a South Korean civilian airliner by a Soviet fighter pilot, and the bombing death of 241 U.S. marines in Lebanon, the absence of public hearing on the question of diplomatic relations with the Vatican went unnoticed. Also forgotten was the blatant anti-Catholicism of the Protestant fundamentalist preachers who so loudly praise Ronald Reagan, in stark contrast to their attacks on candidate John Kennedy in 1960 because of his presumed subservience to the pope. No member of the 1983 Congress was indelicate enough to recall the unequivocal stand on religion and politics taken by Kennedy in this response to his fundamentalist critics:

> I believe that the separation of church and state is fundamental to our American concept and heritage and should remain so. I am flatly opposed to appointment of an ambassador to the Vatican. Whatever advantages it might have in Rome, and I am not convinced of these, they would be more than offset by the divisive effect at home.[21]

The absence of any debate or widespread public criticism of the change in federal law and subsequent appointment of an ambassador to the Vatican confirmed Reagan's judgment that the time was ripe for such a move. Congress reinforced that conclusion when both Senate and House bills authorizing the exchange of ambassadors were sponsored by an assortment of Republicans and Democrats rarely found in the same legislative camp. Republican Senators Lugar, Laxalt, Hatch, and Helms were joined by Democrats Kennedy, Moynihan, Pell and Tsongas; and in the House, Democrats Zablocki, Solarz, and Levine stood side by side with Republican cosponsors Hyde, Ireland, and Lagomarsino. When the nomination of William Wilson as ambassador was put to a vote in the Senate, a call of the roll showed 81 in favor, only 13 opposed, and 6 abstaining.[22] Arguments against diplomatic relations submitted by representatives of such disparate groups as the American Civil Liberties Union,

American Jewish Congress, Baptist Joint Committee on Public Affairs, Christian Civil Liberties Union, Church of Christ, National Association of Evangelicals, National Council of Churches, and Seventh-day Adventists were faithfully recorded in the Wilson hearings, but they made not the slightest impression on the Senate, which was overwhelmingly committed to the Reagan position. Wilson's inept handling of his assignment failed to weaken the U.S.–Vatican tie, even after it was revealed that he had held unauthorized talks with Libyan officials. Unabashed by the ambassador's extraordinary departure from administration policy, President Reagan sent his longtime friend into retirement with praise for his productive work in establishing diplomatic relations with the Vatican.[23]

THE DOMESTIC CHALLENGE
TO ADMINISTRATION FOREIGN POLICY

Resistance to President Reagan's foreign policy has been far more volatile on issues unrelated to the establishment of diplomatic relations with the Vatican. From the outset of his presidency, Reagan has faced serious objections to his program for expanded nuclear armament, his support of overtly undemocratic governments like those in South Africa and the Philippines under Marcos, and his undeclared war on the Sandinista government in Nicaragua. U.S. involvement in Central American politics has also given rise to a direct challenge of federal law in the form of a Sanctuary movement, aimed at aiding refugees from U.S.-supported governments. U.S. churches and church officials are deeply involved in the debate over all of these issues; some clerics are critical of administration policies, and others vigorously support them.

In general terms, the divided camp of religious opinion is accurately described by an interfaith organization called Clergy and Laity Concerned (CALC), which allies itself with those who call for a freeze on nuclear rearmament, an end to U.S. support of repressive (but anticommunist) governments, and abandonment of the practice of ''looking the other way when 'opposition' leaders [in 'friendly' dictatorships] are jailed, deported or murdered.''[24] CALC identifies the religious Right as its opposition on all of these questions.

Division of church opinion on the nuclear arms race antedates Reagan's presidency; but, since his election, the debate has sharpened considerably. What the Episcopal Committee of Inquiry on the Nuclear Issue called, in a 1985 report, *The Nuclear Dilemma*, has brought expressions of concern from most religious organizations. In common with many critics of administration policy, the Episcopal committee opposes all programs, including the Strategic Defense Initiative, that it believes will stimulate the nuclear arms race without adding materially to the defense capability of the United States.

More significant in terms of the number of people affected was a pastoral letter, dated April 29, 1986, approved by the unanimous vote of the Council of Bishops of the United Methodist Church. Surpassed in membership only by Baptist and Catholic congregations, more than 9 million Methodists were warned that the expanding arms race and "the increase in hostile rhetoric and hate among nations" means "Creation itself is under attack," threatened by a nuclear winter. Charging that the theory of "just war" is invalidated by the great-power arms race, which squanders the world's resources and threatens global destruction, the bishops concluded that "When governments themselves become destroyers of community and threats to Creation, when they usurp the sovereignty which belongs to God alone, they are rightly subject to protest and resistance."

Less specific on these points, but equally disturbing to the administration, are the doubts expressed by the National Conference of Catholic Bishops Committee on War and Peace. As early as 1981, the bishops began drafting a pastoral letter on the nuclear arms race. Successive drafts were submitted to the White House for comment. Invariably, the response consisted of a strong defense of administration policy and a charge that the proposed document "does not describe either the facts of the impact of the Soviet buildup. . . . [or] any of the many past unilateral initiatives taken in the last decade by the United States." Undeterred, the bishops approved the final draft in May 1983 and, by a vote of 238–9, called all Catholics to join in an effort to prevent "counterpopulation warfare." Challenging the administration's refusal to disavow the first-strike concept, the letter asserted: "We do not perceive any situation in which the deliberate initiation of nuclear warfare, on however restricted a scale, can be morally justified."[25] To the extent that the letter expressed "conditional moral acceptance" of the concept of nuclear arms as a deterrent to war, the bishops decided in 1986 to reexamine that particular question.[26]

The movement for an arms freeze brought a more mixed response. Gaining momentum in 1981 when a flurry of freeze resolutions were introduced in Congress, the campaign continued to build during 1983, with both religious and lay organizations joining in.[27] U.S. Protestants participated in a World Council of Churches assembly that endorsed both a

UN settlement of the Afghanistan occupation by the Soviets and "a mutual and verifiable freeze" on the testing and deployment of nuclear weapons.[28]

Other evidences of the international impact of the nuclear threat on the world's Christian community were the subject of a 1983 report in the London *Economist*, which noted this significant change in church attitudes:

> Less than a decade ago the churches were still part of the western consensus on defence, including nuclear defence. Today anti-nuclear movements enjoy the wholehearted backing not only of many men-and-women-in-the-pew but of many members of the churches' establishment: pastors, ministers, moderators, bishops, even cardinals.[29]

Even evangelical Christians in the United States were divided on the issue, according to a Gallup poll that, in 1983, found more than half in favor of a verifiable freeze. This was despite the strong opposition of evangelical leaders like Jerry Falwell who, shortly before the Gallup poll, took out a full-page newspaper ad criticizing freeze advocates and inviting readers to follow the president's advice and "cast your ballot today for Peace Through Strength." Six weeks prior to the 1984 election, the president called on all Americans to observe National Peace through Strength Week in rallies organized by the Coalition of Peace through Strength and the American Security Council, two of the most ardent supporters of Reagan's big-stick foreign policy.[30]

President Reagan's reaction to demands for an arms freeze ranged from the scornful suggestion that proponents were "dupes" of the Soviet Union to pity for those poor souls who simply didn't understand the situation.[31] In the heat of these exchanges, the 1982 elections revealed that voters in 10 states, 15 counties, and 23 cities approved resolutions for an immediate, mutual, and verifiable freeze in the nuclear arms race.[32]

As Reagan campaigned for a second term, showing signs of a willingness to abandon rhetoric for serious personal involvement in talks with the Soviets, the freeze movement abated. However, on another front, activity increased among religious groups debating administration attitude toward human rights in particular countries. Celebrating Human Rights Day, the president cited "alien dictatorships" in Afghanistan and Cambodia, and repressive regimes in Angola, Cuba, and Nicaragua—comparing these countries with El Salvador, Grenada, Honduras, and Guatemala, where, he said, "considerable progress toward observance of human rights" had been made. To demonstrate that his administration protests abuses of human rights "wherever they occur," he declared South Africa's apartheid to be "abhorrent" and added that "In Chile and the Philippines, too, we've shown our strong concern when our friends deviate from established democratic traditions."[33]

The philosophy underlying Reagan's policy in the matter of human rights was provided by his first ambassador to the UN, political science professor Jeane J. Kirkpatrick. In an article written before Reagan's election to the presidency, Kirkpatrick distinguished between communist dictatorships and what she called "moderate autocracies." The latter should be supported by the United States, she argued, because over a few decades—or centuries—they may evolve into democracies. Citing the Iranian and Nicaraguan revolutions as the result of mistaken U.S. policy, she glossed over the repressive character of the prerevolutionary governments that the United States had put into power in those countries, and failed to mention the devastating result of U.S. intervention elsewhere, notably in Chile and Guatemala. People in autocracies can become accustomed to poverty, illiteracy, disease, and torturous repression of opposition (which she referred to as "alleged"), she argued, as long as their rulers do not interfere with their religious practices and other "normal" living habits.[34]

On this foundation, which supported Reagan's previously formed opinion that there would be no revolutions anywhere if not for communists, the president has constructed a global policy based on what he calls a realistic view of both world politics and human rights. The Reagan Corollary is that any government that declares itself to be anti-communist must be considered a friend of the United States, regardless of its repressive character. Critics of this concept insist that the documented excesses of governments regarded by the administration as friendly should be treated as seriously as the equally well-documented repressions of communist regimes. In response, Reagan claims to defend human rights against "tyranny in whatever form, whether of the left or the right," an assertion that is belied by the administration's practice of linking human rights and commercial agreements in dealing with Soviet Eastern Europe, and its refusal to apply similar restrictions to the "moderate autocracies" it calls its friends.

For religious groups, this is a particularly sensitive point. Assistant Secretary of State Langhorne Motley acknowledged as much, when he was asked to specify the sources of support for aid to the contras and replied, "Certainly not from the churches."[35] His irritation shows the extent to which religious opposition to Reagan's Central American policy has spread among literally hundreds of Protestant, Catholic, and Jewish groups. Some have joined a Sanctuary movement to take in and shelter refugees that the State Department will not admit, because they come from "friendly" countries. Spurred initially by the murders of priests, nuns, and the archbishop of El Salvador, these groups offer no defense of Nicaragua's harassment of churchpeople, but they point to the more deadly effect of the uncontrolled murder of clerics and innocent civilians by government forces in El Salvador and to the history of near-genocidal slaughter of the native Indian population of Guatemala. By May 1985, the National Council of Churches had joined in the criticism of U.S. policy in Central America, going so far as to suggest that member churches "give serious consideration to the Sanctuary Movement as an expression of the Christian's duty to the suffering stranger."[36] In doing so, the Council acknowledged the risk of criminal prosecution, which the government had warned might follow. In fact, arrest, prosecution, and conviction of Sanctuary workers had begun in January of that year. This did not slow the activity of other participants, including Benedictine monks, Franciscan friars, Quakers, and Methodist, Presbyterian, and Lutheran ministers. As one trial of Sanctuary participants drew to a close, with two Catholic priests, an Episcopalian minister, a nun, and four others found guilty of smuggling and harboring illegal aliens, Governor Toney Anaya declared New Mexico a "state sanctuary" for refugees whom the churches were helping to escape from Central America.[37]

U.S. relations with South Africa have stirred equally strong feelings in religious circles, which have been aroused not only by the general issue of democratic morality but by the clear and unequivocally racial character of South African law and government. For his first four years in office, President Reagan attempted to follow the almost noncommittal approach of the 1980 Republican platform, which simply said that "a Republican administration will not endorse situations or constitutions, in whatever society, which are racist in purpose or effect." The first fruits of this process (called "constructive engagement") appeared early in 1982 when Donald S. deKieffer, a former lobbyist for the Republic of South Africa, was sent to that country as Reagan's trade representative. DeKieffer's assignment was to inform the South African government of Reagan's decision to lift restrictions on the sale of nonmilitary material to South African military and police forces, which had been embargoed by the Carter administration.[38] Resisting the growing demand for commercial disengagement, State Department spokesmen insisted that restricting trade would "undo an avenue of positive effort" in which U.S. employers in South Africa could demonstrate to the government of that country the advantages of equal treatment of blacks and whites. In this way, Washington hoped to encourage evolutionary change rather than revolution, which the State Department believes "will likely leave little worth fighting over."[39]

On the question of apartheid, President Reagan has been consistently critical of the policy. Nevertheless, he has refused to approve successive UN resolutions condemning South Africa's so-called reforms in which separate parliamentary representation has been permitted for "colored" people of mixed race and for East Indians, but none for the majority black population.[40] Washington expressed greater anger when South Africa raided Angola, calling it "an unfriendly act" because it penetrated to within a few hundred yards of a U.S. oil company's installation (an economic investment by Gulf Oil tolerated for four years by the Reagan administration as previous administrations had).[41]

South Africa's relations with Angola and Namibia further complicate the situation on that continent. Although the UN declared South West Africa free of South African control in 1966 (a decision supported three years later by the International Court of Justice), President Reagan and his State Department refer to the former trust territory as "South African territory" and "Africa's last colony."[42] The presence of Cuban troops in Angola, sent to support that country's Marxist government, had long been condemned by the United States. Their presence was perceived as a threat by South Africa also, to itself and to its control over Namibia, and was used to justify repeated military incursions into Angola and overt support for former Marxist Jonas Savimbi, leader of the UNITA rebels in Angola.

Assuming a mediator's role in 1984, Reagan insisted that Jonas Savimbi and his rebel forces were an internal problem and not a party to the negotiations that the United States was attempting to develop between Angola and South Africa.[43] A year later, in a complete about-face, Reagan told reporters in an interview not published in the Weekly Compilation of Presidential Documents that he had decided on convert (sic) aid to UNITA's effort to overthrow the government of Angola.[44] Two months after this announcement, the president was host to Savimbi in a Washington welcome that, short of a 21-gun salute, was equal to that afforded many heads of state.[45]

Church efforts to influence U.S. policy in Africa have met with Washington's approval, or disapproval, depending on whether the action supported or opposed the president's stand. After meeting with South African President Botha, Jerry Falwell announced his unswerving support for Reagan's "quiet diplomacy" and Botha's "racial reforms." Bishop Tutu's refusal to meet with Botha, only a month after Botha had rejected Tutu's request for a meeting, earned him the title of "phony" from Falwell and a "tactful rebuke" from White House officials, who insisted they had been "equally critical of President Botha."[46] When Tutu, winner of the 1984 Nobel Peace Prize for his nonviolent campaign for equal rights for South African blacks, spoke at the UN, U.S. Ambassador Kirkpatrick expressed satisfaction at the opportunity to hear "the eloquent views of a great exponent of human rights."[47] In his subsequent meeting with President Reagan, however, Tutu's eloquence fell on deaf ears, as the president rejected the request for more than constructive engagement, a policy the bishop insisted had not worked. The president cited the release of 21 black labor leaders, which he said had been brought about by his quiet diplomacy, a claim that South Africa's President Botha promptly denied.[48]

As evidence accumulated to show that the reforms of the South African government would involve no basic change in either the power structure or the repressive treatment of blacks, pressure on the Reagan administration to face this reality mounted. Violent confrontations between South African blacks and security forces increased, as Tutu had predicted. Had criticism of the administration's quiet diplomacy been limited to church leaders, it might well have been ignored. However, the growing demand for action spread from public groups to universities and politicians in both major parties. Congress forced the issue in the summer of 1985, when overwhelming majorities in both the Republican-controlled Senate and Democratic-dominated House voted in favor of economic sanctions, including some of those Tutu had urged Reagan to consider.[49] Refusing to sign the congressional bill, the president announced on September 9 the issuance of Executive Order 12532, which would ban the importation of South African gold coins and prohibit the supplying of nuclear materials, computers for security forces, and monetary loans to the South African government. In taking this limited action, Reagan made clear that his purpose was to encourage peaceful change in accordance with his ongoing policy of opposing "the machinery of apartheid without indiscriminately punishing the people who are the victims of that system."[50]

This slap on the wrist, as critics called it, satisfied neither political nor religious supporters of more far-reaching penalties. The reaction of both was expressed in a resolution adopted December 6 by the World Council of Churches, which highlighted demands for the release of political prisoners like Nelson Mandela and for the refusal to reschedule South Africa's $14 billion foreign debt. A month later, leaders of some major Protestant churches in the United States proposed that 1986 be "the year of action by U.S. churches against apartheid."[51]

Before the halfway mark of that year, the crisis reached new heights. Revocation of the hated "pass laws," hailed in Washington as "a major milestone on the road away from apartheid," was followed by South Africa's military invasion of three neighbors—Botswana, Zambia, and Zimbabwe—on the grounds they were harboring African National Congress (ANC) terrorists. All further press coverage of military and police activity was curtailed by a declaration of emergency, with practically no limit on police powers of arrest and detention, and the issuance of press restrictions that defined as subversive any report that authorities decided would "have the effect of inciting the public ... to resist or oppose the Government" in any way, or "of engendering or aggravating feelings of hostility." Under cover of this media blackout, raids conducted on Anglican, Methodist, and Catholic churches were reported to include the use of tear gas, bullwhips, and mass arrests. The inevitable result was a renewal of demands in the U.S. Congress and among British Commonwealth nations for economic sanctions, which President Reagan and Prime Minister Thatcher continued to resist as harmful to "the very people we want to assist." For President Reagan, the final blow fell on October 2, 1986, after his own congressional party leaders disavowed his South African policy and joined a coalition of Republicans and Democrats to override the president's veto of a new sanctions bill.[52]

Unlike South Africa's apartheid, Philippine politics made few headlines prior to the 1983 assassination of Benigno Aquino, principal opponent of President Ferdinand Marcos—although Vice-President George Bush earned an occasional jibe for his 1981 televised testimonial to Marcos that "we love your adherence to democratic principles."[53] When Marcos visited the United States in 1982, he was welcomed by President Reagan, who praised the Philippine dictator as "a voice for reason and moderation in international forums" and a leader responsible for "a record of solid economic growth ... hospitable attitude toward free enterprise [and] dedication to improving the standard of living of your people."[54] This fun-house-mirror view of the government and economy of a nation of poverty-stricken peasants, which for 20 years had been ruled with an iron hand by a tiny, corrupt minority, was not shaken by Aquino's murder the following year. Two months after that event, Reagan assured Marcos in a personal letter that "Our friendship for you remains as warm and firm as ever."[55]

Notwithstanding this evidence of support from his most powerful ally, Marcos was forced by both domestic and foreign rage at Aquino's assassination to name a civilian board of inquiry to investigate the killing. After a year of examining witnesses and the physical evidence of a murder that took place within a circle of military guards presumably sent to the Manila airport to protect Aquino on his arrival from exile in the United States, the commission chairman concluded that "one of the military group . . . was the triggerman" and was part of "a criminal plot to assassinate Senator Aquino on his way from the airplane to the SWAT van." Obligated to bring the accused military officers to trial, a court of three judges, long since selected for their loyalty to Marcos, exonerated all of the accused. Hailing this evidence of the innocence of his military protectors, Marcos immediately called for a presidential election to demonstrate that he still retained the trust of the Philippine people.[56]

This sequence of events was more than even the U.S. State Department could swallow. A department spokesman acknowledged that the Philippine court's verdict did not square with the commission's finding that Aquino's murder had been "the work of Philippine military personnel," and not, as the government insisted, the act of a communist terrorist.[57]

Debate in the United States followed a predictable pattern: media appeals on the one side, for a hard line against an unrelenting dictatorship, and on the other side, support for a regime that welcomed U.S. military use of its territory to "protect the independent nations of the region" and thereby to defend U.S. interests.[58]

Corazon Aquino, widow of the murdered Benigno Aquino, responded to the call for an election by announcing that she would run against Marcos to rid the country of a corrupt and brutal dictatorship that had kept most Philippinos in abject poverty. Subsequent debates between Marcos and Aquino were joined by leaders of the predominantly Catholic clergy. In startling contrast to the public praise accorded Marcos by the Reverend Jerry Falwell, Philippine Archbishop Jaime Cardinal Sin denounced the Marcos court's dismissal of charges against the military plotters responsible for Senator Aquino's death. The court's finding, Sin said, "threatens to push our country to the brink of despair." When Corazon Aquino was joined by Salvador H. Laurel, leader of the major opposition party, in a bid for the presidential and vice-presidential posts, the Catholic Bishops Conference of the Philippines issued a pastoral letter giving effective, if indirect, assistance to the Aquino–Laurel ticket by urging a vote against the "conspiracy of evil" that would otherwise continue to dominate the nation.[59]

Despite widespread popular enthusiasm for Mrs. Aquino, the government's control over all Philippine television stations, and most radio stations and newspapers, meant that voters would see only Marcos rallies and hear or read only Marcos speeches.[60] Still, support for Aquino spread to the point that Marcos was stirred to create thousands of new jobs and to authorize sudden raises in government workers' salaries. These conditions, added to the fact that the entire voting process, the army, and the police were all under tight government rein, led most U.S. analysts to believe that Aquino had only an outside chance of victory.

In the United States, Reagan's philosopher of realism, Jeane Kirkpatrick, assured readers of her newspaper column that people in the Philippines could more freely engage in criticism of their government and the use of speech, press, and assembly than could the citizens of most other Third World countries.[61] She derided charges of election fraud by the Marcos government, citing the "swarm" of reporters and other observers whose presence made such manipulation unlikely. Her account ignored reports from journalists and observers sent by President Reagan and from an international group led by a member of the British Parliament that only the activities of Marcos backers gave evidence of fraud, intimidation, and murder.[62] Instead, Kirkpatrick called on the administration in Washington to put an end to its "interference" with the political process in the Philippines and to accept whatever result the election might bring.

What might have been a sad end to this affair was suggested by President Reagan's retreat from his earlier optimistic view of the election to the position urged in the Kirkpatrick articles. On January 30, 1986, Reagan was bright with assurance: "To safeguard the process [of election] the National Citizens' Movement for Free Elections, or Namfrel, as it is called, will field hundreds of thousands of citizen election observers on February 7."[63] Two weeks later, he ignored completely NAMFREL reports of massive irregularities by Marcos forces, stammering in response to a reporter's inquiry about fraud and violence, "it could have been that all of that was occurring on both sides." Refusing to acknowledge that his own investigative team had given him more than "an interim few remarks," he made it plain that their report on how the election was conducted would be withheld until *after* the final results had been announced by the Philippine National Assembly, two-thirds of whose members were Marcos supporters.

At one point in his February 11 news conference, he declared, "We're neutral", at another point, "We're backing the forces of democracy." The bottom line was this near-perfect rendition of Kirkpatrick's position:

> What we have to say is that the determination of the Government in the Philippines is going to be the business of the Philippine people, not the United States. And we are going to try and continue, as I said before, the relationship, regardless of what government is instituted there by the choice of the people.[64]

Not a single reporter present at the February 11 news conference questioned Reagan's extraordinary conjecture about fraud and violence "from both sides," a charge made by no observer other than Marcos.

In the Philippines, Reagan's "neutrality" was received with open dismay by Aquino forces and equally obvious satisfaction by Marcos adherents, both sides taking the U.S. president's words as evidence of his continuing support for the Marcos government. At home, Senator Lugar's comment was that the president was "not well informed," but an aide indicated that Lugar's inspection team saw no fraud or violence by Aquino backers and could not have reported such actions to the president. The fact that Reagan had met with Lugar cast serious doubt on the president's characterization of their exchange as "an interim few remarks." Lugar himself attested to the inaccuracy of this statement when he told a subcommittee of the House Foreign Affairs Committee that he had advised the president of the unreliability of official voting tallies, pointing out that "an audit trail was there through the NAMFREL for a Mrs. Aquino win, probably a better one than through the government COMELEC count that had come under question after 30 young people left, testifying that they were being asked to cook the figures in the count."[65]

Reagan's refusal to accept the evidence of his own inspection team brought protests from senators on both sides of the aisle. Normally supportive of presidential defense policy, Dole and Nunn ignored Reagan's plea to further delay any judgment until his special emissary to the Philippines, Philip C. Habib, returned from a fact-finding mission. They assumed that Marcos had stolen the election and proposed that any declaration of victory by the Philippine dictator should be followed by termination of all aid and by consideration of U.S. military removal from Clark Field and Subic Bay.

In the end, the Philippine people decided the issue, facing down the tanks and rifles of the presidential military guard in peaceful but massive demonstrations that led Marcos' defense minister and armed forces chief of staff to declare their acceptance of the public verdict that Corazon Aquino had won the election. Abandoned by his military supporters, Marcos accepted President Reagan's offer of sanctuary in Hawaii, taking with him two planeloads of retainers and as many millions in cash and other valuables as he could gather quickly, leaving behind a richly appointed palace that has become a monument to the corrupt opulence of the Marcos dictatorship.[66]

All of the countries discussed in this chapter have one thing in common: Christian churches predominate. In the Philippines, as in Central America, most of the people are Catholic. More than half of all Angolans have been converted to Christianity, and the great majority of these are Catholic. The reverse is true in South Africa, where the ruling white population is largely Protestant and the black Christians are divided between Catholics and Protestants.

For Reagan's foreign policy, the impact of church opinion in these countries is far more serious than he realizes or will acknowledge. Only in Central America and in some—not all—white Protestant churches in South Africa does he find a sympathetic audience. Even then, he is faced with the Vatican's flat denial of papal approval of his Nicaraguan policy and the pope's own forthright and unconditional condemnation of apartheid.

Challenges to U.S. policy in other parts of the world come not only from worshipers of Marx and Lenin but from the followers of Mohammed. President Reagan sees the latter threat only in terms of the terrorist activity of radical Muslim sects encouraged by political leaders in Iran, Libya, and Syria. However, the problem goes deeper than that. The unyielding character of the ethical pattern prescribed by the Koran lends itself to a more strict fundamentalist interpretation than that of any other religion. With the increasing influence of fundamentalists in the predominantly Christian United States and the Middle East's one Jewish state, politics within and among nations have been infected by a new and dangerous virus that Reagan not only fails to recognize but unwittingly helps to foster.

11

The New Crusaders

From the time of Pope Urban II's call to arms in 1095 A.D. to the fall of the last Frankish strongholds in Lebanon in 1291 A.D., the Crusades united the Christian nations of Europe against the Muslim rulers of North Africa and southwest Asia. Two centuries later, that unity was destroyed by the Protestant revolt. As the challenge to Catholicism spread to Great Britain and northern Europe, new "defenders of the faith" arose to challenge the authority of the pope. Evolving almost simultaneously with the spirit of nationalism, Protestantism failed to achieve any kind of unity, each nation erecting its own established church, often enforcing religious conformity with the same degree of brutality used to maintain the political power structure.

During the centuries that followed, Protestantism was further splintered by sectarian differences, each sect having its own interpretation of the Bible's message or its own conception of the proper form of worship. Nowhere was this diversity so evident as in the North American colonies, which ultimately attained both religious and political independence under a constitution that made illegal any national control over, or interference with, religion. By comparison, religious faiths in other parts of the world faced no such restrictions. Roman Catholicism continued to enjoy government support in southern Europe and the countries colonized by Spain and Portugal. Islam remained the dominant religion throughout North Africa and the Middle East, notwithstanding the conquest of these areas by the Christian nations of western Europe. The Russian tsars remained closely tied to the Eastern Orthodox church, while in the Far East, the rulers of China and Japan associated themselves even more directly with the deity.

Nineteenth-century industrialization produced a new crusader, whose appeal to the have-nots of the world would ultimately shake the foundations of government everywhere. The message preached by Karl Marx was aimed, not at religion as such, but at the power structure created by the concentration of wealth and physical resources in relatively few hands. In his attacks on the capitalist system, however, Marx made clear that he believed religion to be the ally of capitalism when he castigated the politics of German Christian Socialism as "the holy water with which the priest consecrates the heartburnings of the aristocrat."[1] This anti-clerical attitude, which persisted long after Marx's dream of the good society had been buried under the brutal dictatorship of Josef Stalin, ensured church opposition to any government characterized as Marxist.

TWENTIETH-CENTURY CRUSADERS

Contrary to Marx's basic principle—that capitalism would crumble first in the industrialized nations that fostered it—the first revolutionary movement to produce a communist government occurred in the least industrialized of Europe's major powers. Devastated by the drain of World War I on its manpower and resources, Russia was ripe for the revolution that broke out in 1917. In the subsequent struggle for power, the victory of the Bolshevik (majority) faction of the Social Democratic Party and the signing of a peace treaty with Germany incurred the wrath of the Allies, who were still battling German and Austrian troops. When, despite Allied military intervention in Russia, the Bolsheviks retained control and established a government dedicated to Marxism-Leninism, the ground was laid for two entirely different anti-communist coalitions: one supporting free enterprise within a democratic political framework; the other permitting free enterprise within the constraints of a fascist dictatorship. As these trends emerged, the hope for lasting peace that had prompted U.S. President Wilson to join in a war to make the world "safe for democracy" faded rapidly.

Leading the fascist crusade for world domination by a "super race," Adolph Hitler forged a domestic military machine and an international alliance with fascist Italy and imperial Japan that might well have achieved his dream of a "thousand year Reich" if he had been able to follow his conquest of Austria and Czechoslovakia with an attack on Russia, rather than Poland. Most of the western Allies would have been

delighted to stand aside and hope the world's two most powerful dictatorships would destroy one another. Instead, the combined efforts of the
Soviet Union and the western Allies were necessary to subdue Hitler's war
machine. Then, when a Japanese crusade under the nominal leadership of
Emperor-God Hirohito began with an attack on Pearl Harbor, the world
was again aflame, thanks not only to competing political ambitions but to
the fundamentally antagonistic philosophies that drove the contending
nations.

Even as the Allies were conducting what General Eisenhower later
called their "Crusade in Europe,"[2] nationalist movements in lands held
or captured by the Allies were given new impetus. To the Allies' dismay,
these yearnings for independence were stimulated both by visions of the
kind of freedom already attained in western democracies and by communist exhortations to eliminate capitalist oppressors and make the
resources of each nation available to the masses of common people. The
United States viewed this latter appeal as a Soviet threat to the
democratic world, and the cold war between these two countries
dominated the foreign policies of both for decades after World War II.
Important as that contest was, however, other forces were at work, which,
in Washington at least, were not given the attention they deserved.

India's drive for independence from Britain provided one of the
earliest battlegrounds for the many ideological conflicts of the postwar
period. Although President Truman virtually ignored that country's problems, and President Eisenhower saw them principally in terms of a communist threat, the issue that tore that region apart was basically a
religious one.[3] Mohandas K. Gandhi and Jawaharlal Nehru were unable
to convince Islamic leaders that Muslims would be treated fairly in a nation ruled by a 3-1 Hindu majority. The threat of open revolt over this
issue forced the separation of India into two nations: Pakistan, controlled
by Muslims; and India, by Hindus. This did not end the tension, which
broke into open warfare when a revolt against the repressive administration in East Pakistan, aided and abetted by India, led to the loss of that
territory and its replacement by the Republic of Bangladesh. In the war
and subsequent succession of coups and attempted coups that have
plagued Bangladesh, tens of thousands of Muslims and Hindus have been
slaughtered.

Within India, discontent was evident among Sikhs, who were vocal in
their demand for an autonomous Indian state. When their more radical
leaders were found to have stored guns and ammunition in the sect's most
holy Golden Temple, Indian troops outraged the entire Sikh population

by bombarding the shrine, killing at least 250 and capturing some 450 of its defenders.[4] The subsequent assassination of Prime Minister Indira Gandhi by one of her Sikh guards brought retaliation by Hindus who turned in fury on Sikhs in scattered Indian communities—stoning, burning, and killing hundreds of people who had no part in the activities of their militant co-religionists.

Westward of Pakistan the influence of Islam has been a major factor in both the domestic and international politics of the area. From Afghanistan through Iran, Turkey, the "fertile crescent" of the Tigris and Euphrates rivers, Arabia, Palestine, and most of North Africa, the over-whelming majority of the population has for centuries been Muslim. However, a common core of religious belief never brought the countries of this Afro–Asian community together on any issue, with one exception: opposition to the establishment and continued presence of the state of Israel. Other political questions are approached by these countries with little regard for democratic institutions or the threat of Soviet invasion, matters the United States considers vitally important.

Sharing a border with the Soviet Union makes a difference, of course. Iran's fear of Russian territorial ambitions, which dates back to the days of the tsars, prompted Shah Mohammed Reza Pahlevi to appeal to the UN when Soviet troops refused to withdraw from the Iranian supply corridor opened during World War II.[5]

Ultimate resolution of this problem did not end Anglo–American involvement in Iran. When a leftist government under Prime Minister Mohammed Mossadegh nationalized the oil industry—with the Shah's approval—and evicted the Anglo–Iranian Oil Company, both Britain and the United States assumed this to be the first step in a Soviet takeover. With President Eisenhower's approval, the CIA joined British intelligence agents in a plan to overthrow the Mossadegh government, restore the Shah to power, and support as new prime minister the anti-communist but pro-Nazi General Fazlollah Zahedi, handpicked by the British for the post. The CIA carried out the plan in the summer of 1953.[6]

Twenty-six years after its successful coup, the United States harvested the bitter fruit of that action, in which its top-level Middle East specialists completely misjudged the importance of the religious influence in Iranian politics. Kemit Roosevelt, leader of the CIA team that toppled Mossadegh, recalls his estimate of the situation in 1953 as follows:

> [A]s the Communist Tudeh gained more power through their influence
> on Mossadegh, these "religious" elements were greatly weakened in

their position. No longer were they *the* leaders of opposition to the Shah. They became in effect a third party, uncommitted to either side. Now, in 1953, we were making an effort to win their support. They hedged, tried to bargain. We certainly did want help wherever we could find it. But I did not believe them worth the time, trouble and, most important apparently to them, the money that would be required. So we decided to go ahead without them, and they lost the opportunity—which was not to come again—to give H.I.M. [His Imperial Majesty, the Shah] some reason to feel obligated to them.[7]

Readers of Roosevelt's evaluation of the religious factor may be excused a degree of astonishment at the fact that Roosevelt made no reference to Ayatollah Khomeini in an account published in 1979, when Muslims under Khomeini's leadership were in the process of bringing down the government installed by the CIA. An earlier report by another CIA agent indicated that a new revolt, under the exiled Shiite leader, "one Ayatollah Ruhollah Khomeine," was still likely.[8] More recently, another analyst has concluded that publication of Roosevelt's book led directly to the 1979 attack on the U.S. embassy in Teheran: "Iranian radicals," he writes, "refused to believe that publication could not be postponed. They perceived it as attempted intimidation, the threat of another coup, best averted by occupying the embassy from which Roosevelt had operated" [in 1953].[9]

Interpretations of this sort are given no credence among officials of the Reagan administration, who persist in arguing that the Shah would still be the leader of a nation friendly to the United States if he had not been abandoned by President Carter. No deviation from this line has emerged, even in the face of clear evidence that the overwhelming majority of Iranians support Khomeini's crusade, not just against the United States but against all opponents of his Shiite dogma, including communists, the Sunni government of Iraq, and Israel.

COMMUNISM, DEMOCRACY, AND OIL

As in Iran, the politics of oil has been at least as important as defense of democracy in U.S. attitudes toward the Middle East. Recently, however, Americans have been conscious of the impact of religion on both national and international politics in that part of the world.[10] On the other hand, except for England's World War I tentative recognition of Jewish pleas for a homeland in Palestine, the empire nations showed little sympathy for either religious or nationalist feelings. The post-World War I transfer of power in Syria, Iraq, Lebanon, and Palestine from the decaying Ottoman Empire to Britain and France brought no immediate hope of independence to the peoples of that area. However, by World War II the concept of self-determination was beginning to eat away at the foundations of the European empires. In the Middle East, independence was achieved, one nation at a time, beginning in 1943. However, the same fervor that had fired separate Arab revolts prevented development of a pan-Arab nationalism that some hoped would bring the separate Arab countries into one political family.

U.S. policy had a substantial influence in this changing atmosphere. Unlike the period following World War I, when England and France simply ignored President Wilson's plea for self-determination as a basic principle, those countries emerged from World War II with sharply diminished power compared to the United States and the Soviet Union. If the United States felt obliged to temper its criticism of British and French imperialism, as Presidents Truman and Eisenhower did, it was through fear of communist influence in areas of revolt. U.S. support for dependent nations was most pronounced in the Middle East, where, without that support, the state of Israel might never have come into existence, Britain being reluctant to give up the mandate in Palestine conferred upon her by the League of Nations. The armed conflict between Arabs and Jews that followed the establishment of Israel in 1948 did not cause Washington to alter its position, but it did raise new fears of Soviet involvement.

In 1950, the United States, Great Britain, and France joined in a Tripartite Declaration aimed at keeping the USSR out of the Middle East by holding down arms shipments to both Arabs and Jews, and in this way avoiding new problems between Israel and her neighbors.[11] When Egypt turned to the Soviet Union for arms, England assumed that this freed her from any obligation under the Tripartite Declaration. In defense of her lifeline through the Suez Canal, she proceeded in 1956 to plan secretly with France and Israel a combined military operation against Egypt, which had nationalized the canal. Eisenhower considered the attack mounted by this trio a double cross that would not only bring the Soviets into the Middle East but would give Premier Bulganin an opportunity to renege on the pledge he had just made to withdraw from Hungary. In fact, Bulganin did order a massive invasion of Hungary only five days after the Israeli army drove into the Sinai and British planes began bombarding Egyptian installations.

That near-fateful two-week period (28 October–11 November 1956) also saw Britain and France veto a U.S.-sponsored Security Council resolution asking all UN members to refrain from the use of force in the Middle East, a Soviet veto of a resolution calling for Russian withdrawal from Hungary, and Eisenhower's unannounced decision to use nuclear weapons against the Soviet Union if hostilities widened into a third world war.[12]

In the face of worldwide condemnation and loss of U.S. support, British, French, and Israeli troops gradually gave way to a UN peacekeeping force. In Washington, however, fear of Soviet intrusion persisted. Eisenhower sought insurance against another Middle East crisis by proposing that Congress give him blanket authority, without further explicit approval, to send money, arms, or U.S. troops "to secure and protect the territorial integrity and political independence of such nations [as request aid] against overt armed aggression from any nation controlled by International Communism."[13] In effect, this Eisenhower Doctrine extended to the Middle East the protection initiated by the previous president's Truman Doctrine.

WAR IN THE HOLY LAND

Recognizing the Arab-Israeli conflict as the major contributor to disruption in the Middle East, Eisenhower evidenced no understanding of the religious aspect of the three-way tangle of Muslim, Christian, and Jewish interests in that part of the world. His attention continued to focus on the Soviet threat, even after his first opportunity to use the power given him under the Eisenhower Doctrine came as a direct result of Lebanon's Christian President Camille Chamoun's attempt to extend his eligibility for office by altering that country's constitution. In a nation whose population and political representation were almost equally divided between Christians and Muslims, this provoked an immediate uprising that Eisenhower, with no evidence whatever, ascribed to communist influence. Notwithstanding the fact that the Eisenhower Doctrine was directed specifically at external aggression, rather than internal revolt, Eisenhower set a dangerous precedent by sending U.S. troops into a country far from the American continents. His action was as unnecessary as it was dangerous, since Chamoun had already renounced his intention to run again for president, and the Lebanese army had regained control. It succeeded only in arousing the ire of Arab Syria and Egypt, which, less than a year later, announced their federation into a United Arab Republic.[14]

The ostensible purpose of U.S. troops in restoring stability to Lebanon proved to be no lasting resolution of that country's problems. The civil war that resumed in 1975 revealed the continued antagonisms that beset the area. Added to Syrian discontent at having lost the Lebanese sector of its former territory were deep divisions between Christians and Muslims, between western-oriented (largely Christian) politicians and Arab nationalists, and between the Lebanese government and the Palestine Liberation Organization (PLO), which had established its headquarters in the midst of several hundred thousand refugees from the Arab–Israeli wars. As fighting became more intense, Syria entered the fray, alternating between peacemaker and combatant, its military operations aimed principally at keeping the PLO from assuming a dominant role in Lebanon.[15]

U.S. participation in Middle East politics abated during the relatively quiet period between Lebanon's civil wars, when Presidents Kennedy, Johnson, and Nixon faced more immediate and pressing problems in Cuba and Vietnam. Attempts to bring Israel and her Arab neighbors to the peace table did not succeed until Egypt's President Anwar el-Sadat decided that his country could achieve more by peace with Israel than by continuing the warfare that had drained Egypt's economy and brought ignominious defeat to her armed forces. With President Carter's encouragement, the peace process, after "ten months of tortuous, acrimonious diplomacy," was concluded with an agreement forged at Camp David and six months later in a formal peace treaty between Egypt and Israel.[16]

The great expectations aroused by the Camp David accord were never realized. Muslim fundamentalists in Egypt were as bitterly opposed to peace with Israel as were the governments of Syria, Jordan, and Libya. Sniping border attacks by Libyan troops began even before Sadat's assassination in October 1981 by members of his own military establishment. Sadat's successor, President Hosni Mubarak, though pledging to keep the peace, renewed his country's ties with Arab League nations and grew ever frostier in his attitude toward Israel. The so-called peace initiative announced by Reagan in September 1982 did nothing to gain new friends in the Islamic world. Nor did it serve to improve the U.S. position as against that of the USSR. At no point did President Reagan show any appreciation of the evidence that, among Muslim fundamentalists, the United States is feared and hated more vehemently than the Soviet Union. As one analyst has pointed out, to the deeply committed followers of Muhammed, the crusading character of U.S. foreign policy is regarded as a renewal of the invasions initiated by Christian Crusaders in the eleventh and twelfth centuries.[17]

In Israel, too, a stiffening stand on the problem of peace with its Arab neighbors was largely the result of pressure from the religious

Right. Just like their Muslim counterparts, the more strictly orthodox members of the Jewish community proved to be the most aggressive supporters of Israel's outright annexation of the West Bank and the least amenable to peaceful settlement except on their own terms. For agreeing at Camp David to an autonomous West Bank, Prime Minister Menachem Begin was denounced as a traitor by some of his erstwhile comrades in the militant (sometimes terrorist) Irgun Zvai Leumi who had fought with him against British occupation. Opposing the opening of Israel's border with Egypt and return of the Sinai, these critics led the drive to replace West Bank Arab communities with Jewish settlements, and they showed no compunction about forcibly dispossessing and/or killing Arabs who resisted these incursions. Claiming the right to all of Judea and Samaria (ancient names of lands occupied by Hebrew tribes 2,000 years ago), Israel's religious zealots appeal to the kind of patriotism that has fostered both church-dominated government and armed conflict all through history.[18] Some, like Rabbi Meir Kahane, applaud the killing of Arab enemies and declare flatly that between the alternatives of Zionism and western democracy Jews must choose the former. When offering his views to U.S. readers, Kahane uses the language of reason and logic; but in Jerusalem he does not hesitate to characterize the Christian Phlange massacre of Palestinian refugee Arabs in the Beirut camps of Sabra and Shatila as "divine retribution," and to state that this action was what the Jews themselves should have done.[19]

Yet this advocate of terror was sent to the Israeli parliament (Knesset) by some 26,000 voters, who were part of a resurgent movement that materially strengthened the religious parties in the election of 1984. Although Israeli courts have sent Jewish terrorists to prison, these sentences have been widely criticized. Equally ominous are the attacks on the peace proposals of Prime Minister Shimon Peres by opposition members Ariel Sharon and David Levy, who were ministers in the Peres coalition cabinet. Moderates who saw prospects for peace improved by the return to power of Labor Party leader Peres could not forget that this change in leadership was made possible, not by Labor Party gains in the 1984 election, but by defections from former Prime Minister Begin's Likud coalition to parties of the religious Right.[20] Before relinquishing the prime ministership to Yitzhak Shamir in 1986, the last-ditch effort of Peres to revive the peace process with the help of King Hassan II of Morocco took place against a background of violent conflict between militant orthodox and secular Jews within Israel.[21]

The Arab–Israeli struggle is not the only fire smoldering in the Middle East. The war between Iran and Iraq has two aspects that are of concern to the rest of the world, both stemming from the revolutionary character of the

Iranian government, which has been as forthright as any Marxist regime in declaring one of its purposes to be "export of the Islamic Revolution." Iran's Ayatollah Khomeini is quoted by a University of Virginia scholar as declaring, "We should try hard to export our revolution to the world," explaining that Islam does not distinguish between Islamic and non-Islamic countries in its defense of oppressed peoples everywhere.[22] Another Middle East expert, testifying before a congressional committee, sums up Iranian leadership objectives as "to consolidate clericalism at home and export its revolution to other countries."[23]

Ironically, the countries with most to fear from Iran are its Muslim neighbors. Like Iraq, these nations are ruled by dictators or hereditary monarchs who are Sunni Muslims and who refuse to accept either the leadership or doctrinal dogma of Khomeini and his Shiite followers, who have established Islamic Revolutionary Movements in the Arabian peninsula as well as in Iraq.[24]

Notwithstanding these divisive forces within the Muslim world, it is significant that Muslims dominate the politics of some 40 countries, from central Africa to Indonesia, comprising in most cases from 70 to 100 percent of the population. Their total, which is approaching 1 billion of the world's 4.8 billion people, is exceeded only by the world's 1.1 billion Christians, who are more seriously divided than Muslims by doctrinal disputes.

The absence of wide support for a world Islamic community does not discourage radical groups, many of which can be traced to Iran.[25] In attempting to deal with these radicals, whose primary weapon is terrorism, the United States has made few, if any, friends in Muslim territory. Egypt continues to depend on U.S. financial aid, and Saudi Arabia still looks to the United States for weapons, but both are put off by Washington's reluctance to take a harder line with Israel in attempts to settle the West Bank dispute. Elsewhere, U.S. support for Israel has brought reactions ranging from the cold diplomacy of Syria to the heated rhetoric and openly expressed enmity of Iran and Libya. In return, Washington vaunts its military might by sending warships into the eastern Mediterranean, the Persian Gulf, and the Gulf of Sidra, conducting periodic exercises off Libya's coast in a futile and puerile display of big-stick mentality. The excuse that these maneuvers are intended only to demonstrate the right of all nations to "innocent passage" in waters outside the 12-mile limit, and that they are not designed to provoke Libya's Qaddafi into retaliatory measures, does not stand even casual scrutiny. If one voyage is not sufficient to establish the right of innocent passage, surely two or three would do. When Reagan decided to test the Soviet Union on innocent passage, only two ships were sent on a single cruise through Soviet waters in the Black Sea, an incident that made news principally because the action was part of an announced plan to move a much larger fleet of ships and planes into the Gulf of Sidra. In the latter area, by the administration's own admission, it had sent warships into the Gulf of Sidra 7 times, and planes 18 times, from 1981 to 1986.[26]

As to the provocative nature of the naval maneuvers by the U.S. Mediterranean fleet, a New York *Times* report of March 26, 1986, revealed that the president had approved the plan at a March 14 meeting of the National Security Council *after* being told that his military advisors expected the Libyans to "come after us" with missiles from a coastal installation well known to U.S. intelligence. When Libyan pilots and shore batteries did fire on U.S. ships and planes maneuvering in the gulf, they "made Reagan's day," allowing his fleet commander to follow standing orders to return fire whenever attacked.[27]

The destruction of two Libyan patrol boats and a radar installation not only failed to teach Qaddafi a lesson, it worsened the already troubled relations between the United States and the Arab nations. Anti-American attitudes became even more vehement after U.S. planes bombed Libyan bases in retaliation for a terrorist bombing that destroyed a German nightclub, killing a U.S. soldier and a number of civilians. Fulminations from Syrian and Iranian media were accompanied by broadsides from such friendly countries as Egypt, Jordan, and Kuwait, where opinion was uniformly and bitterly critical of Reagan's "cowboy" policies and the massacre of Libyan civilians. Even among our NATO allies, the view of two-thirds of all Europeans that the military strike at Libya was a bad move reflected not only a fear of new terrorist attacks on European targets but more direct involvement by the Soviet Union.[28] In that same connection, Washington could take little comfort from the Arab League's rejection of Libya's demand for an end to diplomatic and economic ties with the United States. Although most League members refused to sacrifice the trade-and-aid benefits of association with the United States, they nevertheless approved a resolution in which they strongly condemned U.S. aggression against Libya.[29]

A further reality is the particular danger that arises when unshakable faith in a particular belief, religious or otherwise, is supported by the awesome power of nuclear weapons.

CRUSADERS WITH NUCLEAR SWORDS

Crusaders of any variety tend to create conflict. To the extent that this stimulates open, nonviolent expressions of opinion and indepth examination of opposing views, the results can be highly beneficial. However, when a nation's policy is guided by people with an unyielding dedication to an unalterable doctrine, the danger of conflict escalating to open warfare increases at an alarming rate. In these circumstances it is not enough for more temperate leaders to decry the use of weapons that, unlike those used over past centuries, are capable of destroying all life on earth. The threat calls for action that will curtail the proliferation of nuclear weapons. This is far more urgent than a Soviet–American agreement to reduce superpower nuclear stockpiles, which will never bring accumulated reserves below the level of mutual destruction.

The inevitability of mutual destruction in nuclear war seems to have penetrated the minds of both U.S. and Soviet civilian leaders, although the same cannot be said of the military in either country. In addition to repeated acknowledgment by U.S. and Soviet heads of state of the need to avoid nuclear war, both governments have ratified the 1968 international Treaty on the Non-Proliferation of Nuclear Weapons (NPT).[30] Both insist that they have adhered faithfully to the letter and spirit of the treaty. Unfortunately, this is not true of either. Under cover of assisting in the development of peaceful uses of nuclear power, both countries have contributed to weapons development in nations whose stability or aggressive tendencies pose a serious threat to peace. Soviet exports of equipment and technology are aimed exclusively at making or keeping friends. U.S. aid has been used for the several purposes of securing friendships (Argentina, South Africa), defending against Soviet influence (Pakistan, China), maintaining a balance of regional power (Argentina and Brazil, India and Pakistan), and simply assisting U.S. firms to compete in the international market for nuclear equipment.

It may be technically true, as an official U.S. analysis says, that as of 1982 "No nuclear-weapon state party to the Treaty has transferred nuclear explosive devices or has assisted any nonnuclear-weapon state in acquiring or manufacturing a nuclear explosive device."[31] However, the weakening of export controls under the Reagan administration has certainly made it easier for nonnuclear nations to expand their peaceful nuclear construction into weapons research and development. Senator John Glenn was one of the first to warn against this retreat from the more strict enforcement of treaty and statutory controls. In a 1981 Senate hearing, he cited administration efforts to eliminate provisions of the Arms Export Control Act, which restricted the release of nuclear enrichment and reprocessing technology usable in the production of nuclear explosives. Glenn's suspicions were further aroused by President Reagan's refusal to consider or even discuss a Senate resolution, passed by a vote of 88–0, asking him to take up the question of nonproliferation at an international meeting in Ottawa. The senator's questions regarding administration policy decisions, directed to Department of State and Department of Energy officials, elicited only evasive answers and references to classified documents or matters that were privileged in the executive branch.[32]

This first congressional hearing on the Reagan administration's policy with respect to nuclear nonproliferation was held in November 1981. Little was learned at that time, other than the fact that the president and his advisors believed President Carter's approach to controls should be revised. The nature of the proposed revisions was revealed the following year, not in congressional hearings but in reports leaked to the press. In June 1982 the Washington *Post* learned that "a major reversal of the Carter administration's nuclear proliferation policy," aimed at easing controls over the export of plutonium reprocessing technology, had been set forth in a classified State Department document.[33] Three months later Secretary of State George Shultz established a new office to deal with nuclear proliferation problems, taking that responsibility away from James L. Malone, the assistant secretary for international scientific affairs, whose plan for a freer hand in licensing nuclear exports had been concealed by his evasive testimony before the Senate committee. If nongovernment observers thought that this meant a retreat from the Malone plan, they soon discovered this was not the case. Almost simultaneously with the appointment of Richard T. Kennedy to head the new office (which, incidentally, disappeared three years later) came news of an administration decision to reconsider the ban on nuclear equipment to South Africa.[34]

Concern over the retreat from strict enforcement was not lessened by explanations from special advisor Kennedy. Insisting that "our policy seeks to inhibit the spread of sensitive technology, facilities, and material which could lead to the production of weapons-usable material, particularly where there is a risk of proliferation," Kennedy nevertheless made it clear that the administration's approach was "to open a dialogue" with countries that disagree with U.S. restrictions, favoring "dialogue over confrontation, persuasion over intimidation, and common sense over iron dogma."[35] These meaningless phrases did not prepare the U.S. public for subsequent White House decisions to sell "heavy water" to Argentina (which has consistently refused to permit UN inspection of any suspect nuclear facilities), to modify export regulations by removing some items from the proscribed export list, and to approve some 57 export licenses for the sale of nuclear technology to Argentina, India, Israel, and South Africa—all countries that have failed to ratify the Non-Proliferation Treaty or to permit the inspections called for under that treaty.[36]

Never acknowledged as a factor in administration decisions, but lurking in the background, is the knowledge that, if U.S. companies do not sell nuclear products abroad, their foreign competitors will. For a time, shipments to Pakistan were forbidden by the United States because that country refused to permit UN inspection of its research and development facilities. In 1982, however, after French, Italian, and West German suppliers had demonstrated that they faced no such barriers, the United States exempted Pakistan from the law's restrictions. Similarly, an agreement to exchange peaceful nuclear technology with China was delayed in 1982 because it was believed that that country was supplying proscribed material to Pakistan, which excuse disappeared when the United States took over the supplier's role.[37]

In 1983 the United Nations Association (UNA), a private organization established during World War II to promote the concept of an international peacekeeping organization, published a report that opened with this warning:

> The spread of the capability of making nuclear weapons to more and more countries poses a grave threat to world security and U.S. interests. While existing international institutions and treaties have had some success in containing the spread of nuclear weapons, a dangerous complacency has now set in. Not only is superpower arms control stymied, but there is a growing number of governments entering the nuclear "twilight zone"—that is, with untested but very real nuclear-weapons capability. Some of these regimes are radical or may be unstable over the long run. One or two are suspected of being just a turn of the screwdriver away from having nuclear weapons. With violent confrontation commonplace in much of the world and international terrorists growing increasingly sophisticated in their methods, it is only realistic to assume that unless determined efforts are made by the U.S. and other nations, sooner or later, somewhere, a nuclear weapon will be used.[38]

In the Senate committee considering this report, Senator Glenn recalled that during the 1980 presidential campaign, "Ronald Reagan made the amazing comment that 'Non-proliferation is none of our business,'" and that as president in 1983 he said that his policy had accomplished "if not entirely eliminating nuclear proliferation, holding it down to where a country might have a weapon or two."[39] The extraordinary naivete of this statement, which indicated the president's failure to comprehend that, if a nation can make one or two weapons, it can, in time, make one or two hundred, made little impact outside the committee hearing room. Unfortunately, only Senators Charles H. Percy and John Glenn were present to consider the testimony of UNA representatives. Certainly, Secretary of State George Shultz showed no sign of concern in a speech on "Preventing the Proliferation of Nuclear Weapons" made before the United Nations Association a few months later. Parroting the administration slogan, "we are realistic," the secretary cited only the Middle East and South Asia as "regions of instability and proliferation concern." Remarkably, this was followed immediately by the statement that "Our $3.2 billion package of economic and security assistance to Pakistan" illustrated how the administration was "striving to reduce the motivation of some states to acquire nuclear explosives by working with them to improve regional and global stability."[40] His further claim of success in convincing South Africa, Argentina, and Brazil of the need to establish firm controls over nuclear development was unsupported by any evidence whatever, as was his assurance that progress in this area was being made with the Soviet Union and China. Shultz referred in passing to a meeting of nuclear suppliers, held secretly in Luxembourg in July 1984, but failed to reveal that Eastern European members of what was known as the London Suppliers Club had not been invited to attend. Nor did he explain that Pakistan and Libya were major concerns at this meeting, or that Libya's potential suppliers included not only the Soviet Union but the U.S. NATO ally, Belgium, as well.[41]

Following President Reagan's reelection in November 1984 there was a noticeable soft-pedaling of anti-Soviet speeches and a stiffening attitude toward nuclear proliferation. The latter problem had received only brief mention in the lengthy 1984 Republican platform, taking a single paragraph to praise Reagan's imaginary achievements in this critical area.[42] Many years will pass and many memoirs and now-secret files must be released before we learn whether President Reagan decided he could not finish his presidency with a record of failure in reducing Soviet–American tensions and nuclear proliferation, or if he was reacting to Democratic charges of having "relaxed controls on nuclear proliferation" and having been "the first president since the Cold War to preside over the complete collapse of all nuclear arms negotiations with the

Soviets.''[43] In any event, the Reagan–Gorbachev summit meeting in November 1985, however inconclusive, represented a sharp turnabout from the uncompromising verbal exchanges of the previous four years. Significantly, these talks included recognition of the nonproliferation problem and reaffirmed the commitment both powers had undertaken when they signed the Non-Proliferation Treaty.[44] They followed by two months President Reagan's application of economic sanctions against South Africa that included a ban on the export of "goods or technology which are to be used in a nuclear production or utilization facility."[45]

Typically, Reagan denied that the summit meeting and his action against South Africa represented changes in policy.[46] However, the first indication of a shift from Evil Empire rhetoric to the possibility of an easing of Soviet–American relations by way of a summit meeting came in a statement prepared in cooperation with West German Chancellor Kohl on November 30, 1984.[47] Moreover, only a month before he was forced by Congress to apply some kind of sanctions to South Africa, Reagan was standing by his repeated claim that "the results that we've had in this constructive engagement with South Africa justifies our continuing on that score."[48]

As the United States and the Soviet Union pursue their global struggle for ideological and military supremacy, the years of nuclear experiment conducted by these two giants have demonstrated even to their most aggressive leaders the futility of a nuclear contest. Beyond that, each faces a secondary threat of self-destruction by bleeding the country to death in an effort to support a never-ending drive for more powerful deterrent weapons and more sophisticated and expensive inner- and outer-space defenses. In other parts of the world, both friends and foes of the United States have reason to be apprehensive about U.S. plans, when they consider not only that this is the one country that has used nuclear weapons against another nation, but that according to published records every president from Truman to Carter has seriously considered the use of such weapons in actual and prospective confrontations with North Korea, North Vietnam, China, Iran, and the Soviet Union.[49] Notwithstanding President Reagan's recent acknowledgment that there would be no winner in a nuclear war, his militarist approach to foreign policy and his refusal to disavow the tactic of first strike encourages existing suspicions that he might not refrain from resorting to the ultimate weapon in a crisis.

Public fears of nuclear holocaust tend to focus on the threat posed by superpower antagonisms; but some newcomers to the nuclear family represent an equally grave threat. Most dangerous of all are those countries whose leaders combine a messianic fervor with an implacable hatred of their enemies and an unshakable resolve to destroy those enemies regardless of the cost to themselves. Iranian Khomeini, Libyan Qaddafi, and an Israeli like Kahane are not likely to be deterred from using every weapon at their command in a contest with enemies whom they consider to be the devil's disciples bent on destroying God's chosen people. Iran already has a research reactor, built by the former Shah with U.S. aid; and, while the Shah was still in power, this stalwart U.S. ally was negotiating secretly with Israel for missiles that could accommodate nuclear warheads. Khomeini put an end to that association, but he has since been host to a German team sent to explore the possibility of expanding the country's nuclear facilities.[50]

Israel is believed to have reached the stage of nuclear weapons production, and it has shown its determination to prevent similar progress in enemy Arab countries by its attack on Iraq's unfinished nuclear plant. French indifference to the problem of proliferation made nuclear construction in Iraq possible in the first place, and French contractors lost no time promising to repair the damage done by Israeli planes.[51] Enmities in other parts of the world may be less menacing in the near term, but the ongoing contests between India and Pakistan and between China and the Soviet Union—all with nuclear weapons or weapons capacity—cannot be disregarded.

The threat posed by Libya's Muammar al-Qaddafi is somewhat different. An anti-America, anti-Israel zealot, he demonstrated during the 1986 skirmish with U.S. planes and ships in the Gulf of Sidra that he will not risk obliteration in direct combat with an overwhelmingly superior force. Instead, his call for a "holy war" against the United States in all parts of the world suggests the nature of the campaign he will conduct. Given the nuclear capability that his oil revenues can buy, a concealed strike with nuclear explosives smuggled into the United States—preferably one that would appear to implicate the Soviet Union or some other "enemy" of the United States—would not be uncharacteristic of this would-be international revolutionary. Thanks to the macho we'll-take-no-guff-from-anyone atmosphere generated by President Reagan and Secretary of Defense Weinberger, the "Black Bag" control of nuclear weapons theoretically maintained by the president might not prevent a red alert and release of U.S. missiles, which false alarms have nearly provoked in the past. Even less stable and more dangerous are those members of terrorist organizations like the Muslim

Party of God and communist Red Brigades, who may rely on sympathetic governments for weapons and hiding places, but who have no responsibility for the well-being of any nation or people.[52]

The danger of nuclear war starting by mistake was the subject of a 1982 UN study. As the authors pointed out, specialists have recognized "from the very beginning of the nuclear arms race" that random incidents—"an electrical circuit might shortcut, a relay stick, a switch fail, or that a button might be pressed accidentally, a message misunderstood, an aurora borealis, meteor or flock of geese be mistaken for an attack"—might lead to irreversible military action. Even more dangerous than mechanical failure (which complex safeguards are designed to prevent) is "unauthorized action, human error or sheer madness" inspired by personal judgment as to the needs of the moment, actions politely referred to as "dysfunctional behavior."[53]

Contrary to the popular notion that no nuclear missile can be released without a direct order from the president, there are many situations, particularly on nuclear submarines, in which the unlocking and launching of a missile can be accomplished without a presidential order.[54] Although the United States has taken considerable pains to devise controls that would prevent any unauthorized release of a nuclear missile, we have no firm information as to the precautions taken by other nuclear powers. When one considers the dubious quality of both civilian and military leadership in countries that are only now acquiring nuclear capability, there is little ground for an optimistic view of their ability or will to develop and stress the need for fail-safe controls over weapons that may ultimately destroy this planet. Moreover, encouragement given by governments like Iran, Libya, and Syria to terrorist organizations in other countries increases the likelihood that, ultimately, one of these groups will explode a stolen or contrived nuclear weapon and thereby set off an international conflict they can neither control nor profit by. These are the threats from which U.S. policymakers must not be distracted by a single-minded crusade against communism.

12

Where Are We Heading?

Among Americans of the United States, there is an almost unanimous belief that Abraham Lincoln effectively and concisely expressed the goal of a free people as a "government of the people, by the people, for the people."[1] Even so, bitter disagreements have marked debates over the best method of achieving or retaining this most desirable state. In large part this is because, as world history has demonstrated time and again, freedom involves many rights other than the right to vote. If, as Shakespeare put it, the past is prologue, the experience of this and other countries should be scrutinized with special care to identify those views of the good society that have either fostered or hindered freedom—including (but not limited to) government of, by, and for the people.

Identification of the barriers to freedom is often easier than defining the conditions that make freedom possible; but recognition of even the most obvious dangers requires an ability to distinguish between fact and fancy, reality and myth. President Reagan speaks glibly of "facts" and "realities", but his superficial knowledge of history, shaped by his inability to critically examine either the events he has witnessed personally or the ideas he so readily commits to memory from the printed page, has led him down a road that may prove disastrous for the United States. Convinced of the infallibility of his view of this country's past and the world's present problems, he seeks to convince all of us that the nation's salvation depends on what he regards as a return to the political and religious beliefs of the Founding Fathers.

The implications of Reagan's philosophy are seen in his approach to both domestic and foreign affairs. At home, he persists in associating his policies with the fundamentalist Christian doctrine that in the Bible "lie all the answers to all the problems that man has ever known."[2] Abroad, he sees the world as a battleground in the struggle between good and evil, represented respectively by Bible-based U.S. democracy and godless communism. Repeatedly he urges his fellow citizens to regard themselves as "a special breed," going so far as to adopt Bernard De Voto's concept of Americans as "a people who believed we were chosen by God to create a greater world."[3]

The "Reagan Doctrine" permits no penetration of evidence indicating that the president's "Crusade for Democracy" is as unattainable on a global scale as is the Soviet dream of world socialism. The unrelenting forces of nationalism, race, and religion may be manipulated by both sides in the ideological war, but they will also prevent either side from achieving its objective. Further, Reagan's interpretation of Soviet strategy fails to take account of the demonstrable fact that Soviet leadership has never carried its crusade to lengths that would involve substantial domestic sacrifice. The Kremlin will subsidize friendly governments wherever and whenever that investment seems useful to its cause. However, since Stalin's 1924 victory over Russia's leading international revolutionary, Leon Trotsky, Soviet dictators have never willingly entered a contest that might threaten or weaken the homeland. On the contrary, the only situations in which they have been unreserved in aggressiveness have been in countries on the borders of the USSR. Unlike the United States, which has risked its youth and wealth in such geographically remote areas as Korea and Vietnam, Soviet leaders have been content to leave adventures of this kind to their "friends," supporting them only so long as the benefits seem worth the cost.

Far greater risks have been taken by national leaders following a different star. Countries whose rulers have adopted the Koran as their fundamental law accept Mohammed's command that every true believer must be prepared to defend and advance the cause of Islam by force of arms. As faith knows no national boundaries, the potential for violent confrontations between these countries and their neighbors is ever present. Even within national borders, governments have found it impossible to contain open conflict between Muslim and non-Muslim groups or, for that matter, between different Muslim sects. The fanaticism that fosters unending warfare between Iran and Iraq encourages terrorism as an expression of political belief, and is matched only by the tenacity with which political strong men in Muslim countries resist efforts to "purify" their governments. This uncompromising spirit also plays on the bitterness that blocks resolution of the Arab–Israeli dispute. In Lebanon, the contest for power has degenerated into terrorist warfare in which individual acts of terrorism mushroom into military campaigns aimed at obliterating both the people and property of the enemy.

The explosive mixture of personal ambition, ethnic, racial, and religious antagonisms is by no means confined to the Middle East. In every corner of the globe, contests for control of the government have pitted tribe against tribe, race against race, and culture against culture. In most cases the outcome has been a type of dictatorship that offers little hope of improvement for the overwhelming majority of the population. Thus, of the 51 African nations surveyed in the State Department's *Country Reports on Human Rights Practices for 1985*, 30 are characterized by Freedom House (a private agency) as not free, 19 as partly free, and only 2—Botswana and Mauritius—as free.

Asia presents a picture only slightly more encouraging, with India, Japan, Papua New Guinea, and the tiny Fiji republic standing out as free nations. With a little bit of luck, the Philippines may join that select group, but the remaining countries range in character from the partly free societies of Thailand and Taiwan to the iron theocracy of Iran and the brutally repressive government of Cambodia. Kampuchea, as Cambodia is now known, has not yet recovered from the horror of the Khmer Rouge's takeover in 1975, in which almost one-third of the population was slaughtered. Moreover, that country is not the only one in which near-genocidal killing has been practiced. Government-instigated killings of men, women, and children in Indonesia, as well as those in Cambodia, were cited by Amnesty International as "among the most massive violations of human rights since the Second World War."[4] Against this background, Reagan's assertion that "the winds of freedom are blowing" seemed inappropriate as an introduction to his 1986 tour of the Far East, which began with a visit to Indonesia's President Suharto, "a long-time friend of the United States."[5] Like these Asian nations, dozens of countries on every continent except Australia have been found to have used torture as "part of the state-controlled machinery to suppress dissent."[6]

The challenge to totalitarian barbarism has, in recent years, been strongest in the Western Hemisphere. Nevertheless, in much of Latin America, the heritage of brutality and greed demonstrated by its conquerors is still evident. From the viceroys of colonial days, Latin American countries graduated to homegrown dictators, who assumed absolute authority under so-called republican constitutions. This pattern has been unaffected by the substantial racial integration that occurred in countries like Brazil, Chile, Mexico, and much of Central America.[7]

IDEOLOGICAL TURMOIL IN THE WEST

Catholicism remained dominant in Latin America throughout successive changes in political leadership, although the church lost much of its power after the Spanish and Portuguese colonies won their independence in the first quarter of the nineteenth century. Almost the sole source of comfort for the poverty-stricken majority of the population, the church never extended its spiritual role to support uprisings against the brutal dictators who, for more than a century, succeeded one another with bewildering rapidity in most Central and South American nations. Not until the most recent decade was the church's nonpolitical stance challenged by some of its own clergy as well as by members of the congregation.

Beleaguered by the political polarization engendered by Soviet–U.S. antagonisms and by internal dissension over questions of economic and social policy, the Catholic church now faces its most serious test since the Protestant Reformation. In attempting to deal with modern problems, the clergy—from Pope John Paul down to the lowest level of the priesthood—has been drawn into the political arena. From the pope's open support of Solidarity in Poland and unequivocal condemnation of apartheid in South Africa to his rejection of liberation theology in Latin America and abortion legislation everywhere, the political implications are inescapable.[8]

Within the United States, the Vatican faces equally serious challenges to papal doctrine from members of the clergy who cannot accept the order that forbids diversity of views on birth control and abortion, and from those in educational institutions who fear that church efforts to maintain doctrinal integrity in teaching will result in the dismissal of hundreds of teachers and loss of accreditation for many Catholic colleges. Protests took the form of a newspaper campaign when, on October 7, 1984, a Catholic Statement on Pluralism and Abortion was published as a full-page advertisement in the New York *Times*. Among the signers were 97 academics and 25 priests, brothers, and nuns, who joined lay members of the church in insisting that the constitutional right to free speech should permit them to express their differences with church doctrine. On March 2, 1986, eighteen months after the first statement appeared, a second full-page ad declared the signers' continued solidarity and protested the threats and penalties that had followed their original dissent. Before the month was out, the Washington *Post* of March 28 reported that 235 presidents of U.S. Catholic colleges and universities had protested a proposed order that would require dismissal of all teachers who failed to accept as their principal responsibility "the salvific mission of the church," which makes "spreading the message of Christ" equally as important as "seeking and disseminating truth."

The problems faced by the Roman church, and the heated debates they have stirred up, are almost identical to those that divide the U.S. public. What is most striking is the difference in solutions proposed by the pope, on the one hand, and the president, on the other. United in their unreserved opposition to communist ideology and such social practices as abortion, Pope John Paul and President Reagan part company on issues scarcely less vital. Where Reagan insists that Milton Friedman's notion of uninhibited free enterprise is the foundation of a free democratic society, the Vatican's definition of "Christian freedom" challenges the primacy of the profit motive in these terms: "the person of the worker is the principle, subject and purpose of work. . . . The priority of work over capital places an obligation in justice upon employers to consider the welfare of the workers before the increase of profits. . . . The right to private property is inconceivable without responsibilities to the common good. It is subordinated to the higher principle which states that goods are meant for all." Where Reagan administration policies are shaped by and for the well-to-do, the church declares its "preference for the poor" and "clearly affirms that man is worth more for what he is than for what he has."[9] In a televised address to the people of Canada on September 17, 1984, Pope John Paul went further, denouncing the injustice of what he called the "imperialist monopoly" of the rich nations in the face of worldwide poverty. He was promptly taken to task by a confirmed Catholic, William F. Buckley, Jr. Accusing the pope of talking like a Third World politician in the United Nations, Buckley recommended that, in economic matters, the world—and presumably the pope—should look to President Reagan for guidance in making "the correct Christian decision."[10]

Typically, President Reagan ignores the differences when he frequently identifies his own views with those of the pope. Similarly, he ignores or disparages any opposition from U.S. Protestant clergy. In this regard, his support comes largely from groups and leaders who are, if anything, more fundamentalist than the pope, and who stand solidly behind Reagan's economic doctrines and his championing of assorted right-wing dictators around the world. Even in those instances in which "friendly" tyrants have been overthrown (as in Haiti and the Philippines), Reagan is viewed as having instigated these "victories for democracy," despite the incontrovertible evidence of his continued support for the old regime up to the very moment when the success of a popular revolt was assured.[11]

Information from his own investigators that the revolts against Duvalier and Marcos were inspired by a sincere desire to replace a tyrannical regime with a democratic one did not lead Reagan to grace the insurgents in Haiti and the Philippines with the title "freedom fighters." That honor he extends only to revolutionaries who, regardless of their other qualifications, are dedicated to the overthrow of left-wing governments. Reagan's selective use of the term "freedom fighters" reveals the weakness of his claim to be opposed to all dictatorships, whether right or left. Further, as he denounces the barbarities of their enemies, he lauds freedom fighters who he says avoid civilian targets because they "don't want to hurt the people," a stand belied by the on-site evidence of murder, torture, and destruction of civilian facilities gathered by Americas Watch, Amnesty International, and church officials in Nicaragua and Angola.[12] Similarly, Reagan accepts the Savimbi-Botha alliance without apology, going so far as to put his own words into the mouth of South African President Botha, saying, "he has agreed with us that he finds the past system repugnant and is trying to get changes as quickly as possible."[13] By this patent falsification of Botha's publicly expressed defense of apartheid, Reagan gives the impression that his South African counterpart is at heart a freedom fighter. At the same time, he refuses to apply that title to those blacks who are actively resisting the repressive policies of Botha's government.

It is this habit of distorting history and justifying policy decisions with a combination of truths, half-truths, and flat lies that has led as conservative an observer as James Reston to express his fears for U.S. democracy in these terms:

> We are seeing more than ever before, or so I believe, a distortion of the theory of representative government. Increasingly, the executive branch, with its dominance of television, tends to evade the doubts of Congress by theatrical appeals to the people on the theory that what's popular is right . . .[14]

Comparing Reagan's manipulation of the press and public opinion with that of previous presidents, Reston points out that "The main difference now is that Ronald Reagan is better than any of them at reading speeches other people write." The media contribute to the administration campaign of disinformation, Reston says, by failing to challenge most of the so-called facts and figures turned out by Reagan's monstrous federal public relations machine. He sums up the result by saying, ". . . in over 40 years in Washington I can't remember a period when so much obvious nonsense, even so many distortions of fact, have gone by unchallenged or been dismissed with scarcely more than a whisper by the public." An example that demonstrates both of Reston's points occurred the very day his article was published, when Reagan's falsification of Botha's position was not challenged by a single one of the room full of reporters at his news conference.

This media lethargy was shed with startling suddenness after Bob Woodward revealed in the Washington *Post* the existence of a memorandum from the president's national security adviser, Vice Admiral John M. Poindexter, that described a two-month-campaign in which the media had been used to circulate false information that would lead Qaddafi to think the United States was planning further military moves against him. In a brief press conference on October 2, 1986, the president said, "I challenge the veracity of that entire story." But he never responded directly to repeated questions about the existence of the memorandum referred to in the *Post*, or to the accuracy of the quotations taken from it. In typical Reagan fashion, he closed the questioning with the quip that he had "come to the conclusion that Mr. Woodward is probably Deep Throat," an obvious reference to the anonymous informant in the Washington *Post*'s Watergate investigation.[15] The president's credibility in this matter suffered a further shock when Bernard Kalb, the State Department's official spokesman, resigned to protest over "the reported disinformation program" which he felt called into question "faith in the word of America."[16]

That faith was put to an equally severe test a month later when a new storm arose over the discovery that for 18 months administration representatives had been negotiating secretly with Iranian officials for the release of U.S. hostages while simultaneously supplying munitions to a nation that Reagan had repeatedly charged with fostering terrorism. Few observers accepted either the accuracy or the reasonableness of the president's televised account of his attempt to establish relations with Iranian moderates or his denial of any connection between arms shipments and the release of hostages. The comments of his friends and colleagues were more revealing than those of his critics. George Will, the president's most ardent journalistic supporter, called Reagan's explanation "artless," and Secretary of Defense Caspar Weinberger was found to have written on the secret memorandum that initiated the plan, "this is absurd." Equally significant was the after-the-fact opposition of Secretary of State George Shultz who, under Admiral Poindexter's extraordinary interpretation of the security "need to know" rule, had not been apprised of the negotiations with Iran.[17]

THE REAGAN LEGACY

In the first six years of Ronald Reagan's presidency, the U.S. public has seen the White House transformed into a combination of Theodore Roosevelt's "bully pulpit," a fundamentalist chapel, a Hollywood stage, and a Madison Avenue public relations office. The tragedy of those years has been an erosion of belief in the individual freedom that Reagan talks about incessantly, and just as persistently undermines by attempting to alter the basic framework of the Constitution to accommodate his fundamentalist religious principles. Although he has failed in the attempt to accomplish this by formal constitutional amendment, he has largely achieved his goal by extraconstitutional means.

First and foremost has been his performance on television and in hundreds of personal appearances before carefully selected audiences. He has demonstrated a skill and effectiveness that surpasses his finest Hollywood production, combining personal charm with the technique of old-time comedians, whose motto was "always leave 'em laughing." Often he will turn away a serious question with a facetious answer, and he will frequently conclude a nontelevised speech with a joke aimed at some domestic or foreign adversary.

Bedazzled by this superb acting performance, a large segment of the public has been taken in by Reagan's evangelistic appeals in which he artfully combines morality with patriotism. This approach follows the pattern adopted by Jerry Falwell, Tim LaHaye, and some other churchmen whose definition of freedom embodies the will-destroying doctrine of absolute submission to the principles—and presidential opinions—that these self-anointed professors of Christianity insist are reflections of God's holy purpose.

The international impact of Reagan's evangelism is as significant as its effect on domestic affairs. His indiscriminate anti-communist, anti-socialist, anti-leftist-of-any-sort crusade, although tempered somewhat in his discussions with Gorbachev, has given aid and comfort to nearly every noncommunist dictator throughout the world. Only after his staff had read repeated challenges, at home and abroad, of the assumption that communism is at the root of all revolts against right-wing governments did Reagan finally acknowledge that this is not necessarily the case. In a rare reversal, he once acknowledged that "Most of the world's turbulence has indigenous causes, and not every regional conflict would be viewed as part of the East–West conflict."[18] However, this momentary lapse was followed by a lengthy exposition of the threats to democracy that support his standard view of the global contest between East and West. Moreover, this single concession has not affected his policy of support for any government or revolutionary leader who professes both anti-communism and friendship for the United States.

In the course of his global crusade, Reagan has assumed a level of executive power never achieved by any president in any peacetime period of U.S. history. By way of justification, he has cited military engagements undertaken by other presidents, from Thomas Jefferson's undeclared war against the Barbary pirates to more recent uses of U.S. forces in Asia, the Middle East, Central America, and the Caribbean.[19] In all of these cases, however, the actions were based either on authorizing congressional resolutions, treaties, or to protect U.S. lives and property against direct attack.[20] No previous president has presumed, as Reagan has, that, in the absence of a declaration of war, his authority to engage in military action anywhere in the world is purely a matter of his own discretion. Even Lyndon Johnson, in his single-minded conduct of the undeclared Vietnam War, solicited and received prior approval from Congress to assist any member of SEATO that requested aid.[21] The massive escalation of hostilities that followed this blank check, and the ultimate failure of the U.S. effort in Vietnam, led Congress to cancel its grant of unrestricted executive authority[22] and to restore a semblance of the traditional system of checks and balances by means of the War Powers Act of 1973.[23] This law severely limits the introduction of U.S. armed forces "into hostilities, or into situations where imminent involvement in hostilities is clearly indicated by the circumstances."

Repeated complaints from members of Congress regarding President Reagan's use of the armed forces in contravention of the War Powers Act have been ignored or rejected as unfounded. Congressional ire, expressed by Republicans as well as Democrats, has been aroused more by military or paramilitary adventures taken without consultation with Congress than by the actions themselves. This was true of the mining of Nicaraguan harbors, the Grenada invasion, and the attacks on Libya. Criticism of the Nicaraguan harbor operation was especially bitter when it was learned that CIA officials had not only concealed their agency's part in the attack, but had deliberately ignored briefing requests from the Senate committee responsible for overseeing covert actions. When this was revealed by the staff director of the Senate Select Committee on Intelligence, the CIA demanded that he be disciplined. This final display of arrogance caused the committee's vice-chairman, Daniel Patrick Moynihan, to resign in protest.[24]

In all of these cases, Reagan has avoided calling for a declaration of war, a measure advocated as the preferred approach to Cuba and Nicaragua by William F. Buckley, Jr., the writer-publisher whom the president says he admires above all others.[25] Instead, he has based his use of U.S. military units on the right of self-defense or on his own finding of a national emergency. Using the latter ploy in both Nicaragua and Libya, he carefully refrained from any reference to the War Powers Act, which defines a national emergency as one created by an attack on U.S. territory or armed forces. Instead, he cited legislation that was never intended to extend war-making power to the president.[26] Successive military strikes at Libyan bases, largely supported by the U.S. public because of Qaddafi's long campaign of invective and suspected terror against the United States, were undertaken without so much as a by-your-leave gesture to Congress. Not until the administration's chief Senate supporter, Richard Lugar, publicly complained of actions taken by the executive branch without consulting the legislature did President Reagan condescend to invite selected members of Congress to hear his plans. His concept of self-defense came home to roost only a month later when South African forces invaded three of that country's neighbors for harboring anti-apartheid terrorists of the African National Congress. President Botha announced to the world that this action was based on the same principle as the U.S. raids on Libya, a claim that was angrily denied by the White House.[27]

THE DANGER AHEAD

President Reagan claims to have restored the nation's military and moral strength. If this means that he has gained acceptance of his macho "make my day" attitude toward critics at home and those he designates as enemies abroad, he may be right. Almost every poll of public opinion taken during the first half of 1986 showed that more than 60 percent of the U.S. population believed he was doing a good job. Thus, despite substantial opposition to some of his domestic programs and some aspects of administration foreign policy, the majority of people have reacted enthusiastically to his engaging public image as well as his tough-guy attitude and his appeals to patriotism and national pride. Equally effective is his oft-repeated praise of the extraordinary qualities that make Americans a "special breed," capable of solving any problem and meeting any challenge. Few members of his audience can resist a warming response to such adulation offered them by the highest official of the greatest nation in the world. When he has made his word picture of U.S. fearlessness come alive with bold assaults on Grenada and Libya, the majority of citizens and politicians have cheered him on.

This vision of the United States of America as a nation that needs only a strong, God-fearing leader to establish it as the world's democratic "defender of the faith" is not a delusion that will pass with Reagan's retirement from the White House. Greater than any present danger is the prospect that the U.S. public will continue to look for leaders who will sustain the promise of tough, indomitable leadership and will not compromise what are mistakenly conceived to be American traditions and morals.

Further evidence of the Reagan syndrome appeared when presidential hopefuls began to announce plans to seek their party's nomination for chief executive. All of the early Republican aspirants—George Bush, Jack Kemp, Robert Dole, and the Reverend Pat Robertson—hastened to assure a convocation at the 1986 winter meeting of the Conservative Political Action Conference of their dedication to the principles of the "hard right," including support for CPAC's honored guest, Jonas Savimbi. Front-runner solely by virtue of his two-term vice-presidency, Bush eagerly joined the chorus in an effort to convince CPAC members that he was not the "wimp" some consider him to be.[28] Meanwhile the most enthusiastically greeted CPAC speaker, Jeane Kirkpatrick, continued her newspaper lecturing of the Reagan administration for not learning from past experience in Cuba, Vietnam, and Iran that halfway measures in the use of force are not enough.[29] For her forthright stand on big-stick diplomacy, Kirkpatrick earned the rank of favorite dark horse in Buckley's *National Review*.[30]

Like other Republican candidates, evangelist Pat Robertson appreciates the need for organization in the drive for political recognition. He has established a chain of Freedom Councils in states like Iowa and Michigan where his followers are expected to show enough strength to influence, if not control, the delegations that go to the Republican nominating convention.[31] Like noncandidate Jerry Falwell, Robertson acknowledges that his hope of saving souls goes hand-in-hand with a

campaign for Star Wars and aid to the contras, as well as for constitutional amendments to prohibit abortion and permit prayer in public
schools.[32]

On the Democratic side, Edward M. Kennedy's announcement that
he was out of the running[33] left Gary Hart as the front-runner, with New
York's Governor Mario Cuomo a likely contender. Hart's opening gun in
the 1988 race appeared in the form of a book in which he focuses on the
task of making the United States stronger by reforming its military
organization.[34] However, in speaking about the book, Hart admitted that,
as far as military *policy* was concerned, this was not a current issue.[35]
Neither he nor Cuomo seemed anxious in 1986 to make an issue of
presidential power in the use of military might around the world, or to
cross swords with the administration on the nature of patriotism. On the
contrary, the growing mood of aggressiveness has been manifested in
Democratic applause for every foreign military action mounted by President Reagan, with the exception of CIA action in Central America.

Other signs of Democratic accommodation to unrestricted presidential use of force, subject only to after-the-fact information to Congress,
made their appearance in 1986. A leading Democratic critic of Reagan's
militancy abroad suddenly came out in favor of assassination as a means
of eliminating sponsors of terrorism like Colonel Qaddafi. Democratic
Senator Howard Metzenbaum's acceptance of assassination as simply
"another means" of carrying out national policy (as a former CIA officer
subsequently argued) must have startled his constituents as well as his
congressional colleagues.[36] Three months after rejecting Metzenbaum's
suggestion, the president unleashed an attack on Libyan centers that
clearly had the death of Qaddafi as one of its objectives.

During this period, the Democratic Party was shaken by the
discovery that the followers of right-wing radical Lyndon H. LaRouche
had infiltrated the party to an alarming degree. A three-time candidate
for the presidency, LaRouche had been known to students of politics (but
to few others) as a one-time Marxist whose theoretical concept of violence
was turned to practical application in attacks on the Communist Party of
the United States in 1973.[37] Calling his organization the National
Democratic Policy Committee, LaRouche has run as a Democrat since
1980, supporting maximum military programs, including nuclear
weapons, and inveighing against the "conspiracies" of establishments
ranging from the major media networks to Zionism, the Ford Foundation,
Queen Elizabeth of England, Henry Kissinger, and the Anti-Defamation
League of B'nai B'rith (which LaRouche refers to as the American Drug

Lobby). Democratic complacency over the pinpricks of this little-regarded radical was shattered when, in March 1986, his followers won the Illinois nominations for lieutenant governor and secretary of state on a ticket headed by Adlai Stevenson III.[38] Subsequently, it was discovered that LaRouche had made serious inroads in other states, particularly among Democratic voters disenchanted with their party leadership, most notably in areas of high unemployment and high crime. Ignorance of the real nature of LaRouche objectives, combined with admiration for his "Rambo"-like approach to the problems of crime, communism, and other conditions that he describes as threats to America, have brought voter support for LaRouche candidates from New York to California.[39]

Reactions among Democrats to this assault on the party reflect the seriousness of the situation. Stevenson made an unprecedented appeal to the courts for permission to withdraw his name from the Democratic line and to enter it on another line on the Illinois ballot. Equally significant was a special order in the U.S. House of Representatives to permit a full hour (a lengthy period in the House) for discussion of the LaRouche threat.[40] Congressmen who had taken the trouble to investigate the LaRouche party warned that members of the group had used not only the Democratic Party as their springboard, but had also run candidates for office as Republicans in California, Oregon, and Ohio.[41] Even more startling was the revelation that, until 1983, officials of the LaRouche organization had access to one of President Reagan's assistants on the National Security Council, and another in the Star Wars program, both of whom justified this association on the grounds that LaRouche had "one of the best private intelligence services in the world."[42]

No notice of this unusual House discussion was taken by the press, which was still headlining the previous day's second wave of attacks on Libyan coastal cities. Republicans and Democrats closed ranks behind the president in this response to a bomb explosion in Berlin, which radio intercepts indicated had been instigated by Libya. Presidential candidate Bob Dole introduced into the Senate a bill aimed at eliminating from the War Powers Act all restrictions on a president dealing with what he conceives to be acts of terrorism. Entitled the Anti-Terrorism Act of 1986, the bill's purpose was declared to be that of "clarifying the extent of the President's authority to deal with terrorism, thereby strengthening his hand as he copes with this problem."[43] Denying that he was attempting to give the president new authority, Dole nevertheless defined terrorism so broadly that it would permit the chief executive to take military action for any "activity" he interprets as "intimidation" of a government or its people. More specifically, the bill would permit the use of "deadly force" against "whoever organizes, attempts, commits, procures, or supports the commission of an act of terrorism."[44] The President would be empowered to apply deadly force even when no act has been committed, so long as he believes that one *may be committed*. This is politely referred to as authority "to preempt as well as respond to specific acts of terrorism." Then, to make clear that the U.S. Constitution will be considered no barrier to any action the president may wish to take in foreign lands, the bill contains this soothing guarantee: "Nothing in this Act may be construed as granting any authority to use deadly force *within the United States* which authority would not exist in the absence of this act" (emphasis added).

In the face of the general trend toward acceptance of tough-guy leadership, especially as represented by a president capable of using his television personality to win the hearts, if not the minds, of most people in the United States, it will take rare courage to resist the emotional wave set in motion by President Reagan. Members of Congress may continue to resist administration attacks on domestic programs that they know their constituents wish to have continued, but they show little stomach for challenging the gun-toting, flag-waving character of the Reagan Doctrine. In support of this policy, Reagan recalls the admonition of former British statesman, Edmund Burke, that "the only thing necessary for the triumph of evil is for good men to do nothing."[45] As a good man leading the fight against the evil of communist tyranny, Reagan has also cited America's Founding Fathers on the peril invited by majority oppression of minorities. Yet it is precisely this danger that threatens to undo many of our constitutional protections.

To convince the general public that the path Reagan has chosen will weaken democracy at home and increase the chance of conflict abroad will require an extraordinary degree of courage on the part of those who would turn the country in another direction. It will call for unusual moral strength to resist "going along" on the excuse that "you did it not because of what you thought was right . . .but what somebody else thought was right, contrary to your judgement and contrary to the judgement of those you represent."[46] In the unlikely event that President Reagan were to read this statement in the *Congressional Record*, he would undoubtedly agree with it. It would simply confirm his belief in the rightness of his cause and the reason for public support of his single-minded approach to what he conceives to be the defense of democracy.

Few contest the accuracy of the well-phrased declaration of Reagan's speechwriters that "the struggle between freedom and totalitarianism today is not ultimately a test of arms or missiles, but a test of faith and spirit."

However, there are those who question Reagan's method of conducting "this spiritual struggle [for] the Western mind."[47]

To dispel public doubt raised by critics of administration goals and tactics, Reagan encourages public distrust of those branches of the media that report opposition views, charging them with distortion of the news and lack of patriotism, especially in dealing with military questions. Criticism of the president's military and paramilitary ventures is made even more difficult by the veil of secrecy drawn by executive agencies to prevent publication or discussion of unauthorized information. When all else fails, there is always the threat of prosecution for disclosure of intelligence information or sources, as proposed by CIA Director William J. Casey.[48]

In the longer term, there is the prospect of a federal judiciary so dominated by Reaganesque ideologues that defense of free speech, personal privacy, freedom of information, and even freedom from government enforcement of religious concepts will be severely curtailed. That this is no idle threat is evident from the character of Reagan's choices for positions on the federal bench. The declining quality of these candidates is reflected in ratings by the American Bar Association, as staid and nonrevolutionary an organization as any in these United States. Of 28 persons considered in the early part of Reagan's second administration for appointment to the appellate level (one step below the U.S. Supreme Court), 14 were assigned the ABA's minimum qualification rating, and most of these were classified at the questionable level of "qualified/unqualified."[49] Although the ABA does not publicize the details of its assessments, other observers have provided sufficient information about specific candidates to demonstrate the type of judicial mind that Reagan prefers. The "second American revolution" promised by President Reagan can surely be expected to include a drastic reshaping of constitutional law and individual rights if the federal courts are dominated by jurists like these:

> Robert A. Bork, legal scholar and advocate of Attorney General Meese's interpretation of the Founders' original intent; member of the Court of Appeals in Washington, D.C., and favorite candidate of the far Right for appointment to the Supreme Court.[50]

> Lino A. Graglia, professor of law who writes that the Constitution has contributed little to the nation's well-being, and who entertains his students with references to "pickininnies" and "known subversives," all of whom he finds among women's organizations and minority groups.[51]

Alex Kozinsky, fundamentalist attorney for the Merit Systems Protection Board (MSPB) and protége of Herbert E. Ellingwood, who failed to get Senate approval for appointment to Assistant Attorney General in charge of judicial appointments because of his religious fundamentalist approach to the administration of MSPB.[52]

Daniel A. Manion, appointed to the Court of Appeals in Chicago; a long-time supporter of the John Birch Society; his lack of judicial experience at any level and demonstrated incompetence in the preparation of legal documents brought protests from two Republican members of the Senate Judiciary Committee, the Chicago Council of Lawyers, and 40 law school deans—none of whom had questioned the purely technical competence of earlier Reagan nominees.[53]

Antonin Scalia, elevated by President Reagan from the appellate level to the Supreme Court; considered by his peers to be a brilliant protagonist of administration views on First Amendment questions, his decisions in that area led William Safire to label Scalia "the worst enemy of free speech in America today."[54]

Jefferson B. Sessions III, who considers the National Association for the Advancement of Colored People and National Council of Churches un-American, but whose only criticism of the Ku Klux Klan is that some of its members are pot smokers.[55]

After hearings on Sessions' qualifications, the Judiciary Committee refused to submit his name to the full Senate for consideration. This one rejection, following approval of the previous 269 Reagan nominees, proved only a temporary setback in the campaign to "reform" the courts, as the Senate's subsequent approval of Daniel Manion demonstrated.[56]

Despite widespread opposition to Reagan's attempt to recast the Constitution and the courts in an ideological mold reminiscent of early Puritan days, his public image has not suffered. On the contrary, public opinion polls continue to show a high positive response to the question of whether or not he has done a good job overall.[57] However, these polls do not reveal the extent of public understanding of Reagan's plans for the federal judiciary. Even the widespread publicity attending the battle over Daniel Manion's nomination seemed to excite only readers of editorial and op-ed pages, notwithstanding reports of Reagan's resort to the crude politicking he so often disparages in order to win two badly needed votes, promising Senators Slade Gordon and Daniel J. Evans a free hand in selecting a federal district court judge in their state of Washington.[58]

The congressional elections of 1986, in which majority control of the Senate passed from Republicans to Democrats, signaled the end of automatic confirmation for subsequent Reagan nominees. Nevertheless, changes in the federal judiciary already effected by the president may assure the success of this element of the Reagan Revolution. After winning the battle for Manion's appointment, Reagan boldly predicted that, before he leaves the White House, 45 percent of all federal judgeships will be held—for life—by his appointees.[59] He did not have to add that the coincidence of these jurists' views with his own on civil rights, in general, and First Amendment protections, in particular, will shape the administration of justice in those areas for years to come. In this fashion, Reagan may well bring about the kind of constitutional revision that a majority of the country's 535 elected members of the national legislature have refused to approve and that even his adoring public (given a clear-cut choice) probably would reject. Certainly the biblical fundamentalism on which his concept of constitutional reform is based is not the reason for his popularity among voters, who, nationwide, do not look favorably on political candidates who make a campaign issue of their religious beliefs.[60] Only his fundamentalist supporters attempt to convey the impression that, like historian Carlton Hayes's "typical Christian" of seventeenth-century England, Reagan demonstrates "by external conduct that his particular religion inculcate[s] a higher moral standard than any other."[61]

Of those who would succeed Ronald Reagan in the White House, only Pat Robertson is clearly dedicated to assuming the mantle of defender of the faith, a true Christian who will lead us all in the path of righteousness. This will not bring him the presidential nomination at the Republican convention in 1988. However, if Robertson controls enough delegates to swing the election to a candidate acceptable to the religious Right, that candidate will find it difficult, if not impossible, to depart from the course charted by the party's leader over the previous eight years.

Contenders for both Republican and Democratic nominations, unable to match the incumbent president as a television personality, will attempt to convince convention delegates and the general public that their more substantive talents are needed to deal with the many critical problems Reagan will leave behind. It remains to be seen whether the winner in 1988 will have either the will or the courage to convince the U.S. people that neither the welfare of this country nor the cause of democracy will be served by continuing to pursue the fundamentalist reformation initiated by President Reagan in the conduct of both domestic and foreign affairs.

Notes

A Word about Sources

Because this book deals with critical periods and events in American history, particular care has been taken to document all references to the words and actions of individuals and organizations that have played a significant part in this history. The original spelling and punctuation used in very old documents have been retained except where the terms or arrangement would be unintelligible to the modern reader.

Most of the sources referred to can be found in any large public or university library. The author and title are given in full the first time a work is cited, and in abbreviated form thereafter. A bibliography of materials used appears immediately after the notes. The following abbreviations are used for sources that appear repeatedly in the notes:

Commager—Henry Steele Commager, *Documents of American History.*
CR—U.S. Congress, *Congressional Record.*
Documents—Charles C. Transill, ed., *Documents Illustrative of the Formation of the Union of the American States.*
Elliot—Jonathan Elliot, ed., *The Debates in the Several State Conventions on the Adoption of the Federal Constitution as Recommended by the General Convention at Philadelphia in 1787.*
Farrand—Max Farrand, ed., *The Records of the Federal Convention of 1787.*
Letters—Library of Congress, *Letters of Delegates to Congress, 1774–1789.*
NYT—New York *Times.*
Poore—Ben Perley Poore, *The Federal and State Constitutions, Colonial Charters, and Other Organic Laws of the United States.*
Schwartz—Bernard Schwartz, *The Roots of the Bill of Rights.*
WCPD—Office of the Federal Register, *Weekly Compilation of Presidential Documents.*
WP—Washington *Post.*
WTROM—Ronald Reagan, with Richard G. Hubler, *Where's the Rest of Me?*

CHAPTER 1

1. Lewis Browne, *This Believing World,* pp. 294–98.
2. Matthew 22: 21; Mark 12: 17.
3. Exodus 20: 3.
4. Geoffrey Barraclough, ed., *The Christian World: A Social and Cultural History,* p. 51.
5. Ibid., p. 109. See also Charles Diehl, *Byzantium: Greatness and Decline.*
6. *The Koran,* trans. by N. J. Dawood, pp. 105, 123, 319, 422, 317.
7. Ibid., p. 34.
8. Zoé Oldenbourg, *The Crusades,* pp. 84–85.
9. Ibid., p. 85.

10. Ibid., p. 137.

11. Ibid., pp. 249–53.

12. Ibid., pp. 428–30.

13. Harold J. Grimm, *The Reformation Era: 1500–1650.*

14. Quotations from Henry Gee and William John Hardy, *Documents Illustrative of English Church History,* pp. 1, 75, 79–80.

15. Carlton J. H. Hayes, *A Political and Cultural History of Modern Europe,* 1:173.

16. Ibid., 1:174–83, 432–53. The extreme measures adopted by the Spanish Inquisition brought protests from more than one pope.

17. Barry Coward, *The Stuart Age: A History of England, 1603–1714,* p. 91.

18. Ibid., p. 240.

19. Schwartz, 1:41–46.

CHAPTER 2

1. Poore, 2:1379.

2. Ibid., 2:1888.

3. Ibid., 1:922; 2:1893.

4. Ibid., 2:1893.

5. Ibid., 1:774.

6. Ibid., 1:922.

7. Ibid., 1:931.

8. Ibid., 1:932.

9. Ibid., 2:1328.

10. Ibid., 2:1310.

11. Ibid., 1:811. The charter issued to Lord Baltimore was written in Latin. An English translation can be found in Commager, pp. 21–22.

12. Poore, 2:1379–90.

13. Ibid., 2:1507. For the early history of Pennsylvania, see William Mason Cornell, *The History of Pennsylvania, from the Earliest Discovery to the Present Time.*

14. Poore, 2:1594–95.

15. Ibid., 1:249–58.

16. Ibid., 2:1270–75. Poore's footnote regarding the king's Commission for New Hampshire mistakenly gives the date of that document as 18 September 1779, rather than 1679.

17. Ibid., 1:270–73.

18. Ibid., 1:369.

19. Commager, pp. 2–3.

20. The baptism of Jesus is recounted in each of the first four books of the New Testament: Matthew 3:13–16; Mark 1:9; Luke 3:21; and John 3:23.

21. Numerous histories have been written of the various Christian churches. Those used here include: R. W. Albright, *A History of the Protestant Episcopal Church;* G. G. Atkins and F. L. Fagley, *History of American Congregationalism;* W. T. Hanzsche, *The Presbyterians;* Philip Hughes, *A Popular History of the Catholic Church;* H. E. Luccock and Paul Hutchinson, *The Story of Methodism;* Elbert Russell, *The History of Quakerism.*

H. C. Vedder, *A Short History of the Baptists*; and A. R. Wentz, *A Basic History of Lutheranism in America.*

22. A fascinating, if slanted, history of early Virginia is found in an account written by a maverick member of that province, first published in London in 1705: Robert Beverley, *The History and Present State of Virginia.*

23. Poore, 2:1902.

24. Matthew Page Andrews, *History of Maryland: Province and State*, p. 10.

25. Commager, pp. 21–22.

26. Schwartz, 1:68.

27. Andrews, *History of Maryland*, pp. 92–93, 697. The somewhat misleading title of Toleration Act is used in some histories and documentaries, including Commager, p. 31.

28. Poore, 2:1382.

29. Ibid., 2:1406–08.

30. Ibid., 2:1397n.

31. Harold E. Davis, *The Fledgling Province: Social and Cultural Life in Colonial Georgia, 1733–1776*, p. 15.

32. Poore, 2:1518–27.

33. Ibid., 2:1536–40.

34. The term Scotch-Irish refers to Scots who first settled in Northern Ireland and whose descendants later migrated to the colonies.

35. Richard P. McCormick, *New Jersey from Colony to State*, pp. 18–23, 43.

36. The New York Charter of Libertyes and Privileges is reproduced in Schwartz, 1:163–68. For a general history of the state, see David M. Ellis, et al., *A Short History of New York State.*

37. Albert Hart, *Commonwealth History of Massachusetts*, 1:23.

38. Poore, 1:932–42.

39. Known as the Cambridge Agreement, this document is reproduced in Commager, p. 18.

40. Hart, *Commonwealth History*, 1:104–106.

41. For full text, see Schwartz, 1:71–85.

42. The English background and Massachusetts experience with witchcraft are described in Hart, *Commonwealth History*, vol. 2, ch. 2. *The Minutes of the Provincial Council of Pennsylvania*, 1:93–96, report that state's trial of Margaret Mattson and Yeshro Hendrickson, which resulted in a jury verdict of "Guilty of having the Common fame of a witch, but not guilty in manner and forme as Shee stands Indicted." Each husband was fined fifty pounds and the wives put on good behavior for six months.

43. For more detail, see Paul R. Lucas, *Valley of Discord: Church and Society along the Connecticut River, 1636–1725*; and Jere R. Daniell, *Colonial New Hampshire.*

44. Poore, 2:1270–74.

45. Ibid., 1:249–52.

46. Ibid., 2:1594–95.

47. Carl Bridenbaugh, *Fat Mutton and Liberty of Conscience; Society in Rhode Island, 1636–1690*, p. 5.

48. Hart, *History of Massachusetts*, 1:85.

49. Ibid., 1:286.

50. Mary Hewitt Mitchell, *The Great Awakening, and Other Revivals in the Religious Life of Connecticut*, p. 3.

51. Alan Heimert and Perry Miller, eds., *The Great Awakening: Documents Illustrating the Crisis and Its Consequences*, p. v.

52. Ibid., p. v.

53. Ibid., p. vi.

CHAPTER 3

1. John Adams' account of the case presented in court by James Otis is recorded in Schwartz, 2:189–91.

2. Charles S. Hyneman and Donald S. Lutz, *American Political Writing during the Founding Era, 1760–1805*, 1:6, 15.

3. Ibid., 1:38–44, 92–96, 110–159.

4. See Silas Downer's "Discourse at the Dedication of the Tree of Liberty" and Daniel Shute's sermon, ibid., 1:98–136.

5. Gad Hitchcock, in an election day sermon, ibid., 1:282–89.

6. Simeon Howard, "A Sermon Preached to the Ancient and Honorable Artillery Company in Boston," ibid., 1:185–208.

7. Some of the protests are recorded in Commager, pp. 71–78; and in Henry Steele Commager and Robert B. Morris, *The Spirit of 'Seventy Six: The Story of the American Revolution as Told by Participants*, pp. 17–37.

8. Commager and Morris, *Spirit of 'Seventy Six*, pp. 16–17.

9. *Letters*, 1:38. The official record of the first Congress, which was the only federal authority recognized by the colonies from 1774 to 1789, is contained in the *Journals of the Continental Congress*. For an understanding of the depth of personal feelings on the issues debated in Congress, a more revealing source is the Library of Congress documentary collection of *Letters*. As of June 1986, eleven volumes of this series had been published, covering the period 29 August 1774 to 31 January 1779.

10. *Letters*, 1:27–32.

11. Ibid., 2:23.

12. Ibid., 2:21. Zubly's emphasis.

13. Ibid., 1:575. The "disaffected people," known as the Regulators, had been in revolt since 1768.

14. Elizabeth I. Nybakken, ed., *The "Centinel": Warnings of a Revolution*. John Adams' letter to Jedidiah Morse, 2 December 1815, is quoted on unnumbered seventh page.

15. Arthur M. Schlesinger, Jr., *Prelude to Independence: The Newspaper War on Britain, 1764–1776*, pp. 12, 32. See also Silas Deane to Elizabeth Deane, 23 June 1775, *Letters*, 1:537.

16. Thomas Nelson to John Page, *Letters*, 3:249.

17. Schlesinger, *Prelude to Independence*, p. 11.

18. *Letters*, 1:318, 325n2.

19. A. James Reichley, *Religion in American Public Life*, p. 98.

20. Francis Lightfoot Lee to Landon Carter, 20 November 1775; Edward Rutledge to Thomas Bee, 25 November 1775; and Richard Smith's diary, 5 February 1776—all in *Letters*, 2:366, 390, 3:204.

21. Commager and Morris, *Spirit of 'Seventy Six*, p. 61.

22. Commager, p. 96.

23. John Adams to James Warren, 15 May 1776, *Letters*, 3:676-79. A copy of the resolution appears on p. 677.

24. The sequence of events leading to the Declaration of Independence can be found in Commager and Morris, *Spirit of 'Seventy Six*, ch. 8. The text of the Declaration is in Commager, pp. 100-02.

25. John Adams to his wife, Abigail, 19 March 1776, *Letters*, 3:389; David Freeman Hawke, *Paine*, p. 50.

26. Hyneman and Lutz, *American Political Writing*, 1:333.

27. John Adams to Mercy Warren, 16 April 1776, *Letters*, 3:538.

28. Poore, 2:1279-81.

29. Ibid., 2:1620-27.

30. Schwartz, 2:231-43.

31. James Madison, *The Papers of James Madison*, 8:298-304.

32. Thomas Jefferson, *The Papers of Thomas Jefferson*, 2:546.

33. Poore, 2:1313.

34. Schwartz, 2:344-54.

35. Ibid., 2:355-67.

36. Poore, 2:1413.

37. Anson Phelps Stokes, *Church and State in the United States*, 1:405.

38. Poore, 2:1338-39.

39. Ibid., 2:1594-1603.

CHAPTER 4

1. A record of the delegates chosen to attend each congress, and the days of their attendance, is included in the several volumes of *Letters*.

2. Jonathan Elliot, ed., *The Debates in the Several State Conventions on the Adoption of the Federal Constitution as Recommended by the General Convention at Philadelphia in 1787*, 1:55. This is one of two classic studies of the Constitutional Convention and the struggle for ratification. The other is Max Farrand, ed., *The Records of the Federal Convention of 1787*. A handy and reliable one-volume compilation of constitutional documents is Charles C. Transill's *Documents Illustrative of the Formation of the Union of the American States*. As explained above, these reference works are cited here as Elliot, Farrand, and *Documents*.

3. Copies of John Dickinson's and Josiah Bartlett's drafts of the Articles of Confederation are reproduced in *Letters*, 4:233-50.

4. Elliot, 1:74; *Documents*, pp. 27-37.

5. Article XIII, *Documents*, p. 35.

6. *Letters*, 4:234-35, 253n3.

7. Article III, *Documents*, p. 27.

8. The dates on which the several states signed the Articles are reported in *Documents*, pp. 36-37.

9. *Letters*, 4:290, 308, 311, 326-27.

10. Ibid., 4:419–20, 433–37.

11. Elliot, 1:106–15.

12. *Debates and Proceedings in the Convention of the Commonwealth of Massachusetts, Held in the Year 1788*, p. 155.

13. *Documents*, p. 38.

14. Ibid., pp. 39–43. James Madison later attested to Hamilton's authorship of this report; see James Madison, *The Papers of James Madison*, 9:127.

15. *Documents*, p. 46.

16. Farrand, 3:558n2.

17. For Madison's view of this refusal, see ibid., 3:547.

18. *Documents*, p. 67.

19. Farrand, 1:17.

20. Ibid., 1:10.

21. Views of these and other opponents of the Constitution are reported in Elliot, vol. 1; and Jackson Turner Main, *The Anti-Federalists: Critics of the Constitution, 1781–1788*.

22. Main contends, ibid., that pro-constitutionalists should have been called Nationalists, and opponents, Federalists.

23. At one point in the Virginia debates, the reporter summarized: "Here Mr. Henry strongly and pathetically expatiated on the probability of the President's enslaving America, and the horrid consequences that might result." Elliot, 3:60.

24. Farrand, 2:587–88.

25. *Documents*, pp. 1009–59.

26. *Massachusetts Debates*, pp. 279–80.

27. These papers have been republished many times. The volume used here is the Modern Library edition: Alexander Hamilton, John Jay, and James Madison, *The Federalist*.

28. Elliot, 3:281–83, 222.

29. Ibid., 3:22.

30. Madison, *Papers*, 11:12–13.

31. These letters are in Madison, *Papers*, 11:226, 231, 237, 254–55, 257. For a further analysis of this problem, see Wilbur Edel, *A Constitutional Convention: Threat or Challenge?* ch. 1–2; and Wilbur Edel, "James Madison on a Second Convention," U.S. Senate, Judiciary Subcommittee on the Constitution, *Hearings: Constitutional Convention Procedures*, pp. 90–99.

32. *Documents*, pp. 716, 726.

33. Ibid., p. 716.

34. Farrand, 2:334–35.

35. Ibid., 2:461.

36. Ibid., 3:78–79.

37. Ibid., 2:616.

38. For state certification dates, see *Documents*, pp. 1009–59.

39. Ibid., pp. 1018–20; Poore, 1:957.

40. *Massachusetts Debates*, pp. 190, 251.

41. Farrand, 3:227.

42. Elliot, 3:317, 330, 587.

43. *Documents*, 1027–34.

44. Ibid., pp. 1034–37.

45. Ibid., p. 1026; Poore, 2:1281.

46. *Documents*, p. 1021, italics added.

47. Elliot, 4:191–200, 208, 215.

48. Loc. cit.

49. *Documents*, pp. 1044–51.

50. Ibid., pp. 1052–65.

51. The problems of the first federal Congress, and Madison's part in initiating the first ten amendments to the Constitution, are described in Madison, *Papers*, 12:52–209.

CHAPTER 5

1. Geoffrey Barraclough, ed., *The Christian World: A Social and Cultural History*, p. 50.

2. *The Koran*, p. 376.

3. Ibid., p. 216.

4. James Walvin, *Slavery and the Slave Trade*, ch. 1.

5. Ibid., p. 9.

6. Elizabeth Donnan, *Documents Illustrative of the History of the Slave Trade to America*, 1:5.

7. Ibid., vol. 2.

8. Ibid., 1:346–51.

9. Walvin, *Slavery*, chapter 3.

10. Ibid., p. 35.

11. Robert Beverley, *The History and Present State of Virginia*, p. 48.

12. Donnan, *Slave Trade Documents*, 4:1–2; Willie Lee Rose, *A Documentary History of Slavery in North America*, p. 15.

13. Donnan, *Slave Trade Documents*, 3:1–4.

14. U.S. Department of Commerce, *Historical Statistics of the United States*, 2:1168.

15. Rosser H. Taylor, *Ante-Bellum South Carolina: A Social and Cultural History*, pp. 2–3.

16. Ibid., p. 7.

17. David M. Ellis, et al., *A Short History of New York State*, p. 62.

18. See Rose, *A Documentary History*, pp. 16–25, on the similarity of treatment accorded slaves and servants, black and white, in the early years of the English colonies.

19. Schwartz, 1:81.

20. Donnan, *Slave Trade Documents*, 3:25–27.

21. Ibid., 3:108.

22. Ibid., 4:21.

23. Ibid., 4:257.

24. Ibid., 4:592.

25. Abdel R. Wentz, *A Basic History of Lutheranism in America*, p. 162.

26. Anson Phelps Stokes, *Church and State in the United States*, 2:121.

27. Elbert Russell, *The History of Quakerism*, pp. 246–48.

28. Stokes, *Church and State*, 2:129; Russell, *History of Quakerism*, p. 203.

29. Charles S. Hyneman and Donald S. Lutz, *American Politcal Writing during the Founding Era, 1760–1805*, 1:183.

30. Ibid., 1:217–30.

31. Donnan, *Slave Trade Documents*, 3:289.

32. Hyneman and Lutz, *American Political Writing*, 1:305–17.

33. See Jefferson's lengthy digression in a section on "Laws" in his "Notes on the State of Virginia" written in 1781–82. Thomas Jefferson, *The Papers of Thomas Jefferson*, 7:207–221.

34. *Letters*, 4:359; Jefferson, *Papers*, vol. 6.

35. Poore, 1:277.

36. Ibid., 2:1859.

37. Stokes, *Church and State*, 2:129.

38. See Jefferson, *Papers*, 6:581–615, for background.

39. Elliot, 3:452–53.

40. Farrand, 1:486.

41. Ibid., 1:579–88.

42. U.S. Constitution, Art. 1, sec. 9, par. 1, in Poore.

43. Farrand, 2:221–22.

44. Ibid., 2:370.

45. Ibid., 3:210.

46. *Debates and Proceedings in the Convention of the Commonwealth of Massachusetts Held in the Year 1788*, 208, 217, 251.

47. Elliot, 3:454.

48. Ibid., 4:100, 272.

49. Ibid., 2:203–04.

50. Alexander Hamilton, John Jay, and James Madison, *The Federalist*, No. 42.

51. Hyneman and Lutz, *American Political Writing*, 2:723.

52. Commager, p. 197.

53. Ibid., p. 401.

54. Leonard D. White, *The Jacksonians*, p. 5.

55. H. C. Vedder, *A Short History of the Baptists*, p. 321.

56. H. E. Luccock and Paul Hutchinson, *The Story of Methodism*, p. 217.

57. Ibid., p. 327.

58. Loc. cit.

59. Ibid., pp. 327–31.

60. Ibid., pp. 352–55.

61. Donald Bruce Johnson, *National Party Platforms*, 1:3–9.

62. This televised speech to the black people of Cameroon was aired on 13 August 1985 by all major networks in the United States.

63. Thomas Bokenkotter, *A Concise History of the Catholic Church*.

64. Gaius Glenn Atkins and Frederick L. Fagley, *History of American Congregationalism*.

65. James T. Addison, *The Episcopal Church in the United States*, p. 192.

66. Ibid., pp. 194–95, 198–99.

67. Wentz, *Lutheranism in America*, pp. 161–67.

68. W. T. Hanzsche, *The Presbyterians*, pp. 104–13.

69. Vedder, *History of the Baptists*, pp. 346–47.

70. Garrison's views were circulated in his newspaper, *Liberator*, which he published from 1831 to 1865.

71. Addison, *U.S. Episcopal Church*, p. 191.

72. Taylor, *Ante-Bellum South Carolina*, p. 172.

73. Wentz, *Lutheranism in America*, p. 163.

74. Hanzsche, *Presbyterians*, p. 106.

75. Wentz, *Lutheranism in America*, p. 169.

76. Dr. Samuel Seabury, quoted in Addison, *U.S. Episcopal Church*, p. 194.

77. National Council of the Churches of Christ in the United States of America, *Yearbook of American and Canadian Churches, 1985*, pp. 229–35.

CHAPTER 6

1. Territory gained by the Louisiana Purchase of 1803, the Adams-Onis Treaty of 1819, accession of Texas in 1845, and the 1848 Treaty of Guadelupe-Hildago.

2. U.S. Department of Commerce, *Historical Statistics of the United States*, 1:11–12, 139. The figure for agricultural employment includes slaves.

3. Ibid., 1:139.

4. Ibid., 1:105–11.

5. Robert T. Hardy, ed., *Religion in the American Experience*, pp. 193–94.

6. Quotes are from Leonard D. White, *The Republican Era*, ch. 17.

7. Ibid., pp. 365–66.

8. Ibid., p. 379.

9. Quoted in Munn v. Illinois, 94 U.S. 113 (1877).

10. Gibbons v. Ogden, 9 Wheaton 1 (1824).

11. Brown v. Maryland, 12 Wheaton 419 (1827).

12. 3 Stat 587, quoted in Munn v. Illinois (see note 9).

13. Munn v. Illinois (see note 9).

14. The U.S. lost its first anti-trust case, U.S. v. E. C. Knight, 156 U.S. 1 (1895); but was upheld in Northern Securities v. U.S., 193 U.S. 197 (1904); Swift & Co. v. U.S., 196 U.S. 375 (1905); and Standard Oil Co. of N.J. v. U.S., 221 U.S. 1 (1911).

15. Hammer v. Dagenhart, 247 U.S. 251 (1918); and Duplex Printing Press Co. v. Deering, 254 U.S. 443 (1921).

16. Donald Bruce Johnson, *National Party Platforms*, 1:35.

17. For details, see Joseph B. James, *The Framing of the Fourteenth Amendment*.

18. Commager, 2:14.

19. For evidence of widespread opposition to the Fourteenth Amendment, see James, *Framing* and *The Ratification of the Fourteenth Amendment*.

20. James, *Ratification*, pp. 296–98.

21. James, *Framing*, p. 192.

22. San Mateo County v. Southern Pacific R.R., 116 U.S. 138 (1882).

23. Santa Clara County v. Southern Pacific R.R., 118 U.S. 394 (1886).

24. Howard J. Graham, "The Conspiracy Theory of the Fourteenth Amendment," 47 *Yale Law Journal* 371–403.

25. James, *Framing*, chap. 6.

26. Slaughterhouse Cases, 16 Wallace 36 (1873).

27. Edward S. Corwin, ed., *The Constitution of the United States of America: Analysis and Interpretation*, p. 974.

28. Mugler v. Kansas, 123 U.S. 623 (1887).

29. Ibid.

30. Muller v. Oregon, 208 U.S. 412 (1908). But as late as 1923, in Adkins v. Children's Hospital, 261 U.S. 525, the court declared a federal law establishing minimum wages for women in Washington, D.C., unconstitutional under the Fifth Amendment.

31. Lochner v. New York, 198 U.S. 45 (1905).

32. Adair v. United States, 208 U.S. 161 (1908).

33. G. G. Atkins and F. L. Fagley, *History of American Congregationalism*, pp. 252–53.

34. Ibid., pp. 253–56.

35. W. T. Hanzsche, *The Presbyterians*, p. 136.

36. James T. Addison, *The Episcopal Church in the United States*, pp. 280–81.

37. Ibid., pp. 286–87, 311, 322–23.

38. Hanzsche, *Presbyterians*, pp. 152–53.

39. H. C. Vedder, *A Short History of the Baptists*, p. 341.

40. H. E. Luccock and Paul Hutchinson, *The Story of Methodism*, pp. 466–69.

41. Edwin S. Gaustad, *A Documentary History of Religion in America since 1865*, pp. 121–22.

42. Winthrop S. Hudson, *Religion in America*, p. 246.

43. Thomas Bokenkotter, *A Concise History of the Catholic Church*, pp. 360–61.

44. Quoted material from articles in Gaustad, *Documentary History of Religion*: Sheldon, pp. 113–15; Huntington, pp. 115–16; Rauschenbusch, pp. 120–21; Gibbons, pp. 117–19; Ryan, pp. 132–34; rabbis, p. 123.

45. Leonard J. Arrington and Davis Bitton, *The Mormon Experience: A History of the Latter-Day Saints; The Book of Mormon*, 1921 ed., unnumbered pages headed "Origin of the Book of Mormon."

46. *Book of Mormon*, Jacob 2:24–29. These paragraphs proscribe polygamy in no uncertain terms.

47. Arrington and Bitton, *Mormon Experience*, pp. 70, 195, 199–200.

48. Samuel W. Taylor, *Rocky Mountain Empire: The Latter-Day Saints Today*.

49. Reynolds v. U.S., 98 U.S. 145 (1879).

50. Two brief paperbacks are Paul G. Kauper, *Religion and the Constitution*; and Richard C. McMillan, ed., *Education, Religion, and the Supreme Court*.

CHAPTER 7

1. See Chapter 3 for specifics.

2. Poore, 2:1430.

3. Ibid., 1:839.

4. Ibid., 1:278.

5. Ibid., 1:975.

6. Ibid., 1:276.

7. Ibid., 2:1543.

8. Ibid., 2:1313–14.

9. Barron v. Baltimore, 7 Peters 243 (1833).

10. Permoli v. New Orleans, 3 Howard 589.

11. Constitutions of states admitted to the Union prior to 1878 are in Poore. Those of states admitted later are published in *Constitutions of the United States, National and State.*

12. Poore, 1:101–02; 2:1672–74.

13. Chicago, B & Q.R. Co. v. Chicago, 166 U.S. 226 (1897).

14. Gitlow v. New York, 268 U.S. 652 (1925).

15. Near v. Minnesota, 283 U.S. 697 (1931).

16. DeJonge v. Oregon, 299 U.S. 353 (1937).

17. James A. Beckford, *The Trumpet of Prophecy: A Sociological Study of Jehovah's Witnesses.*

18. Details from Cantwell v. Connecticut, 310 U.S. 296 (1940).

19. Quotations are from Terminiello v. Chicago, 337 U.S. 1 (1949). Emphasis is Terminiello's.

20. Chaplinsky v. New Hampshire, 315 U.S. 568 (1942).

21. Feiner v. New York, 340 U.S. 315 (1951).

22. Kunz v. New York, 340 U.S. 290 (1951).

23. Davis v. Beason, 133 U.S. 333 (1890).

24. Schenck v. U.S., 249 U.S. 47 (1919).

25. Elbert Russell, *The History of Quakerism*, pp. 244–46.

26. United States v. Seeger, 380 U.S. 163 (1965).

27. Vietnam brought the question of "just war" to the court in Gillette v. United States, 401 U.S. 205 (1972).

28. Cummings v. Missouri, 4 Wallace 277 (1867).

29. Ex parte Garland, 4 Wallace 333 (1867).

30. Minersville School District v. Gobitis, 310 U.S. 586 (1940).

31. Dies Committee activities are reviewed in Arthur M. Schlesinger, Jr., and Roger Bruns, eds., *Congress Investigates, 1792–1974*, pp. 287–323.

32. West Virginia v. Barnette, 319 U.S. 624 (1943).

33. Walz v. Tax Commission of the City of New York, 397 U.S. 664 (1970).

34. Quoted in Anson Phelps Stokes, *Church and State in the United States*, 2:51.

35. Spiller v. Woburn, 12 Allen 127 (1866).

36. Quoted in Abington v. Schempp, 374 U.S. 203 (1963).

37. Pierce v. Society of the Sisters, 268 U.S. 510 (1925).

38. In Wisconsin v. Yoder, 406 U.S. 205 (1972), the court went further in upholding the Amish view that, for them, parental guidance was adequate after completion of the eighth grade.

39. Everson v. Board of Education, 330 U.S. 1 (1947).

40. Illinois ex rel. McCollum v. Board of Education, 333 U.S. 203 (1948).

41. Zorach v. Clauson, 343 U.S. 306 (1952).

42. NYT, 22 April 1986. At this writing the protest had not been calendared for court action.

43. Lemon v. Kurtzman, Early v. DiCenso, 403 U.S. 602 (1971).

CHAPTER 8

1. Proverbs 22:6.

2. *Documents*, p. 296.

3. Engel v. Vitale, 370 U.S. 421 (1962), Jefferson's reference to a wall of separation was cited by the court in Everson v. Board of Education, 330 U.S. (1947).

4. Abington Township v. Schempp, 374 U.S. 203 (1963).

5. WP, 27 September 1985. A parent's challenge of this practice has not yet reached the federal courts.

6. U.S. Congress, Congressional Research Service, "State Applications, January 1963 to April 3, 1973."

7. CR, vol. 119, index, p. 327.

8. Ibid., vol. 121, index, p. 303.

9. CR (daily), 28 January 1980, p. E138.

10. Ibid., 29 January 1980, p. 5539.

11. Ibid., pp. H295, H388, H2464.

12. WP, 30 July 1980.

13. Statement by Richard Viguerie in *MacNeil-Lehrer Report*, aired by PBS-TV on 6 May 1982, transcript no. 1724, p. 4.

14. CR, vol. 127, pp. S13399–13407.

15. Reported in WP, 20 March 1982.

16. Ibid., 25 May 1982; NYT, 7 October 1982.

17. NYT, 25 June 1982.

18. See *MacNeil-Lehrer Report* cited in note 13.

19. Richard Cohen, "Prayer," WP, 21 October 1982.

20. U.S. Congress, Public Law 97-280, 96 Stat. 1211, signed 4 October 1982.

21. NYT, 14 July 1982.

22. McLean v. Arkansas Board of Education, 529 F. Supp. 1255 (E.D. Ark. 1982).

23. Tim LaHaye, *The Battle for the Mind*.

24. See David Bollier, *Liberty & Justice for Some*.

25. Reported in WP, 10 May 1982.

26. For specific cases in 48 states see NYT, 21 January 1984.

27. Ibid., 15 September 1985.

28. Quoted in *Christian Science Monitor*, 17 July 1985.

29. Wayne Moyer, "Put Evolution Back in the Books," *U.S.A. Today*, 16 September 1985.

30. Board of Education, Island Trees School District No. 26 v. Pico, No. 80-2043 (slip opinion), decided 25 June 1982.

31. Excerpts from counsels' arguments reported in WP and NYT on 3 March 1982.

32. Emphasis by the court. The final sentence is from the Supreme Court's decision in West Virginia v. Barnette (1943).

33. Events reported in NYT, 15 and 21 February 1984; and Nat Hentoff's column, WP, 25 July 1984 and 11 January 1986.

34. James A. Speer, "The New Christian Right and Its Parent Company: A Study in Political Contrasts," in David G. Bromley and Anson Shupe, eds., *New Christian Politics*, pp. 33–34.

35. Quoted in "Jerry Falwell's Crusade," *Time*, 2 September 1985, p. 49.

36. WP, 19 October 1985.

37. LaHaye, *Battle for the Mind*, ch. 4.

38. Ibid., ch. 8, p. 142.

39. Ibid., p. 211.

40. Ibid., ch. 13 and appendix A.

41. WP, 26 September 1984.

42. NYT, 10, 11, and 13 October 1980.

43. Ibid., 21 August 1985.

44. Quoted from a variety of sources in full-page advertisement, People for the American Way, "The Gospel According to Four Religious Leaders," NYT, 10 May 1982.

45. NYT, 12 November 1985; aired on Philippine government TV.

46. WP, 2 June 1986; *Newsweek*, 30 June 1986, p. 70.

47. Edwin S. Gaustad, *A Documentary History of Religion in America since 1865*, p. 540.

48. Ibid., p. 541.

49. WP, 2 November 1985.

50. Losers were Democrats Frank Church, Birch Bayh, John Culver, John Durkin, George McGovern, and Gaylord Nelson; winners were Alan Cranston, Gary Hart, and Thomas Eagleton. For evangelical strength, see A. J. Reichley, "Religion and the Future of American Politics," *Political Science Quarterly*, 1986, pp. 26–27.

CHAPTER 9

1. Ronald Reagan, *Ronald Reagan Talks to America*, pp. 3–18.

2. WTROM, pp. 9–10.

3. Ibid., p. 15.

4. David R. Shepherd, ed., *Ronald Reagan: In God I Trust*, p. 14.

5. Lou Cannon, *Reagan*, p. 25; WTROM, p. 23.

6. Shepherd, *In God I Trust*, pp. 6, 15; televised debate of 9 October 1984.

7. Anson Phelps Stokes, *Church and State in the United States*, 1:767.

8. WTROM, p. 10.

9. Loc. cit.

10. Ibid., pp. 8–9, 64.

11. Ibid., pp. 138–39, 141.

12. Cannon, *Reagan*, p. 79.

13. Ronnie Duggan, *On Reagan: The Man and His Presidency*, pp. 11–12.

14. Ibid., p. 13. Cannon, *Reagan*, p. 96.

15. Cannon, *Reagan*, p. 97.

16. Ibid., p. 94.

17. Holmes Tuttle, quoted in Duggan, *On Reagan*, p. 15.

18. WTROM, pp. 200–01.

19. Reagan's association with the FBI was revealed in documents secured by the San Jose *Mercury News* under the Freedom of Information Act and published 25 August 1985.

20. WTROM, pp. 257, 259, 266.

21. Ibid., pp. 297–98.

22. Reagan's letter was discovered in the Nixon papers and released by Walter Mondale, NYT, 24 October 1984.

23. Interview with Ben Wattenberg, the substance of which was reported in NYT 23 December 1981. For Ickes' views on communism, see Harold L. Ickes, *The Secret Diaries of Harold L. Ickes*, 2:349, 428, 492–93, 683–85.

24. Reagan, *Talks*, p. 15.

25. NYT, 16 October 1971.

26. Veterans Day speech, 11 November 1968, Reagan, *Talks*, p. 123.

27. Statement to *Wall Street Journal* reporter, quoted in Hedrick Smith, *Reagan, the Man, the President*, p. 100.

28. Message to Congress, 17 May 1982; meeting 13 October with Christian organization leaders.

29. Farrand, 1:450–52.

30. WP, 5 November 1984, by the Arthur S. DeMoss Foundation.

31. Speech accepting the Republican nomination, 17 July 1980.

32. Stephen E. Ambrose, *Eisenhower*, 2:291; WCPD, vol. 20, p. 1748.

33. Richard B. Morris, ed., *The Early Republic*, pp. 51–52.

34. Winton U. Solberg, *Redeem the Time: The Puritan Sabbath in Early America*, pp. 114, 169.

35. Shepherd, *In God I Trust*, p. 18; WCPD, vol. 21, p. 213.

36. Speeches at Dallas church gathering, 22 August 1980.

37. Shepherd, *In God I Trust*, pp. 40–44.

38. Remarks at White House ceremony, 7 May 1982.

39. Political commercial televised nationwide on 31 October 1982.

40. Acceptance speech, 17 July 1980.

41. Speech to Baptist Fundamentalism '84 Convention, 13 April 1984; to similar groups on 31 January, 9 March, and 13 October 1983 and 7 March 1984.

42. NYT, 28 September 1984.

43. Ibid., 19 August 1984.

44. Ibid., 17 September 1984.

45. WP, 14 July 1984.

46. Statement released to the press on 14 October 1984.

47. Released on 12 November 1984.

48. Report excerpted in NYT, 8 November 1984.

49. Ibid., 29 October 1984.

50. WCPD, 2 September 1984, vol. 20, p. 1212.

51. Ibid., vol. 20, p. 1161.

52. Reported by Anthony Lewis, NYT, 8 October 1984.

53. Quoted by Anthony Podesta in Cleveland *Plain Dealer*, 26 July 1984.

54. NYT, 21 January 1985.

55. WCPD, vol. 20, p. 980. For a more accurate report of Winthrop's statement and purpose, see Martin E. Marty, *Pilgrims in Their Own Land: 500 Years of Religion in America*, p. 63.

56. NYT, 8 August, 12 November 1985.

57. WCPD, vol. 21 (21 October 1985), p. 1278.

58. Compare opinions of Laurence H. Tribe and Patrick McGuigan, NYT, 22 October 1985, and *Time*, 4 November 1985, p. 77.

59. NYT, 19 November 1985.

60. Text of speech given 9 July 1985, supplied by Justice Department's public affairs director, Terry Eastland.

61. Members of the conservative majority that decided the case of Gitlow v. New York (1925), to which Meese referred.

62. Joseph B. James, *The Framing of the Fourteenth Amendment*, pp. 137, 185–86.

63. Address to Federal Bar Association, 23 October 1985.

64. Ronald Brownstein and Nina Easton, *Reagan's Ruling Class*, p. 643; WP, 26 August 1985.

65. Quoted in Los Angeles *Times*, 28 August 1985.

66. WP, 30 August 1985.

CHAPTER 10

1. Robert Browder, *The Origins of Soviet–American Diplomacy.*

2. Address to joint session of Congress, 20 February 1985.

3. Laurence Beilenson, *The Treaty Trap*, cited by President Reagan in address at West Point, 28 May 1981.

4. See, for example, WCPD, vol. 20, p. 815, and index to Soviet noncompliance re evidence that remains classified, in report to Congress, 23 January 1984. For other CIA–White House disputes, see NYT 6 April, 29 May, and 16 July 1986.

5. WCPD, vol. 20, pp. 1262, 1859.

6. Ibid., vol. 20, pp. 804–08, 1922.

7. Joint U.S.-Soviet statement, WCPD, vol. 21, pp. 1422–24.

8. Ibid., pp. 1426–29.

9. Ibid., vol. 21, p. 1398.

10. Edith Hamilton, quoted in *Washington Spectator*, 15 January 1985.

11. Released to the U.S. press on 3 September 1984.

12. NYT, 28 October 1984.

13. WP, 18 March 1985.

14. An excellent summary of U.S.–Vatican relations from 1797 to World War II is included in Anson Phelps Stokes, *Church and State in the United States*, vol. 2, ch. 14.

15. Franklin D. Roosevelt, *The Public Papers and Addresses of Franklin D. Roosevelt*, 1939 vol., pp. 606–08.

16. Ibid., 1940 vol., pp. 101–02. For reactions of U.S. churches, see Stokes, *Church and State*, 2:96–105.

17. CR (daily), 7 March 1984, pp. S2384–85; Congressional Research Service Report No. 84-104 GOV, pp. 37–38.

18. WCPD, vol. 21, pp. 417 and 458; WP, Los Angeles *Times*, 19 April 1985.

19. WCPD, vol. 20, p. 638.

20. PL 98-164, sec. 134; House Reports No. 98-130 and 98-563.

21. Cited in U.S. Senate Committee on Foreign Relations, Hearing 98-586 (1984), *Nomination of William A. Wilson*, p. 30.

22. H.R.Res. 315, CR (daily), 30 June 1983, p. H4893; S.1757, CR (daily), 3 August 1983, p. S11444, and 7 March 1984, p. S2390.

23. Reported in the press on 21 May 1986. No reference in WCPD.

24. Undated letter circulated by Reverend John Collins in July 1985.

25. For development of text and comment, see NYT 31 October 1981, 26 October 1982, and 5 May 1983.

26. WP, 1 February 1986.

27. From January to June 1982, 21 arms control resolutions were filed in the House, 13 in the Senate. House Report 97-640; Senate Report 97-483.

28. WP, 11 August 1983.

29. "Church and Bomb," *The Economist*, 5 February 1983, p. 19.

30. NYT, 7 July 1983; WCPD, vol. 20, p. 1350.

31. News conferences, 13 August 1981 and 11 November 1982.

32. Peace Pac, "1982 Election Report"; NYT, 3 November 1982; *Public Administration Times*, 1 December 1982.

33. U.S. Department of State, "Safeguarding Human Rights," Current Policy No. 775, December 1985.

34. Jeane Kirkpatrick, "Dictatorships and Double Standards," *Commentary*, November 1979, pp. 34–45.

35. Message to Congress, 14 March 1986, WCPD, vol. 22, p. 359. For Motley's statement, see WP, 23 April 1985.

36. WP, 18 May 1985.

37. WP, 25 October 1985 and 2 May 1986; NYT, 14 December 1985 and 30 March 1986, letters to ed. 29 December 1985 and 14 Jan. 1986.

38. WP, 27 February 1982.

39. Speech by Under Secretary of State Laurence S. Eagleburger, 23 June 1983, reported in the press the following day.

40. Only the United States and the United Kingdom abstained in Security Council votes on 17 August and 23 October 1984; NYT, 18 August 1984; WP, 1 November 1984.

41. WP, 25 May 1985; no mention in WCPD.

42. Eagleburger speech cited in note 39; Reagan interview 27 November 1984, WCPD, vol. 20, p. 1851.

43. WCPD, vol. 20, p. 1909.

44. NYT, 23 November 1985.

45. Savimbi also met with the secretaries of state and defense; NYT, 30 and 31 January 1986.

46. Ibid., 20 August 1985.

47. WP, 1 November 1984.

48. News conference, 7 December 1984, WCPD, vol. 20, pp. 1879–84; NYT, 8 December and 14 December 1984.

49. NYT, 12 July and 2 August 1985.

50. WCPD, vol. 21, pp. 1048–51; Executive Order pp. 1051–54.

51. NYT, 7 December 1985; WP, 14 January 1986.

52. Developments in this tumultuous period were reported daily in the press from January through July 1986. For specifics: WP, 14 January, 13 and 14 June, 12 July, and 30 September; NYT, 19 and 24 April, 20 and 31 May, 17, 20, and 27 June, 21 July, and 5 and 6 August, 3 October.

53. WP, 4 July 1981.

54. WCPD, vol. 18, pp. 1157–58.

55. Not published in WCPD but reported in NYT 5 October 1983.

56. NYT, 24 October 1984 and 24 January, 3 May, and 3 December 1985.

57. Ibid., 3 December 1985.

58. See contrasting views in op-ed articles, WP, 16 December 1985 and 14 January 1986.

59. WP, 29 January 1986.

60. NYT, 20 January 1986.

61. Jeane Kirkpatrick, "The Magellan Syndrome in Manila," New York *Daily News*, 9 February 1986.

62. NYT, 20 January; WP, 10 and 11 February; AP radio network news, 13 February 1986.

63. WCPD, vol. 22, p. 111.

64. Ibid., p. 214.

65. NYT, 12 and 13 February 1986: House Committee on Foreign Affairs, Subcommittee on Asian and Pacific Affairs, *Hearings and Markup: The Philippine Election and the Implications for U.S. Policy*, 19 February 1986, p. 7.

66. NYT, 14 February 1986, reported protest of Senators Lugar, Dole, Nunn, and Hart. Daily reports followed with details of Marcos' downfall and flight to Hawaii.

CHAPTER 11

1. From the 1848 *Communist Manifesto* of Karl Marx.

2. Eisenhower's title for his history of the war in Europe.

3. Robert J. Donovan's biography, *The Presidency of Harry S. Truman, 1949–1953*, reveals nothing of Truman's views on India's revolt. For Eisenhower's reaction, see Stephen E. Ambrose, *Eisenhower*, 2:209–20, 380.

4. NYT, 7 June 1984.

5. United Nations, *Yearbook of the United Nations 1946–47*, pp. 327–36.

6. Kermit Roosevelt, *Countercoup: The Struggle for the Control of Iran*, pp. 107–23, ch. 10–12.

7. Ibid., p. 71. Roosevelt's emphasis.

8. Reported in *Washington Spectator*, 1 September 1985. Inquiry revealed Barry Stevens as the ex-CIA agent who filed this report.

9. Leonard Bushkoff, "Intelligence Memoirs and Scandalous Occasions," *Foreign Intelligence Literary Scene*, October 1984, p. 7.

10. Central Intelligence Agency, *Issues in the Middle East* (1973).

11. Ambrose, *Eisenhower*, 2:315–16.

12. Ibid., ch. 15.

13. Ibid., 2:382.

14. Ibid., 2:462–75. The United Arab Republic was dissolved in 1971.

15. For an analysis of modern Middle East problems, see Arthur Goldschmidt, Jr., *A Concise History of the Middle East*, ch. 12–21.

16. Seth P. Tillman, *The United States in the Middle East*, ch. 1.

17. Daniel Pipes, "Fundamentalist Muslims between America and Russia," *Foreign Affairs*, Summer 1986, pp. 939–59.

18. Don Peretz, "Israel Confronts Old Problems," *Current History*, January 1985; Fouad Ajami, et al., "Prophets of the Holy Land," *Harper's*, December 1984; Gershom Schocken, "Israel in Election Year 1984," *Foreign Affairs*, Fall 1984; Janet Aviad, "Israel: New Fanatics and Old," *Dissent*, Summer 1984.

19. See op-ed article by Meir Kahane, NYT, 20 December 1985; and news report, WP, 25 October 1982.

20. Schocken, "Israel in 1984"; NYT, 23 July 1985; WP, 23 October 1985 and 14 March 1986.

21. NYT 22, 25, and 26 July 1986; WP, 12 June 1986.

22. R. K. Ramazani, "Iran's Islamic Revolution and the Persian Gulf," *Current History*, January 1985, p. 6.

23. Shahrough Akhavi testimony in U.S. House Foreign Affairs Subcommittee on Europe and the Middle East, *Hearings: Islamic Fundamentalism and Islamic Radicalism* (1985), p. 132.

24. Ramazani, "Iran's Islamic Revolution," p. 7.

25. Augustus Norton, "Political and Religious Extremism in the Middle East," in U.S. House, *Hearings: Islamic Fundmantalism*, appendix 9.

26. NYT, 19, 25 March 1986.

27. For White House reports on the Gulf of Sidra incident, see WCPD, vol. 22, pp. 412, 413, 418, 423.

28. *World Press Review*, May 1986, p. 16, June 1986, pp. 21–26.

29. NYT, 27 March 1986.

30. U.S. Arms Control and Disarmament Agency, *Arms Control and Disarmament Agreements*, 1982 ed., pp. 82–98.

31. Ibid., p. 89.

32. U.S. Senate Governmental Affairs Subcommittee on Energy, Nuclear Proliferation, and Government Process, *Hearings: Nuclear Proliferation Policy and the Implications of New Technology* (1981), pp. 4, 5, 28, 35, 36.

33. WP, 12 June 1982.

34. Ibid., 15 September 1982. The 1985–86 edition of Office of the Federal Register, *United States Government Manual* showed Malone back in charge of nuclear affairs.

35. Richard T. Kennedy, "Nuclear Nonproliferation: Our Shared Responsibility," State Department Current Policy No. 446, 25 January 1983.

36. WP, 18 and 23 March 1983; General Accounting Office report cited in *Critical Mass Bulletin*, December 1983, p. 4.

37. NYT, 19 September and 3 December 1982; WCPD, vol. 21, p. 1506.

38. United Nations Association of the United States of America, *Nuclear Proliferation: Toward Global Restraint*, printed in U.S. Senate, *Hearing: United Nations Association Report on Nuclear Proliferation*, 27 June 1984, p. 47.

39. Ibid., p. 7.

40. George P. Shultz, "Preventing the Proliferation of Nuclear Weapons," State Department Current Policy No. 631, 1 November 1984.

41. See Leslie Gelb's report in NYT, 16 July 1984.

42. CR (daily), 5 September 1984, p. S10755.

43. Democratic platform, ibid., p. S10695.

44. WCPD, vol. 21, pp. 1422–26, esp. p. 1423.

45. Executive Order 12532, 9 September 1985, WCPD, vol. 21, pp. 1051–54.

46. WCPD, vol. 21, pp. 35 (9 January), 1051–52 (9 September 1985).

47. Ibid., vol. 20, p. 1059.

48. Ibid., vol. 21, p. 963.

49. Donovan, *Presidency of Truman*, 2:307-10; Ambrose, *Eisenhower*, 2:205-06, 397; Arthur M. Schlesinger, Jr., *A Thousand Days*, pp. 306-13, 802; NYT, 2 September 1986; interview with Richard Nixon, *Time*, 22 April 1985, pp. 14-15.

50. Iran-Israeli negotiations were unknown in United States until revealed by the Khomeini government to the U.S. press on 1 April 1986. To date, no contract with the German firm has been announced.

51. The Israeli raid of 7 June 1981 was "strongly condemned" on June 19 by a unanimous vote of the UN Security Council.

52. David Krieger, "What Happens If...? Terrorists, Revolutionaries and Nuclear Weapons," *Annals of the American Academy of Political and Social Science*, March 1977.

53. Daniel Frei and Christian Catrina, *Risks of Unintentional Nuclear War*, pp. 155-59.

54. Paul Bracken, *The Command and Control of Nuclear Forces*.

CHAPTER 12

1. Gettysburg Address, Commager, pp. 428-29.

2. Prayer breakfast, 3 Feb. 1983, David R. Shepherd, ed., *Ronald Reagan: In God I Trust*, p. 84.

3. Ibid., p. 139 address to the Conservative Political Action Conference (CPAC).

4. Amnesty International, *Political Killings by Governments*, p. 34. Also cited: Argentina, Guatemala, India, Libya, Uganda.

5. Radio broadcast, 26 April 1986, WCPD, vol. 22, pp. 551-52. The newly freed Philippines was bypassed on this tour.

6. Amnesty International, *Torture in the Eighties*, p. 4.

7. For overview of global population changes, see Colin McEvedy and Richard Jones, *Atlas of World Population History*.

8. A formal instruction entitled "Instruction on Christian Freedom and Liberation" appeared in NYT 6 April 1986.

9. Loc. cit.

10. "The Pope and the Poor Nations," WP, 22 September 1984.

11. See congratulatory message from the national chairman of the Anti-Defamation League of B'nai B'rith, WCPD, vol. 22, p. 312.

12. Quote from WCPD, vol. 22, p. 328. For evidence to the contrary, see: Americas Watch, *Human Rights in Nicaragua, 1985-1986*, pp. 10-13, 111-121; Amnesty International, *Nicaragua: The Human Rights Record*, pp. 5, 25, 32-35; *Oxfam America News*, Spring 1986, p. 3; NYT, 10 April, 8 July, and 19 July 1986; WP, 1, 5, and 29 July 1986.

13. News Conference, 9 April 1986, WCPD, vol. 22, p. 465.

14. James Reston, "Politics and the Press," New York *Times*, 9 April 1986.

15. WP, 20 October 1986; WCPD, vol. 22, pp. 1322-23; "A Bodyguard of Lies," *Newsweek*, 13 October 1986, pp. 43-46.

16. NYT, 9 October 1986.

17. NYT, 5, 7, 11, 15, 17 November 1986; president's televised address to the nation, 13 November 1986; ABC-TV evening news broadcast, 13 November 1986; WP, 18 November 1986; "The U.S. and Iran: The story behind Reagan's Dealings with the Mullahs," *Time*, 17 November 1986, pp. 12-26.

18. Message to Congress, 14 March 1986, WCPD, vol. 22, p. 357.

19. A list of foreign military engagements by U.S. forces, from 1798 to 1975, was compiled by the U.S. Congress, Congressional Research Service and published as *Background Information on the Use of U.S. Armed Forces in Foreign Countries.*

20. See ibid., for legal justification of each mission.

21. The Tonkin Gulf Resolution, based on the Southeast Asia Collective Defense Treaty of 1954, became law PL 88–408, 78 Stat. 384 on 10 August 1964.

22. The Tonkin Gulf Resolution, was repealed in 1972.

23. PL 93–148, 87 Stat. 555, passed over President Nixon's veto on 7 November 1973.

24. NYT, 15 October 1984. Moynihan later reconsidered this action, but has since abandoned his membership in the committee.

25. See Buckley's columns in New York *Daily News* on 7 February 1982; and WP, 18 August 1983, 18 April 1984, and 25 March 1986. Reagan's praise for Buckley was circulated with a 1983 letter soliciting subscriptions to the *National Review.*

26. For declaration of national emergency on Nicaragua, see WCPD, vol. 21, pp. 566–67; on Libya, vol. 22, pp. 21–22.

27. Lugar's protest was aired on 14 April 1986 by ABC-TV news. WP reported Botha's statement and U.S. response, 21 May 1986.

28. *Newsweek*, 10 February 1986, p. 45.

29. Jeane Kirkpatrick, "Our Cuban Misadventures," and "A Loud Voice but No Stick," WP, 29 January and 21 April 1986.

30. "Horses, Dark and Otherwise," *National Review*, 31 January 1986.

31. WP, 12 April 1986; *Newsweek*, 21 April 1986, p. 10.

32. NYT, 17 March 1986; WP, 4 and 12 April 1986.

33. WP, 20 December 1985.

34. Gary Hart, with William S. Lind, *America Can Win: The Case for Military Reform.*

35. NYT, 23 April 1986.

36. WP, 10 January 1986; Richard D. Kovar, "Sometimes, Assassination Is the Right Way," WP, 26 April 1986.

37. LaRouche's political history was reviewed by Patricia Lynch, "Is Lyndon LaRouche Using Your Name?" *Columbia Journalism Review*, April 1985, pp. 42–46.

38. NYT, 20 March 1986.

39. Ibid., 23 March 1986.

40. CR (daily), 17 April 1986, pp. H1975–82.

41. Ibid., H1976.

42. Ibid., H1981–82.

43. CR (daily), 17 April 1986, pp. S4423 and H1131.

44. For the text of the act, see ibid., p. S4425.

45. Remarks made during 1984 visit to Ireland, WCPD, vol. 20, p. 813.

46. Russell B. Long in U.S. Senate, 14 April 1986, CR (daily), p. S4192.

47. Address to the Irish parliament, WCPD, vol. 20 (1984), p. 835.

48. WP, 20 May 1986.

49. NYT, 25 May 1986.

50. Ibid., 19 November 1985; Patrick B. McGuigan, "Judge Robert Bork is a Friend of the Constitution," *Conservative Digest*, October 1985, pp. 91–102.

51. *Student Lawyer*, February 1986.

52. Los Angeles *Times*, 25 December 1985; Senate Judiciary Committee, *Confirmation Hearings on Federal Appointments* (1985), Serial No. J-99-7, pp. 89–100.

53. Senate Judiciary Committee, *Nomination of David A. Manion*, Exec. Rpt. 99-16 (1986).

54. William Safire, "Free Speech v. Scalia," NYT, 29 April 1985. For Scalia's opinions on affirmative action, abortion, and freedom of the press, see NYT, 19 June 1986.

55. Ibid., 1 June 1986.

56. Ibid., 24 July 1986.

57. A Gallup poll reported in NYT on 15 June 1986 showed the president's general approval rate at an all-time high of 68 percent.

58. NYT, 24 July 1986.

59. Speech to Knights of Columbus, WCPD, vol. 22, p. 1049.

60. A nationwide survey reported in WP on 26 July 1986 indicated that only white fundamentalists would vote for an avowed evangelical candidate. Most other voters would resent the association of a candidate's religion with his campaign.

61. Carlton J. H. Hayes, *A Political and Cultural History of Modern Europe*, 1:207.

Bibliography

GOVERNMENT DOCUMENTS AND PUBLICATIONS

Central Intelligence Agency. *Issues in the Middle East.* Washington, D.C.: Government Printing Office, 1973.

Coakley, Robert W., and Stetson Conn. *The War of the American Revolution.* Washington, D.C.: Government Printing Office, 1975.

Corwin, Edward S., ed. *The Constitution of the United States of America: Analysis and Interpretation.* Washington, D.C.: Government Printing Office, 1953.

Edel, Wilbur. "James Madison on a Second Convention." U.S. Senate, Committee on the Judiciary, Subcommittee on the Constitution. *Hearings: Constitutional Convention Procedures.* 98th Cong., 2d sess., 25 April 1984, pp. 90–99.

Kennedy, Richard T. "Nuclear Nonproliferation; Our Shared Responsibility." Department of State Current Policy No. 446, 25 January 1983.

Library of Congress. *Letters of Delegates to Congress, 1774–1789.* Edited by Paul H. Smith. 11 vols. (29 August 1774–31 January 1779). Washington, D.C.: Government Printing Office, 1976–85.

Norton, Augustus. "Political and Religious Extremism in the Middle East." House Committee on Foreign Affairs. *Hearings: Islamic Fundamentalism and Islamic Radicalism.* Appendix 9. 99th Cong., Ist sess., 1985.

Office of the Federal Register. *United States Government Manual, 1985–86.* Washington, D.C.: Government Printing Office.

_____. *U.S. Statutes at Large.* Washington, D.C.: Government Printing Office, 1973–1983.

_____. *Weekly Compilation of Presidential Documents.* Washington, D.C.: Government Printing Office.

Poore, Ben Perley. *The Federal and State Constitutions, Colonial Charters, and Other Organic Laws of the United States.* 2 vols. Washington, D.C.: Government Printing Office, 1878.

Shultz, George P. "Preventing the Proliferation of Nuclear Weapons." Department of State Current Policy No. 631. 1 November 1984.

Transill, Charles C., ed. *Documents Illustrative of the Formation of the Union of the American States*. Washington, D.C.: Government Printing Office, 1927.

U.S. Arms Control and Disarmament Agency. *Arms Control and Disarmament Agreements*. 1982 ed. Washington, D.C.: Government Printing Office, 1982.

U.S. Congress. Congressional Research Service. "State Applications, January, 1963 to April 3, 1973."

————. *Background Information on the Use of Armed Forces in Foreign Countries*. Washington D.C.: Government Printing Office, 1975.

————. Public Law 97-280, 96 Stat. 1211. Signed by President Reagan on 4 October 1982.

————. *Congressional Record*.

U.S. Department of Commerce. *Historical Statistics of the United States*. 2 vols. Washington, D.C.: Government Printing Office, 1975.

U.S. Department of State. "Safeguarding Human Rights." Current Policy No. 775, December 1985.

U.S. House of Representatives. Armed Services Committee. House Report No. 97–640, 1981.

————. Committee on Foreign Affairs. Reports No. 98–130 and 98–563, 1983.

————. Committee on Foreign Affairs, Subcommittee on Asian and Pacific Affairs. *Hearings and Markup: The Philippine Election and the Implications for U.S. Policy*. 19 February 1986.

U.S. House of Representatives. Committee on Foreign Affairs, Subcommittee on Europe and the Middle East. *Hearings: Islamic Fundamentalism and Islamic Radicalism*. 99th Cong., Ist sess., 1985.

U.S. Senate. Armed Services Committee. Senate Report No. 97–483, 1981. Committee on Foreign Relations. *Hearings: Nomination of William A. Wilson*. 98th Cong., 2d sess., 1984.

_____. Committee on Governmental Affairs, Subcommittee on Energy, Nuclear Proliferation, and Government Process. *Hearing: United Nations Association Report on Nuclear Proliferation* (98-909). 98th Cong., 2d sess., 27 June 1984.

_____. *Hearings: Nuclear Proliferation Policy and the Implications of New Technology.* 97th Cong., 1st sess., 1981.

_____. Judiciary Committee. *Confirmation Hearings on Federal Appointments.* Serial No. J-99-7, 1985, pp. 89–100.

_____. *Nomination of David A. Manion.* Exec. Rpt. 99–16, 1986.

_____. Select Committee to Study Governmental Operations. *Alleged Assassination Plots Involving Foreign Leaders.* 94th Cong., 1st sess., 1975.

_____. *Final Report of the Select Committee to Study Government Operations with Respect to Intelligence Activities.* 6 vols. 94th Cong., 2d sess., 1976.

U.S. Supreme Court. *United States Reports.* Washington, D.C.: Government Printing Office, 1985.

Whittier, Charles H. "Religion and Public Policy: Background and Issues in the 80's." Congressional Research Service Report No. 84–104 GOV. 17 October 1984.

PERIODICALS

Christian Science Monitor.
Cleveland *Plain Dealer.*
The Economist.
Los Angeles *Times.*
National Review.
New York *Times.*
Newsweek.
San Jose *Mercury News.*
Student Lawyer.
Washington *Post.*
Washington Spectator.
World Press Review.

(See also the individual by-lines below.)

TV

PBS. *MacNeil-Lehrer Report*. Transcript no. 1724, 6 May 1982.

GENERAL

Addison, James Thayer. *The Episcopal Church in the United States, 1789–1931*. New York: Scribner's, 1951.

Ajami, Fouad. "Prophets of the Holy Land." *Harper's*, December 1984, p. 34.

Albright, R. S. *A History of the Protestant Episcopal Church*. New York: Macmillan, 1964.

Alexander, Yonah, and Allan Nanes, eds. *The United States and Iran: A Documentary History*. Frederick, Md.: University Publications of America, 1980.

Ambrose, Stephen E. *Eisenhower*. 2 vols. New York: Simon and Schuster, 1983.

America's Watch. *Human Rights in Nicaragua 1985–1986*. New York: America's Watch Committee, 1986.

Amnesty International. *Nicaragua: The Human Rights Record*. London: Amnesty International Publications, 1986.

———. *Political Killings by Governments*. London: Amnesty International, 1983.

———. *Torture in the Eighties*. London: Amnesty International, 1984.

Andrews, Matthew Page. *History of Maryland: Province and State*. Garden City, N.Y.: Doubleday, Doran, 1929.

Arrington, Leonard J., and Davis Bitton. *The Mormon Experience: A History of the Latter-Day Saints*. New York: Knopf, 1979.

Atkins, Gaius Glenn, and Frederick L. Fagley. *History of American Congregationalism*. Boston: Pilgrim Press, 1942.

Aviad, Janet. "Israel: New Fanatics and Old." *Dissent*, Summer 1984.

Bailyn, Bernard, and John B. Hench, eds. *The Press and the American Revolution*. Boston: Northeastern University Press, 1981.

Barraclough, Geoffrey, ed. *The Christian World: A Social and Cultural History*. New York: Harry N. Abrams, 1981.

Beckford, James A. *The Trumpet of Prophecy: A Sociological Study of Jehovah's Witnesses*. New York: John Wiley, 1975.

Beilenson, Laurence. *The Treaty Trap*. Washington: Public Affairs Press, 1969.

Beverley, Robert. *The History and Present State of Virginia*. Chapel Hill, N.C.: University of North Carolina Press, 1947.

Bible. King James version. New York: American Bible Society, 1916.

Bokenkotter, Thomas. *A Concise History of the Catholic Church*. Garden City, N.Y.: Doubleday, 1977.

Bollier, David. *Liberty & Justice for Some*. New York: Frederick Ungar, 1982.

Book of Mormon, The. Salt Lake City: The Church of Jesus Chirst of the Latter-Day Saints, 1921 edition.

Bracken, Paul. *The Command and Control of Nuclear Forces*. New Haven: Conn.: Yale University Press, 1983.

Bridenbaugh, Carl. *Fat Mutton and Liberty of Conscience: Society in Rhode Island, 1636–1690*. Providence, R.I.: Brown University Press, 1974.

Bromley, David G., and Anson Shupe, eds. *New Christian Politics*. Macon, Ga.: Mercer University Press, 1984.

Browder, Robert Paul. *The Origins of Soviet-American Diplomacy*. Princeton, N.J.: Princeton University Press, 1953.

Browne, Lewis. *This Believing World*. New York: Macmillan, 1926.

Brownstein, Ronald, and Nina Easton. *Reagan's Ruling Class*. Washington, D.C.: Presidential Accountability Group, 1982.

Burnett, Edmund Cody. *The Continental Congress*. Westport, Conn.: Greenwood Press, 1975.

Bushkoff, Leonard. "Intelligence Memoirs and Scandalous Occasions." *Foreign Intelligence Literary Scene*, October 1984, p. 7.

Cannon, Lou. *Reagan*. New York: G. P. Putnam's Sons, 1982.

Chandler, Ralph Clark. "The Wicked Shall Not Bear Rule: The Fundamentalist Heritage of the New Christian Right." In David G. Bromley and Anson Shupe, eds. *New Christian Politics*. Macon, Ga.: Mercer University Press, 1984.

Cohen, Richard. "Prayer." Washington *Post*, 21 October 1982.

Commager, Henry Steele. *Documents of American History*. 2nd ed. New York: F. S. Crofts, 1940.

Commager, Henry Steele, and Richard B. Morris. *The Spirit of 'Seventy-Six: The Story of the American Revolution as Told by Participants*. New York: Harper & Row, 1975.

Constitutions of the United States, National and State. 7 vols. Dobbs Ferry, N.Y.: Oceania Publications, 1978–79.

Cornell, William Mason. *The History of Pennsylvania from the Earliest Discovery to the Present Time*. Philadelphia: Quaker City Publishing House, 1876.

Coward, Barry. *The Stuart Age: A History of England, 1603–1714*. New York: Longman, 1980.

Daniell, Jere R. *Colonial New Hampshire*. Millwood, N.Y.: KTO Press, 1981.

Davis, Harold E. *The Fledgling Province: Social and Cultural Life in Colonial Georgia 1733–1776*. Chapel Hill, N.C.: University of North Carolina Press, 1976.

Debates and Proceedings in the Convention of the Commonwealth of Massachusetts, Held in the Year 1788. Boston: William White, 1856.

Diehl, Charles. *Byzantium: Greatness and Decline*. New Bruswick, N.J.: Princeton University Press, 1957.

Donnan, Elizabeth. *Documents Illustrative of the History of the Slave Trade to America*. 4 vols. Washington, D.C.: Carnegie Institute, 1930.

Donovan, Robert J. *The Presidency of Harry S. Truman, 1949–1953*. 2 vols. New York: W. W. Norton, 1977, 1982.

Duggan, Ronnie. *On Reagan: The Man and His Presidency*. New York: McGraw-Hill, 1983.

Edel, Wilbur. *A Constitutional Convention: Threat or Challenge?* New York: Praeger, 1981.

_____ . *The State Department, the Public, and the United Nations*. New York: Vantage Press, 1979.

Ehrlich, Anne. "Nuclear Winter: A Forecast of the Climatic and Biological Effects of Nuclear War." *Bulletin of the Atomic Scientists*, April 1984.

Eisenhower, Dwight D. *Crusade in Europe*. New York: Doubleday, 1948.

Elliot, Jonathan, ed. *The Debates in the Several State Conventions on the Adoption of the Federal Constitution as Recommended by the General Convention at Philadelphia in 1787*. 2d ed., 5 vols. Philadelphia: J. B. Lippincott, 1891.

Ellis, David M., et al. *A Short History of New York State*. Ithaca, N.Y.: Cornell University Press, 1957.

Episcopal Diocese of Washington. *The Nuclear Dilemma: A Search for Christian Understanding*. Washington, D.C.: 1985.

Falwell, Jerry. *Listen, America!* 1980 Reprint. New York: Bantam Books, 1981.

Farrand, Max, ed. *The Records of the Federal Convention of 1787*. Rev. ed. 4 vols. New Haven, Conn.: Yale University Press, 1937.

Frei, Daniel, and Christian Catrina. *Risks of Unintentional Nuclear War*. Geneva: United Nations, 1982.

Gaustad, Edwin S., ed. *A Documentary History of Religion in America since 1865*. Grand Rapids, Mich.: William B. Eerdmans, 1983.

Gee, Henry, and William John Hardy. *Documents Illustrative of English Church History*. New York: Kraus, 1972.

Goldschmidt, Arthur, Jr. *A Concise History of the Middle East*. Boulder, Col.: Westview Press, 1983.

Graham, Howard J. "The Conspiracy Theory of the Fourteenth Amendment." 47 *Yale Law Journal* 371–403.

Grimm, Harold J. *The Reformation Era: 1500–1650.* New York: Macmillan, 1954.

Hamilton, Alexander, John Jay, and James Madison. *The Federalist.* New York: Modern Library, n.d.

Hanzsche, Wm. Thomson. *The Presbyterians: The Story of a Stanch and Sturdy People.* Philadelphia: Westminster Press, 1934.

Hardy, Robert T., ed. *Religion in the American Experience.* Columbia, S.C.: University of South Carolina Press, 1972.

Hart, Albert Bushnell. *Commonwealth History of Massachusetts.* 5 vols. New York: States History Co.: 1927–28.

Hart, Gary, with William S. Lind. *America Can Win: The Case for Military Reform.* New York: Adler & Adler, 1986.

Hawke, David Freeman. *Paine.* New York: Harper & Row, 1974.

Hayes, Carlton J. H. *A Political and Cultural History of Modern Europe.* 2 vols. New York: Macmillan, 1932.

Heimert, Alan, and Perry Miller, eds. *The Great Awakening: Documents Illustrating the Crisis and Its Consequences.* New York: Bobbs-Merrill, 1967.

Hudson, Winthrop S. *Religion in America.* 3d ed. New York: Charles Scribner's Sons, 1981.

Hughes, Philip. *A Popular History of the Catholic Church.* New York: Macmillan, 1949.

Hyneman, Charles S., and Donald S. Lutz. *American Political Writing during the Founding Era, 1760–1805.* 2 vols. New York: Harper & Row, 1975.

Ickes, Harold L. *The Secret Diaries of Harold L. Ickes.* 2 vols. New York: Simon and Schuster, 1953.

James, Joseph B. *The Framing of the Fourteenth Amendment.* Urbana, Ill.: University of Illinois Press, 1956.

_____ . *The Ratification of the Fourteenth Amendment*. Macon, Ga.: Mercer University Press, 1984.

Jefferson, Thomas. *The Papers of Thomas Jefferson*. Edited by Julian P. Boyd. 19 vols. Princeton: Princeton University Press, 1950–74.

"Jerry Falwell's Crusade." *Time*, 2 September 1985, p. 49.

Johnson, Donald Bruce. *National Party Platforms*. 2 vols. Urbana, Ill.: University of Illinois Press, 1978.

Jowett, Benjamin. *Aristotle's Politics*. New York: Carlton House, n.d.

Kalb, Madeleine G. *The Congo Cables*. New York: Macmillan, 1982.

Kauper, Paul G. *Religion and the Constitution*. Kingsport, Tenn.: Louisiana State University Press, 1964.

Kearns, Doris. *Lyndon Johnson and the American Dream*. New York: Harper and Row, 1976.

Kennan, George F. *The Decision to Intervene*. Princeton, N.J.: Princeton University Press, 1958.

Kirkpatrick, Jeane. "A Loud Voice but No Stick." Washington *Post*, 21 April 1986.

_____ . "Dictatorships and Double Standards." *Commentary*, November 1979, pp. 34–45.

_____ . "The Magellan Syndrome in Manila." New York *Daily News*, 9 February 1986.

_____ . "Our Cuban Misadventures." Washington *Post*, 29 January 1986.

Koran, The. Translated by N. J. Dawood. 4th ed. New York: Penguin Books, 1983.

Krieger, David. "What Happens If . . . ? Terrorists, Revolutionaries and Nuclear Weapons." *Annals of the American Academy of Political and Social Sciences*, March 1977, pp. 44–57.

LaHaye, Tim. *The Battle for the Mind.* Old Tappan, N.J.: Fleming H. Revell, 1980.

Lucas, Paul R. *Valley of Discord: Church and Society along the Connecticut River, 1636–1725.* Hanover, N.H.: University Press of New England, 1976.

Luccock, Halford E., and Paul Hutchinson. *The Story of Methodism.* New York: Methodist Book Concern, 1926.

Lynch, Patricia. "Is Lyndon LaRouche Using Your Name?" *Columbia Journalism Review,* April 1985, pp. 42–46.

McCormick, Richard P. *New Jersey from Colony to State.* New York: D. Van Nostrand, 1964.

McEvedy, Colin, and Richard Jones. *Atlas of World Population History.* New York: Facts on File, 1978.

McGuigan, Patrick B. "Judge Robert Bork is a Friend of the Constitution." *Conservative Digest,* October 1985, pp. 91–102.

McMillan, Richard C., ed. *Education, Religion, and the Supreme Court.* Danville, Va.: Association of Baptist Professors of Religion, 1979.

Madison, James. *The Papers of James Madison.* Vols. 8–12. Edited by Robert A. Rutland and Charles F. Hobson. Charlottesville, Va.: University Press of Virginia, 1977.

Main, Jackson Turner. *The Anti-Federalists: Critics of the Constitution, 1781–1788.* New York: W. W. Norton, 1961.

Marty, Martin E. *Pilgrims in Their Own Land: 500 Years of Religion in America.* Boston: Little, Brown, 1984.

Marx, Karl. *Communist Manifesto.* Chicago: H. Regnery, 1955.

Minutes of the Provincial Council of Pennsylvania, The. Philadelphia: Jo. Severns, 1852.

Mitchell, Mary Hewitt. *The Great Awakening, and Other Revivals in the Religious Life of Connecticut.* New Haven, Conn.: Yale University Press, 1934.

Morris, Robert B., ed. *The Early Republic, 1789–1828: Documentary History of the United States.* Columbia, S.C.: University of South Carolina Press, 1968.

Moyer, Wayne. "Put Evolution Back in the Books." *U.S.A. Today*, 16 September 1985.

National Council of the Churches of Christ in the United States of America. *Yearbook of American and Canadian Churches, 1985.* Nashville, Tenn.: Abingdon Press, 1985.

Nybakken, Elizabeth I., ed. *The "Centinel": Warnings of a Revolution.* Newark, Del.: University of Delaware Press, 1980.

Oldenbourg, Zoé. *The Crusades.* New York: Pantheon Books, 1966.

Peace Pac. Leaflet. "1982 Election Report." n.d.

Peretz, Don. "Israel Confronts Old Problems." *Current History.* January 1985, pp. 9–12.

Pipes, Daniel. "Fundamentalist Muslims between America and Russia." *Foreign Affairs*, Summer 1986, pp. 939–59.

Plate, Thomas. "Reagan on the American Family." *Family Week*, 10 June 1984.

Ramazani, R. K. "Iran's Islamic Revolution and the Persian Gulf." *Current History*, January 1985, pp. 5–8.

Reagan, Ronald. *Ronald Reagan Talks to America.* Old Greenwich, Conn.: Devin Adair, 1983.

Reagan, Ronald, with Richard G. Hubler. *Where's the Rest of Me?* 1965 Reprint. New York: Karz, 1981.

Reichley, A. James. *Religion in American Public Life.* Washington D.C.: Brookings Institution, 1985.

———. "Religion and the Future of American Politics," *Political Science Quarterly*, Issue No. 1, 1986, pp. 23–48.

Reston, James. "Politics and the Press." New York *Times*, 9 April 1986.

Roosevelt, Franklin D. *The Public Papers and Addresses of Franklin D. Roosevelt.* 13 vols. New York: Macmillan, 1941.

Roosevelt, Kermit. *Countercoup: The Struggle for the Control of Iran.* New York: McGraw-Hill, 1979.

Rose, Willie Lee. *A Documentary History of Slavery in North America.* New York; Oxford University Press, 1976.

Russell, Elbert. *The History of Quakerism.* New York: Macmillan, 1942.

Safire, William. "Free Speech v. Scalia." New York *Times*, 29 April 1985.

Schlesinger, Arthur M., Jr. *Prelude to Independence: The Newspaper War on Britain, 1764–1776.* Boston: Northeastern University Press, 1980.

———. *A Thousand Days: John F. Kennedy in the White House.* Boston: Houghton Mifflin, 1965.

Schlesinger, Arthur M., Jr., and Roger Bruns, eds. *Congress Investigates, 1792–1974.* New York: Chelsea House, 1975.

Schocken, Gershom. "Israel in Election Year 1984." *Foreign Affairs.* Fall 1984, pp. 77–92.

Schwartz, Bernard. *The Roots of the Bill of Rights.* 5 vols. New York: Chelsea House, 1980.

Shepherd, David R., ed. *Ronald Reagan: In God I Trust.* Wheaton, Ill.: Tyndale House, 1984.

Smith, Hedrick, et al. *Reagan the Man, the President.* New York: Macmillan, 1980.

Smith, C. Henry. *The Story of the Mennonites.* Berne, Indiana: Mennonite Book Concern, 1941.

Smith, Wayne S. "A Trap in Angola." *Foreign Policy.* Spring 1986, pp. 61–74.

Solberg, Winton U. *Redeem the Time: The Puritan Sabbath in Early America.* Cambridge, Mass.: Harvard University Press, 1977.

Stokes, Anson Phelps. *Church and State in the United States.* 3 vols. New York: Harper & Brothers, 1950.

Taylor, Rosser H. *Ante-Bellum South Carolina: A Social and Cultural History.* Chapel Hill, N.C.: University of North Carolina Press, 1942.

Taylor, Samuel W. *Rocky Mountain Empire: The Latter-Day Saints Today.* New York: Macmillan, 1978.

Tillman, Seth P. *The United States in the Middle East.* Bloomington, Ind.: Indiana University Press, 1982.

Tracy, Joseph. *The Great Awakening: A History of the Revival of Religion in the Time of Edwards and Whitefield.* Boston: Tappan and Dennet, 1842.

United Nations. *Yearbook of the United Nations, 1946–47.* Lake Success, N.Y.: United Nations, 1947.

Vedder, Henry C. *A Short History of the Baptists.* Philadelphia: American Baptist Publication Society, 1907.

Walvin, James. *Slavery and the Slave Trade.* Jackson, Miss.: University of Mississippi Press, 1983.

Wentz, Abdel Ross. *A Basic History of Lutheranism in America.* Philadelphia: Muhlenberg Press, 1955.

White, Leonard D. *The Jacksonians.* New York: Macmillan, 1954.

————. *The Republican Era.* New York: Macmillan, 1963.

Wise, David, and Thomas B. Roos. *The Invisible Government.* New York: Bantam Books, 1964.

Index

About the Author

Wilbur Edel is Professor Emeritus of Political Science, Herbert H. Lehman College, The City University of New York. He retired in 1976 from the position of Vice-President and Dean of Administration at Lehman.

Dr. Edel is author of *The State Department, the Public, and the United Nations* and *A Constitutional Convention: Threat or Challenge?* His articles on questions of public policy have appeared in *Modern Government*; *State Government*; *Educational Record*; and *Journal of Geography*.

Dr. Edel holds a B.S. from New York University and an M.A. and a Ph.D. from Columbia University.